S0-DXI-923

Development Success

Also by A. Bebbington

THE SEARCH FOR EMPOWERMENT: SOCIAL CAPITAL AS IDEA AND PRACTICE AT THE WORLD BANK (2006, *also edited by M. Woolcock, S. Guggenheim and E. Olson*)

EL CAPITAL SOCIAL EN LOS ANDES (2001, *also edited by V. H. Torres*)

LOS ACTORES DE UNA DECADA GANADA: TRIBUS, COMUNAS Y CAMPESINOS EN LA MODERNIDAD (1992, *also by H. Carrasco, L. Peralvo, G. Ramón, V.H. Torres and J. Trujillo*)

NGOs AND THE STATE IN LATIN AMERICA: RETHINKING ROLES IN SUSTAINABLE AGRICULTURAL DEVELOPMENT (1993, *also by G. Thiele*)

RELUCTANT PARTNERS: NGOs, THE STATE AND SUSTAINABLE AGRICULTURAL DEVELOPMENT (1993, *also by J. Farrington with K. Wellard and D. Lewis*)

Also by W. McCourt

THE HUMAN FACTOR IN GOVERNANCE: MANAGING PUBLIC EMPLOYEES IN AFRICA AND ASIA (2006)

GLOBAL HUMAN RESOURCE MANAGEMENT: MANAGING PEOPLE IN DEVELOPING AND TRANSITIONAL COUNTRIES (2003, *also by D. Eldridge*)

THE INTERNATIONALIZATION OF PUBLIC MANAGEMENT: REINVENTING THE THIRD WORLD STATE (2001, *also edited by M. Minogue*)

Development Success

Statecraft in the South

Edited by
Anthony Bebbington
Professor, Institute of Development Policy and Management, University of Manchester, UK

Willy McCourt
Senior Lecturer, Institute for Development Policy and Management, University of Manchester, UK

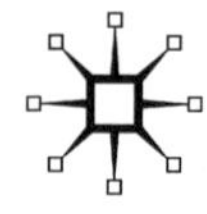

First published 2007 by
PALGRAVE MACMILLAN
Houndmills, Basingstoke, Hampshire RG21 6XS and
175 Fifth Avenue, New York, N. Y. 10010
Companies and representatives throughout the world

PALGRAVE MACMILLAN is the global academic imprint of the Palgrave Macmillan division of St. Martin's Press, LLC and of Palgrave Macmillan Ltd. Macmillan® is a registered trademark in the United States, United Kingdom and other countries. Palgrave is a registered trademark in the European Union and other countries.

ISBN-13: 978–0–230–00821–2 hardback
ISBN-10: 0–230–00821–6 hardback

This book is printed on paper suitable for recycling and made from fully managed and sustained forest sources. Logging, pulping and manufacturing processes are expected to conform to the environmental regulations of the country of origin.

A catalogue record for this book is available from the British Library.

A catalogue record for this book is available from the Library of Congress.

10 9 8 7 6 5 4 3 2 1
16 15 14 13 12 11 10 09 08 07

Printed and bound in Great Britain by
Antony Rowe Ltd, Chippenham and Eastbourne

Anthony Bebbington dedicates this book to Denise, who has been always there to remind me that 'it's the politics stupid,' to Anna and Carmen, who would probably rather I hadn't become involved in this project, and to Tom Carroll, friend and mentor who always insisted that I look for success

Willy McCourt dedicates the book to Glynnis, Róisín and Maya

Contents

List of Figures, Box and Tables

Figures

Box

Tables

Preface and Acknowledgements

This book has its origins in a seminar series entitled 'Statecraft in the South: Public policy success in developing countries.' The series was coordinated by Willy McCourt and Anthony Bebbington, and was supported by the UK Economic and Social Research Council (Grant No. Res-451-26-0266) for which we are very grateful. The series was conducted as a collaboration among four development studies and research centers in the UK: the Institute for Development Policy and Management at the University of Manchester, which served as the coordinating institute; the Institute for Development Studies at the University of Sussex; the International Development Department at the University of Birmingham; and the International Institute for Environment and Development, London. We are grateful for all the support that academic and administrative staff at these centers gave to the seminar series, and in particular to the following: Anne Marie Goetz, Camilla Toulmin, Richard Batley, John Thompson, Debra Whitehead, Susan Johnson, Gerry Stoker, Sam Hickey, Siu Fei Tan, George Larbi and Mark Robinson. Tony Bebbington also thanks the Centres Peruano de Estudios Sociales, Lima, Peru for giving him such a welcoming academic and intellectual home during the preparation of the book, and to the ESRC Global Poverty Research Group whose support gave him time to complete the edition.

The overall aim of the seminar was to explore the conditions under which development policies have been successful in meeting their goals and being sustained, over time, often against the odds. The rationale for this exploration was that accounts of development policy traditionally emphasize failures and problems. We felt that there was need to explore the conditions under which success was possible. This was not with a view to celebrating successes for success's sake, but rather to explore the political, institutional, design and other conditions under which success occurred. Success was understood in both positive and normative terms – namely, success was the achieving of goals over an extended period; but we were also particularly interested in those policies whose goals were to expand human capabilities and reduce poverty.

The four seminars in the series approached this general goal in different ways – one focused on a specific type of policy in distinct contexts, one focused on a type of policy in a specific country context, one focused on governance as a condition of development success in a particular country context, and the first seminar focused more explicitly on conceptual issues. In brief, the first seminar explored questions of success for economic and human development policies more generally; the second seminar explored the conditions under which policies aimed at securing land title and control for resource poor groups in urban and rural contexts were successful. The third seminar then explored conditions of development success in Brazil, and the fourth in Mozambique. The countries were selected because the partner institutions hosting those seminars had a particular concentration of research projects that could speak to the seminar series' issues.

This book brings together several of the papers presented in the seminar series, plus an invited paper from Bert Hofman, Ella R. Gudwin and Kian Wie Thee. We are grateful to the authors for having allowed us to do this, for revising (and re-revising) their papers and for helping make the seminar series such a success. We are also grateful to other colleagues who presented papers in the seminar series which are not included in this collection.

Willy McCourt
Anthony Bebbington

Manchester and Lima

List of Contributors

Anthony Bebbington is Professor in the Institute of Development Policy and Management at the University of Manchester. A geographer by training, he was previously Associate Professor of Geography at the University of Colorado, and has worked at the World Bank, Overseas Development Institute, International Institute for Environment and Development and University of Cambridge. His work addresses the relationships among civil society, livelihoods and development, with a particular focus on social movements and NGOs in Latin America. He is currently an Economic and Social Research Council Professorial Fellow (RES-051-27-0191).

Andrea Cornwall is a fellow at the Institute of Development Studies at the University of Sussex in the UK. A social anthropologist by training, she currently works on the politics of participation, sexuality and women's empowerment. She has published widely on participation and gender, and is co-editor of *Spaces for Change? The Politics of Participation in New Democratic Arenas* (2006).

Merilee S. Grindle is Edward S. Mason Professor of International Development at the Kennedy School of Government at Harvard University. A political scientist with a Ph.D. from MIT, Grindle has focused her recent work on the politics of policy reform and local governance in the wake of decentralization. More broadly, she is a specialist on the comparative analysis of the politics of policymaking and implementation with a particular focus on countries in Latin America.

Bert Hofman is currently heading the Economics Unit of the World Bank in China. Before his current posting, he spent five and a half years in Indonesia, the last three also as head of the economics unit, leading a team of economists and experts in the field of decentralization, poverty, and governance to support the Government of Indonesia in recovering from the Asian Crisis. Besides China and Indonesia, Bert has also worked on South Africa, Russia, Brazil, Zambia, Mongolia, East Timor and Namibia. Before joining the World Bank, he worked at the Kiel Institute of World Economics, the OECD, and ING Bank. He has published on issues of debt and debt overhang, public expenditure management, decentralization, and Indonesia's economic history.

David Hulme is Professor of Development Studies at the University of Manchester and Associate Director of the Brooks World Poverty Institute (University of Manchester), the Chronic Poverty Research Centre and the ESRC Global Poverty Research Group (University of Manchester and Oxford). His research interests include poverty and human development, poverty reduction policies, rural development, the role of NGOs and civil society in development, microfinance and public management. At present he is a Leverhulme Senior Research Fellow preparing a book entitled 'A Contemporary History of Global Poverty and Global Poverty Reduction: Compassion and Self-interest'.

David Jackson has over 20 years of experience in governance and public sector planning and finance. He is interested in the relationship between the citizen and the state, in particular at local levels. His career includes assignments in over 10 countries. He has written a book on the Mozambican planning and budgeting system (*Descentralização, Planeamento e Sistema Orçamental em Moçambique*. Principia, Publicações Universitárias e Científicas S João de Estoril, Cascais, Portugal) and taught at the School of Oriental and African Studies, London University. David Jackson is Decentralization Advisor with the United Nations Development Programme, Indonesia.

Thee Kian Wie is a senior researcher at LIPI (the Indonesia Institute of Sciences). He is author of prize-winning books about the Indonesian economy, and is among the group of economists who studied in the US in the 1960s. He began his career at the National Institute for Economic Research (Lembaga Kajian Ekonomi Nasional – LKEN), which later amalgamated with LIPI. While most of his colleagues have joined the bureaucracy, Thee continues to engage in research and writing in Indonesia Economic History, Industrial Policy, and Competitiveness and Trade. He chairs the board of SMERU Research Institute, an important poverty research center in Jakarta.

Willy McCourt is a Senior Lecturer in human resource management in the Institute for Development Policy and Management at the University of Manchester. He has carried out research and consultancy in Africa and Asia for national governments and development agencies such as the UK Department for International Development and the United Nations. His most recent (2006) book is *The Human Factor in Governance: Managing Public Employees in Africa and Asia*.

Marcus André Melo holds a PhD from Sussex University, and is currently Professor of Politics at the Federal University of Pernambuco

(Brazil), where he directs the Centre for Public Policy (NEPPU). He formerly held visiting appointments at the Massachusetts Institute of Technology where he was also a Fulbright Scholar. He has consulted for the World Bank, IADB, DFID and UNDP. His latest publications are (as co-editor) *Diseño institucional y participación política: experiencias en Brasil contemporaneo,* Flacso, Buenos Aires, 2006; and (as co-author) *Political institutions, policy making processes and policy outcomes in Brazil,* Washington, DC, IADB, 2006.

Diana Mitlin is Senior Research Associate at the International Institute for Environment and Development (www.iied.org) and Lecturer at the Institute for Development Policy and Management at the University of Manchester (www.sed.manchester.ac.uk). The major focus of her work is urban poverty reduction with a particular focus on the areas of secure tenure and basic services, and collective action and local organization. Her recent books include *Empowering Squatter citizen: local government, civil society and urban poverty reduction* (ed. with D. Satterthwaite) 2004 and *Environmental problems in an urbanizing world: finding solutions for cities in Africa, Asia and Latin America* (ed. with J. Hardoy and D. Satterthwaite) 2001.

Karen Moore is a Research Associate with the Chronic Poverty Research Centre, and has been based at IDPM, University of Manchester since 2003. She has undertaken research on microfinance programmes and practice in Bangladesh, with a focus on savings and 'gender empowerment', as well in the southern African context. Currently her research is focused on childhood, life-course and intergenerational poverty, particularly in South Asia. She is presently undertaking doctoral research on risk and resilience among low-income children in urban Bangladesh.

Ella R. Gudwin was a consultant at the World Bank at the time of writing. She has worked for the Population Council, an international non-profit nongovernmental organization working on population and reproductive health issues. She holds a degree from the School for South East Asia Studies of SAIS at Johns Hopkins.

Alex Shankland has worked in Brazil, Peru, Angola and Mozambique as a researcher, NGO manager and social development consultant. His research interests have centred on rights, participation and policy, particularly in the health sector. Formerly the Research Manager of the Development Research Centre on Citizenship, Participation and Accountability, he is currently engaged in fieldwork on the theme of representation and health policy in the Brazilian Amazon for a D.Phil. at the Institute of Development Studies (IDS), University of Sussex.

1
Introduction: A Framework for Understanding Development Success

Willy McCourt and Anthony Bebbington

Why success?

The American singer-songwriter Paul Simon once sang that while he would be the first to admit something going wrong, something going right in his life was apt to take him by surprise because it was 'such an unusual sight'. Admittedly he was thinking rather more about his happy relationship with his wife than about development policy at the time, but his words still tell us something about the subject of this volume.[1] For public policy successes in developing countries – policies that have endured, met their aims and secured the acquiescence of those who initially opposed them – are also a distressingly 'unusual sight'. This has provided fertile ground for those 'negative academics' (Chambers, 1983) – a category that includes most of us for at least some of the time – who, like Paul Simon, sometimes find success harder to deal with than failure; failures *in* development, if not the failure *of* development. The thumping sub-title of a book that was prominent at the time of writing is indicative here (Easterly, 2006). Such work has generated various explanations of failure. Some policies failed because they were ill conceived or poorly designed (Easterly's analysis is that many aid programmes were bound to fail because their goals were utopian and vague). Others failed because they were resisted, unpicked and steadily undermined by groups opposed to them, or because government bureaucracies proved unable to implement them; and so it goes on.

To be fair, focusing on failure has sometimes led to identifying factors that might increase the likelihood of success. Despite its title, James Scott's *Seeing like a state: How certain schemes to improve the human condition have failed* came to strong conclusions about the importance of institutional flexibility and local knowledge, and it inspired worthwhile further research (see, for instance, Pritchett and Woolcock, 2004; and World Bank 2003b). It was in this vein that the former editor of the English liberal newspaper *The Guardian* concluded a book review with the statement that in public policy, 'Failure is so much more instructive than success' (Preston, 2006).

Begging to differ from the editor and those academics who think like him, we propose in this volume to be instructed by success. Let us flag up two paradigmatic cases so that readers know immediately the sort of thing we have in mind. The first is education and health in the state of Kerala in south-western India. Kerala has long been noted for the quality of its health and education relative to the rest of India – for low infant mortality and high literacy rates, for example (Sen, 1992). The second example is the economic development that followed structural adjustment in Mauritius in the early 1980s, analysed by Gulhati and Nallari (1989). The Mauritian economy did indeed stabilize and then get on to a growth trajectory that it has maintained over 20 years, confounding doomsayers like the Nobel prize-winning novelist V. S. Naipaul (1972), who had pointed to a rising population that the economy would not be able to support.

Our second example allows us to recognize that success is rarely if ever unambiguous. For example, a different 'periodization' (to use a historian's term) would give a different version of success in Mauritius. There is an argument for seeing the establishment in 1970 of the island-wide free trade zone as the start of Mauritius' route to prosperity, with structural adjustment merely a hiccup in the longer time scale (Bheenick and Schapiro, 1989). Similarly, the success of the free trade zone came at the expense of working conditions for female employees (Kothari and Nababsing, 1996), while prosperity in general managed to coexist with poor management and widespread patronage in government (McCourt and Ramgutty-Wong, 2003).

With such successes in mind, and with apologies to Scott, our concern is to understand *'How certain schemes to improve the human condition have succeeded, against the odds.'* For development studies, we suggest, still lacks a coherent account of development success: hence, for example, the UK Department for International Development's (2005) multi-country 'Drivers of Change' project that has tried to identify factors that facilitate or constrain social and political change in particular settings. Understanding how development policies come into being and occasionally prosper in the face of external threats and capacity constraints, and in volatile surroundings, is therefore important: for improving the practice of development; for theorizing about develo ment and the role of government in improving the human condition; and for teaching development studies, because students need convincing success stories from which to draw instruction and inspiration as well as sobering accounts of policies that have failed.

The nature of success

One thing or many things?

It could be, though, that our focus on success just shows that we are fools rushing in where angels fear to tread. To take our own examples, what could structural adjustment in Mauritius have in common with social development in Kerala? Ought we not to throw up our hands in the face of 'the embeddedness of social phenomena within the historically specific conditions of real people and places' (Fine, 2001: xv), and confine ourselves to speaking in the singular about this or that individual policy that 'worked' (Davies *et al.*, 2000)? Of course it would be surprising to find that success stories share none of the common features that an enterprise like ours inevitably looks for. But we might still find that those features – 'capacity', say – are a kind of lowest common denominator, while the factors that really count are the unique ones. Success might be a *gestalt*, to use a psychological term, an economic-political-administrative 'whole' that is in some way greater than the sum of its parts. If so, policy elements from which policymakers elsewhere might seek to learn, or that might lend themselves to transfer (we discuss policy transfer and policy learning later on), would lose their value outside the *gestalt* in which they arose. 'Vice may be virtue uprooted' is how the Anglo-Welsh poet David Jones put much the same point (1974: 56).

Our provisional position remains that there is a single thing called development policy, overlapping with public policy. We are going to take a permissive view of policy itself – 'something bigger than particular decisions, but smaller than general social movements' (Heclo, 1972, quoted in Parsons 1995: 13) – allowing contributors to this volume to focus either on a single policy introduced at one point in time or a constellation of policies; for example, either on a particular educational reform or on a trend in education spread out over many years. We think it is still economical for scholars to generalize where we can and for policymakers to learn from experience elsewhere where they can, rather than for all of us endlessly to reinvent the wheel. But we are still obliged as we start this enquiry to leave on the table the null hypothesis that success may be *sui generis*.

view: development as tangible enhancement of lities

established that it is useful to try to generalize about e on to defining it. What we call 'success' will depend we call development, that typically undefined term, apt to fall apart as soon as we examine it (Crush, 1995; Escobar, 1995; Ferguson, 1994), but on which our project requires us to take a view. First, we are interested in development as a purposive activity, as in development policy and programmes, rather than as an immanent, unintentional process, as in "capitalist development" (Cowen and Shenton, 1996; 1998), even while we do not discount the 'informal development' practised by millions of our fellow citizens which may turn out to have been more developmental than our deliberate interventions.[2]

Second, we argue that development is about the enhancement of human capabilities, in particular for the people who have the greatest capability deficits. Development in this sense is a normative term that conveys a commitment to shift the balance of opportunities and investments in society towards the poorer and the excluded (cf. World Bank, 2005). After its eclipse in the 1980s and early 1990s, at least in the Anglo-Saxon countries like the United States, the United Kingdom and New Zealand and, partly as a result, in the IMF and the World Bank, this view has returned to centre stage. It was the focus of the *World Development Reports* of 2000/2001 and of 2006, and it is the ostensible goal of the 'Poverty Reduction Strategy Papers' that have gradually superseded structural adjustment in recent years.

We are therefore interested in policies that have *demonstrably* (a word we flesh out below) improved the human capabilities of a significant population of otherwise disadvantaged people. This may occur through interventions involving direct investments and improvements in their assets – their financial resources, physical assets, health and education, social networks etc.[3] – or through interventions that improve the environments in which poor people pursue their well-being. Examples of the former might include land reform, education, microfinance and health programmes; examples of the latter might include peace building, social inclusion or macroeconomic programmes that have demonstrably helped people.

A consequence of the normative view is that we are not obliged to confine ourselves to success in terms of a policy's satisfaction of its original stated goals. A policy could have a benign effect that is indirect and possibly even unintended. Indeed, it is conceivable that such effects might include creating a constituency that comes to defend the policy's very existence. There can be pro-poor effects without initial pro-poor intentions.

The legitimacy view: public policy as legitimate public action

No sooner, however, do we nail our colours to the mast than we feel the need to lower them by a couple of notches. While the view of development we have just advanced will seem self-evident if not anodyne to many readers, it has a competitor. This is the view that whatever development might be, public policy is, quite simply, whatever a legitimate government decides to do. It is implicit in the UK government Commission for Africa's report which argues that donors should support pan-African organizations

> in a way which enables the organisation to decide and manage its own priorities – in other words, aligned with the organisation's strategies, not donors' particular predilections, priorities and procedures. (Commission for Africa, 2005: 128)

It is conceivable that it was the 'predilection' for pro-poor policies that the Commission had at least partly in mind, given the pro-poor orientation in recent years of so many development agencies, including the UK government's own Department for International Development (DFID).

What we will call the 'legitimacy' view recognizes the right of a legitimate government – increasingly, but still by no means always a democratically elected one – to go to the devil in its own way. Take India as an example: some would argue that its recent economic liberalization, which has increased income inequality, has been at the expense of the poor. In addition, many necessary things that governments do are not so much hostile to the interests of the poor as not primarily concerned with them: reforms to the machinery of government, such as those strengthening meritocracy in public staffing, for example, are only 'pro-poor' in the most tenuous sense. They may be associated with economic growth, as Evans and Rauch (1999) have claimed, but that is not usually why governments introduce them. Growth is a side-effect. It is confidence in the integrity of government among rich and poor alike that they promote. It would seem perverse to exclude from consideration policies based on the belief that 'a rising tide will lift all boats' (in President John F. Kennedy's seductive phrase), or that merit-based staffing is a good thing in itself, because they are not obviously 'pro-poor'.

Durability

However impeccably pro-poor or legitimate a policy happens to be, it only becomes successful when it has endured. For how long? Following Sabatier (1988), we suggest a duration of ten years at least. In a competitive electoral system, there is the additional rider that it should survive a change of government.

Endurance into at least the medium term adds three interesting features to the mix. The first is how the policy adapts or fails to adapt to changing circumstances. Some policies are indeed supple, like the many social funds in Latin America that have changed substantially during their 15 to 20 years' existence. Others, though, have hardened into a 'frozen constraint' (Mahoney and Snyder, 1999: 18) that endures only because it is so well dug in that the game of removing it is not worth the candle. Success can atrophy into entrenched failure.

The second feature is that endurance protects us against the curse of Peters and Waterman (1982). Their account of 'excellent' companies caught the imagination of policymakers, including in developing countries, because it offered a recipe for success, and it is an influence on Grindle (1997) and elsewhere in development studies (see for example Curtis, 1994). Yet some of their 'excellent' organizations notoriously ran into trouble shortly after the book's publication. Our preference for the medium- to long-term allows us to learn from cases that, even were they to lapse into crisis in 2007, would still have been around long enough to have been successes in their time. Moreover, policies that lapse into crisis but then recover are likely to provide particularly interesting lessons.

Recognizing success

The third interesting feature of endurance is that it allows proper evaluation of policy outcomes once teething or other troubles have been resolved. As hinted already, we take the 'consequentialist' position, in philosophical terms, that there is an important sense in which we can only tell if policies are developmental after the fact: we know them by their fruits. Much debate in development studies is precisely about whether a given policy was or was not developmental in this sense. Clearly lots of policies implemented in the name of development have proved to have nothing developmental about them in their effects.

Hypotheses on success

If something that everyone wants is rarely seen, it must be harder to obtain than is generally realized. Having said what we mean by success and how we will recognize it, we wish finally in this section to introduce the discussion of how we might explain it, a discussion that will occupy much of the remainder of the chapter. The literature provides us with a range of hypotheses. Some of them relate to political economy; some to design, organization and management; and some are what might be called serendipitous factors which are hard to theorize. In what follows we outline them in order to develop a framework for understanding development success which we hope will help readers to make sense of the cases that will be reported in this volume. We will return to it in our final chapter when we reflect in the light of our cases on why policies have succeeded in the past, and how they can be made to succeed in future.

A model of development success: from linear to complex

Exogenous shocks and the 'naïve model'

As a preliminary, we should recognize first that policies need the good luck of being spared from exogenous shocks. In the World Bank's analysis, such shocks were responsible for the failure of a substantial portion of the Bank's interventions in the 1980s, with fluctuations in the price of oil being the classic example (Johnson and Wasty, 1993; see also Nelson, 1990: 20).

Second, we should note that inexperienced governments tend to come into power with a naïve model of development success. Overawed by the formal resources of the State, so much greater even in poor countries than what is available to political parties in opposition, it is not surprising if new governments assume that all that is needed is to hand their election manifestos to the civil servants and let them get on with implementing them. '(Tony Blair's) eyes would glaze over at any discussion on how to do things,' complains a jaundiced British civil servant, 'His attitude was: "You lot just get on and deliver." He had no idea that delivery was a complex process' (quoted in Foster, 2005).

The linear model

But the beginning of policy wisdom is the disillusioned recognition that manifesto promises do not always materialize. That is the basis of the linear model of policy that Thomas and Grindle outline, and which is the convenient real starting point for our discussion:

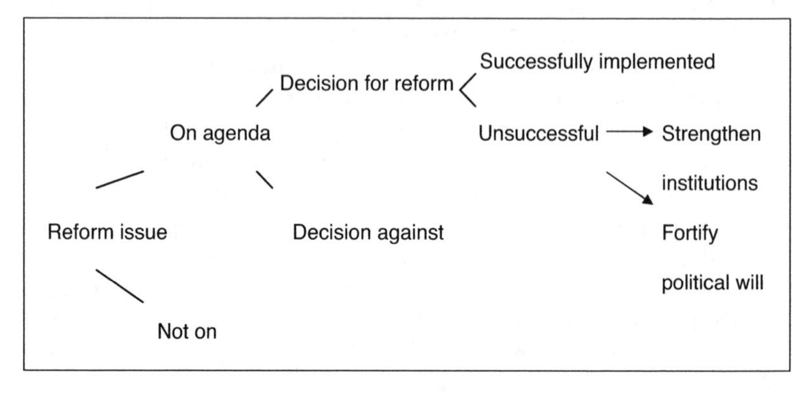

Figure 1.1 The linear model of policy reform
Source: Thomas and Grindle (1990: 1165).

Capacity

This model already provides two suggested explanations of failure – or, conversely, two success factors – which we should not discount because they are universally recognized: institutions and political will. 'Institutions' is Thomas and Grindle's shorthand for the capacity of government to do what it wants to do. Capacity is the hoariest of explanations for success, but that is not a reason to discount it. It has pride of place, for example, in the report of the UK government's Commission for Africa, for which weak capacity is 'a matter of poor systems and incentives, poor information, technical inability, untrained staff and lack of money' (Commission for Africa, 2005: 11), and which calls on donors to make a major investment in it. A discussion of the capacity of implementing agencies must be part of any explanation of success.

'Capacity' and the 'capacity building' which develops it are well established but somewhat vague terms that usually connote a combination of institutions and institutional development on one hand, and of public agency staff and staff development on the other. Actions taken under its banner include strengthening institutions such as the laws governing civil service management and the remit of the central agencies responsible for managing public servants, and also strengthening the capacity of staff themselves, mainly through training programmes (Hilderbrand, 2002; see also Grindle, 1996, which offers an expanded model that includes technical and political factors).

The emphasis on capacity is reinforced by recent research under UN and World Bank auspices which has pointed to the role that an effective bureaucracy plays in government effectiveness, which in turn may contribute to national economic growth. Key elements include meritocratic recruitment, internal promotion, career stability for public servants, salaries that are competitive with the private sector and administrative autonomy (Evans and Rauch, 1999; Hyden *et al.*, 2004; Kaufmann, 1999). We should also point to the overlapping research on industrialized country private companies that has established the importance for the effectiveness of organizations in general of human resource management 'levers' which include performance management in addition to those mentioned already (Guest, 1997; McCourt and Eldridge, 2004).

Political commitment

Of course capacity can be constrained even when it exists, as many discussions recognize. 'The quality of the civil service ... stems from political culture ... Countries get the bureaucracies they deserve and can use,' Gulhati has observed (1990: 1128). This brings us to the second success factor in the linear model, political will. Thomas and Grindle stigmatize it as 'a catch-all culprit, even though the term has little analytic content and its very vagueness expresses the lack of knowledge of specific detail' (1990: 1164), and even writers who deploy it admit that it is 'conceptually difficult' or '*ad hoc*' (Heaver and Israel, 1986; Killick, 1998: 91). Yet it has been the centrepiece of many explanations of policy outcomes, for example in World Bank project evaluation reports (Nunberg, 1997). McCourt (2003), taking account of the criticisms and drawing on a number of studies, has proposed a model of what we should call 'political feasibility' rather than 'political commitment' or 'will', since it contains 'antecedents' that are clearly outside the dictionary understanding of commitment as a personal 'pledge or undertaking'.

The model arguably provides a way of working with the customarily opaque concept of 'will', but it is still only a partial account of development success or failure. It does not spell out what it means by terms like 'political leadership' (see below on this). It is also indifferent to the content of policy, implying that any action is always better than inaction. We can usefully remind ourselves that while *Hamlet,*

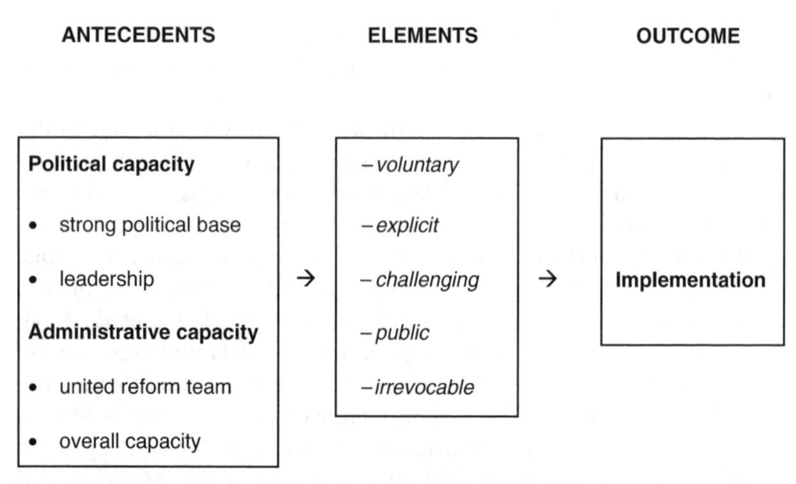

Figure 1.2 A model of political commitment/feasibility
Source: McCourt (2003).

Macbeth and *Othello* are all in part studies in indecision, hesitation or even downright procrastination, the bold murders which their eponymous heroes eventually commit are not terribly well advised. When used by a donor, the notion of 'commitment' is self-serving, insulating the donor against the possibility that the policy it foisted on a government failed because it was foolish. So let us move on to examine the content of policy.[4]

Policy content: innovation, specification and design

We are going to argue further on that there is a political economy of policy which shapes its content. But we cannot read policy off like an algebraic product of stakeholders' interests. We *may* be able to read off the policy problem, but a creative leap will be needed to move from posing the problem to shaping the policies that will address it. There may also be the slightly wistful hope that the creative leap will take policymakers further than mere trimming between rival interests would enable them to go, and allow otherwise intractable political problems to be solved. This, we suggest, is the source of much of the current interest in policy innovation (Government of Singapore, 2004; Government of the United States, 2004; Mulgan and Albury, 2003; NZ Institute of Economic Research, 2002; Pinto, 1998).

Policy specification and design

However innovative a policy may be, one explanation for its success must be that its technical specification was appropriate. Jeffrey Sachs describes with a minimum of undue modesty how in Bolivia he used his historical understanding to propose a remedy for hyperinflation that stopped it virtually overnight at the end of August 1985, in the teeth of those who believed that it could only be reined in gradually over several years (2005, Chapter 5). Less dramatically but still with substantial effects, cotton production in francophone Africa doubled in the four years following devaluation of the CFA franc in 1994 (Gabre-Madhin and Haggblade, 2004). There may indeed be development policies which are 'technically correct', based on evidence that is clear and all but unambiguous, even though political leaders and international institutions may resist them. Most would agree that governments do need a specific policy for dealing with AIDS, notwithstanding Thabo Mbeki's skepticism and Muammar Qadhafi's pinning the blame on Bulgarian expatriates in the Libyan health system (Sarrar, 2005), or central banks that are independent from political control, despite Margaret Thatcher's opposition in the UK throughout the 1980s.

Short of correctness, and at the risk of stating the obvious, some policy designs are better than others.

Policy actors

Policies or organizations?

In setting up our volume we opted for 'policy' as our unit of analysis, implying that the same agency could have a successful and an unsuccessful policy running side by side. But it could be that it is not policy, whether broad or narrow, but the organization responsible for it that is the key variable. Grindle (1997) has provided an account of relatively successful organizations in six developing countries, characterized by their clear sense of mission and by an autonomy that was sufficient to allow managers to manage: to encourage participation, reward good performers, protect staff from political interference and so on. Successful organizations, to paraphrase the emperor Augustus, may be able to transmute policy brick into implementation marble and score success after success. The way we have set up our volume may seem to privilege policy content as the unit of analysis, but that should not be at the expense of organizational and process factors, or, equally, of outcomes.

States, markets and networks

Who does *public*, or *development*, policy? 'Governments' is the answer we no longer give, and no more in industrialized countries than in developing ones. Rhodes (1997) has shown how the attempt to cut the state down to size in the UK following the Conservative election victory in 1979 had the unintended consequence of increasing its complexity through the range of actors who now became involved in state action. Government that had relied on hierarchy – bosses giving orders to trembling minions in an unbroken chain of command running all the way from the Prime Minister in 10 Downing Street to the cleaner in a local hospital – had now conjured the sorcerer's apprentice of markets and networks into being. Markets were the result of contracting services to supposedly more efficient private or voluntary providers, or of introducing competition within the state itself, as between hospitals. Networks were the result of hierarchical managers having to rub shoulders with the new contractors, but also with the plethora of special purpose bodies that the government had created to bypass local authorities which they saw as sluggish and politically unreliable. While the putative advantages and disadvantages of hierarchies are well known, those of networks are not. We reproduce below a list which Rhodes has provided.

Box 1.1 The limits of networks

Networks are effective when:

- Actors need reliable, 'thicker' information
- Quality cannot be specified or is difficult to define and measure
- Commodities are difficult to price
- Professional discretion and expertise are core values
- Flexibility to meet localized, varied service demands is needed
- Cross-sector, multi-agency cooperation and production is needed
- Monitoring and evaluation incur high political and administrative costs
- Implementation involves haggling

Their costs include:

- Closed to outsiders and unrepresentative
- Unaccountable for their actions
- Serve private interests, not the public interest (at both local and national levels of government)
- Difficult to steer
- Inefficient because cooperation causes delay
- Immobilized by conflicts of interest
- Difficult to combine with other governing structures

Source: Rhodes (2000: 355); see also Perkin and Court (2005).

Yet the 'discovery' of non-state provision, networks and 'joined-up government' was different in degree rather than kind from what went before. The success of the 1944 Education Act in the United Kingdom, without which at least a couple of the contributors to this volume would not be sitting where they are now, lay precisely in gaining the enduring assent of the Churches, of local authorities with different political groupings in charge, and not least of the wartime government coalition itself, to what we would now call a 'mixed economy' of state, religious and private schools (Hennessy, 1993). And it must have been managing this kind of heterogeneous network that the Act's author, Rab Butler, had in mind when he famously characterized politics as 'the art of the possible'.

Networks and NGOs in developing countries

Likewise, development intervention has always been the domain of a wide range of actors, whether or not we chose to recognize them: government, civic, private-not-for-profit, and private-for-profit. Non-state providers like 'harambee' schools in Kenya, and mission hospitals almost everywhere, have been around for a long time. Moreover, policy networks play – and always did play? – a vital role in framing and lobbying for policies (Haas, 1992).

Rhodes assumes the continuing power of government in the UK. It was responsible, however accidentally, for the growth of networks in the first place, and Rhodes argues that it is still able to alter the terms on which they trade. The sorcerer's apprentice that has slipped out of its formal control continues to operate under its auspices, at least nominally. But allowing for exceptions like the deliberate creation of a network of water users, suppliers and others in Ceará, Brazil (Lemos and De Oliveira, 2004), the increased prominence of non-state actors in developing countries is rather more a reflection of government impotence, if not outright state failure, as those actors are sucked into a service vacuum rather than deliberately substituted by the state for unsatisfactory but definitely functioning public services. Hence the extreme cases of NGOs standing in for a state that does not properly exist, as in Palestine, or providing what few services citizens actually receive, as in post-conflict Angola in the mid-1990s (Christoplos, 1997). Hence also the less dramatic but steady growth of NGOs through the 1980s and 1990s even in a stable democracy like Bangladesh (Edwards and Hulme, 1992), albeit fuelled by the same practical frustration and ideological dissatisfaction with governments on the part of international donors that Margaret Thatcher had displayed towards British local authorities.

Public policy without public agencies

An NGO or other non-state actor whose actions have developmental effects is effectively involved in 'public' policy, regardless of its legal status. The 'publicness' of a policy ought, then, to be defined by its goal and the structure of access to its benefits, not by the juridical nature of the organization implementing it.

Going a step further, can we call a policy 'public' even when no public agency in the conventional sense is involved in it? We think that we must be able to, if only to allow for those countries where government has all but collapsed and where non-state public policy is just about the only kind there is. But we have to qualify that view. First, the policy must deliver some public rather than purely private benefit, and we will want to take particular notice of whether the beneficiaries are drawn from the ranks of the disadvantaged. Second, the notion of 'public' also contains a sense of scale: there has to be a significant number of beneficiaries. Local authorities and agencies can have policy successes, but the emphasis here is on policies that are multi-regional, possibly spanning national or (in federal systems) state territories. This reflects both the normative view of development and our theoretical and explanatory concerns. Large-scale policies are important because they represent a substantial commitment to the enhancement of human capabilities. But they are also interesting, because the factors that determine their success are more complex than those that determine the success of a local authority or NGO's policy that extends only to a single area. This complexity makes the explanatory task more challenging but also more fruitful for developing theory. Further, this is the scale of policymaking which much development debate and intervention envisages, as in the current case of Poverty Reduction Strategy Papers.

This view of public policy, therefore, allows us to consider large-scale policy implemented through non-state agents. It is particularly relevant to South Asia, where some NGOs – BRAC, Proshika, the Grameen Bank, Sarvodhya – are operating on the same scale as government ministries. Moreover, it brings into play two additional elements: the presence of donor agencies from outside the developing country, and the international activist networks to which developing countries are particularly susceptible, lobbying on issues like human rights and the environment (Keck and Sikkink, 1998). However, it is unclear whether we see anything resembling the sophisticated network management that Rhodes and others discuss in relation to industrialized countries. All too often, developing country public agencies, NGOs and other providers continue to operate in splendid isolation, and complaints abound of NGOs or donors distorting indigenous priorities.

The political economy of policy formation

Policy initiation

There is a political economy of policy which is often neglected. 'Technically correct' policy notwithstanding, policy formation is mostly indigenous, arising in a local political and social process in which power is exercised, alliances are formed and supporters are enrolled. The structural adjustment literature bears this out, including studies emanating from the World Bank: 'Domestic policies set the basic parameters of government efforts', while external support 'emerges as a sometimes necessary, but far from sufficient, condition for implementation' (Nelson, 1990: 344, 347). 'Successful reform depends primarily on a country's institutional and political characteristics' (World Bank, 1998a: 52, 53).

If this is so, in what circumstances are successful policies initiated? There are two traditions in the policy literature: that of continuous, 'incremental' change in the well-known tradition that stems from Lindblom (1959), and discontinuous, dramatic change in the more recent model proposed by Baumgartner and Jones (1993) in which 'New ways of thinking about public problems, rapid mobilizations of new constituencies, changes in institutional structures, and the self-reinforcing effects of these trends occasionally combine to create dramatic and unpredictable policy changes' (Jones *et al.*, 1998: 2; see also John and Margetts, 2003).

Power

Once formed, policies endure when the balance of power supports them. They are more likely to last, we hypothesize, when they have a broad alliance as their base, and when many people benefit from them. Sen (1992) has argued convincingly that the quality of health and education in Kerala, which we offered as an example of success earlier on, is the result of state action which has proceeded from a robust tradition of popular participation and social mobilization (see also Heller, 1996). We might go a step further and say that even when there is an alliance between a domestic interest and a strong external actor, the policy will be unstable without a broader domestic alliance. President Soglo of Benin, as a former regional director of the World Bank, implemented civil service pay reform with enthusiasm and the Bank's wholehearted support, but they did not make up for the opposition of the powerful trade unions, of many members of parliament, and ultimately of the voters, who ejected him in the 1996 presidential election (Kiragu and Mukandala, 2004).

However, we need to recognize that policies may also endure through coercion, as under authoritarian regimes in Latin America, or through the tyranny of the majority, as in Sri Lanka's pro-Sinhala (and anti-Tamil) policies from the late 1950s onwards. But policy survival will depend on a lot of people believing that coercion of fellow citizens is an acceptable price to pay for the benefits they enjoy, possibly because they believe that those fellow citizens have no right to oppose the policy – they might be a 'mere' minority, after all. This then would be a case of policy sustained by an alliance between an autocratic government and a conniving section of the population – by integrative forces of a kind, as well as by coercion.

Coercion or the brute force of the majority weakens a policy's legitimacy; police clubbing demonstrators or a majority riding roughshod over a minority is scarcely the best way to build a broad social alliance. It generates resistance which may topple the policy, and much else besides, as Sri Lanka's Tamil separatist war testifies. In short, and not very surprisingly, win-win stands a better chance than win-lose. In the absence of coercion, policies that emerge from or at least gain the steady support of a broad social alliance are more likely to last.

Varieties of policy

The above examples also illustrate the importance of policy *type*. Our cases will discuss the conditions under which different types of policy succeed, as they are likely to vary. Policies may stand a better chance in areas like health or primary education where resistance is weaker because, for one thing, they don't threaten any elite group. Conversely, policies like participatory governance or land reform that redistribute power or resources seem less likely to succeed. Different policies provoke different distributional conflicts and are therefore more or less likely to generate broad alliances of support.

The hypothesis has an uncomfortable implication for those of us who subscribe to the normative view that development is only development when it addresses the needs of the disadvantaged. The logic of our position is that a policy that coopts the advantaged to support the interests of the disadvantaged is more likely to stick. Their support is liable to come at a price, but it may be one worth paying.

Our Benin example, taken from one specific policy domain, also illustrates the importance of the *scope* of policy. Narrow policies that affect a limited number of stakeholders should, other things being equal, be easier to push through: there are fewer ducks to line up. By the same token, of course, they are less likely to generate a broad alliance that supports them, as fewer people will benefit from them. McCourt (2005b) suggests that the latest in a long line of attempts in Sri Lanka on the relatively narrow issue of civil service reform is fragile specifically because it has few supporters outside the bureaucracy; while by contrast, Tendler (1997) describes the imagination that Ceará displayed in combining merit recruiting with popular participation.

Lastly, there is the question of the *depth* of the policy. The policy may only see the light of day when the policy negotiation that is part and parcel of alliance building has stripped away its most radical features, which could also be its most worthwhile ones. There is an instructive contrast between post-apartheid South Africa's ponderous but broadly supported land reform on one hand and its incisive but confrontational counterpart in Zimbabwe, sustained only through coercion, on the other. The trade-off is that a shallow policy, albeit broadly supported, *ipso facto* delivers less.

State-society relations

Lastly, the literature on state-society synergy in development suggests that policies are more likely to succeed when the organizations responsible for public policy are responsive to the people they serve, so that there is real accountability and a free flow of information from people to institution and back again, enabling policy to adapt to changing social conditions (Evans, 1996). In this way the organization builds up what Scott (1998) has called *mêtis*, that practical knowledge of the flows of social life which informs policies that are more likely to work. Evans (1996) goes on to suggest that the synergy is stronger in a relatively equal society, where trust is higher and the distance between organizations and their clients is lower. Greater equality of opportunity and asset distribution may also facilitate the emergence of policy networks (see above) which cut across social and institutional boundaries.

Leadership and success

Leadership is frequently identified as a key explanation of development success. The leadership of politicians – but also of senior officials – is central to Tendler's (1997) account of successful governance in the state of Ceará in Brazil, and is also a factor in Nelson's (1990) analysis of the politics of structural adjustment in 13 countries. It pervades the practitioner-orientated literature. Yet it is a difficult concept to work with, seeming to depend on the fortuitous emergence of gifted and determined leaders.

We need to distinguish here between bureaucratic and political leadership. We are on fairly firm ground with the former, having the organizational literature on leadership to draw on (for example, Tichy and Devanna, 1986), and Leonard's (1991) rich study of successful managers of rural development in Kenya. But political leadership is not well understood. Grindle provides one of the most detailed analyses, painting a picture of leaders who, against a background of adequate state capacity, have a vision that they are able to communicate, and who build coalitions and use their power of appointment to realize it (1996; see also Nelson, 1990; Wallis, 1999; and Williamson, 1994).

Crucially, we lack an understanding of how much room political leaders have to manoeuvre in their political environments. In theoretical terms, how much weight should we give to (leaders') agency and how much to (political and social) structure (Lewis *et al.*, 2003)? How much does a successful political leader owe to the society from which he or she has emerged? Mahathir Mohamed retired as Malaysia's prime minister in 2003 with his reputation substantially intact (allowing for accusations of 'crony capitalism': see Gomez and Jomo, 1997), yet without underestimating his personal achievement it can be argued that a national predilection for deference to authority makes Malaysian society a peculiarly easy one to lead (McCourt, 2005a).

Implementation

The study of policy implementation, following Pressman and Wildavsky's (1973) classic work, is largely the study of unforeseen consequences and how they are controlled (or not). Thomas and Grindle (1990) have proposed a model in which stakeholders' reactions are anticipated, and policymakers, recognizing the process nature of policy, are 'hands-on' throughout implementation in order to face down any threats that emerge (and the threat could take the form of our old friend, lack of 'capacity').

But anticipation has a limit. Unforeseen consequences might actually be unforeseeable, in which case learning and adaptation *post facto* become very desirable. Policymakers learn better when there is the free flow of information between public organizations and the people they serve that we have already discussed. Indeed, the value of feedback for improving performance is one of the strongest findings in the entire organizational literature (Locke and Latham, 1990). Learning requires some flexibility in the original plan as opposed to an implacable determination, possibly egged on by a donor, to dot every i and cross every t in the dreaded logical framework (Bond and Hulme, 1999).[5]

Following the policy process through to implementation also highlights the problem of political incentives. Thomas and Grindle are right to encourage politicians to involve themselves in implementation, as it takes time for the effects of large-scale policies of the kind we are interested in to work their way through the system. But they may seek incentives for doing so. Hence the policy designs that allow for – resorting to frequently-heard clichés – 'scoring quick wins', 'getting runs up on the board' or 'picking the low-hanging fruit'; or, one way or another, for politicians to have benefits to show to their constituents when elections come round.

The policy diaspora: policy transfer

Despite all we have said, we remain naïve enough to hope that policy learning can occur across national or regional frontiers as well as within an organization, and that policies can sometimes be transferred successfully, in however amended or truncated a form. Dolowitz and Marsh have developed a model for this special form of policy learning. Significantly, they relate policy transfer to policy success, pointing out that in successful transfers the original policy is properly understood and appropriate to the location to which it is being transferred (2000, see especially p. 9).

There is a similar interest in policy diffusion, the way in which public agencies acquire policies 'off the peg' from elsewhere (Mintrom, 1997), whether ubiquitous microfinance (see Chapter 5), client's charters, adopted from Britain in Botswana, Malaysia and Mauritius among other countries, or anything else. There is also an interesting intermediate position between innovation and diffusion which McCourt (2002) has labeled 'refraction', where governments do adopt policies from elsewhere, but in doing so adapt them to their political, institutional and cultural circumstances.

Coercion reappears in Dolowitz and Marsh's model as one of the reasons why policies get transferred, opening up the question of whether a policy imposed from outside rather than adopted voluntarily can ever succeed. The experience of structural adjustment, as we know, suggests that success under such conditions is unlikely.

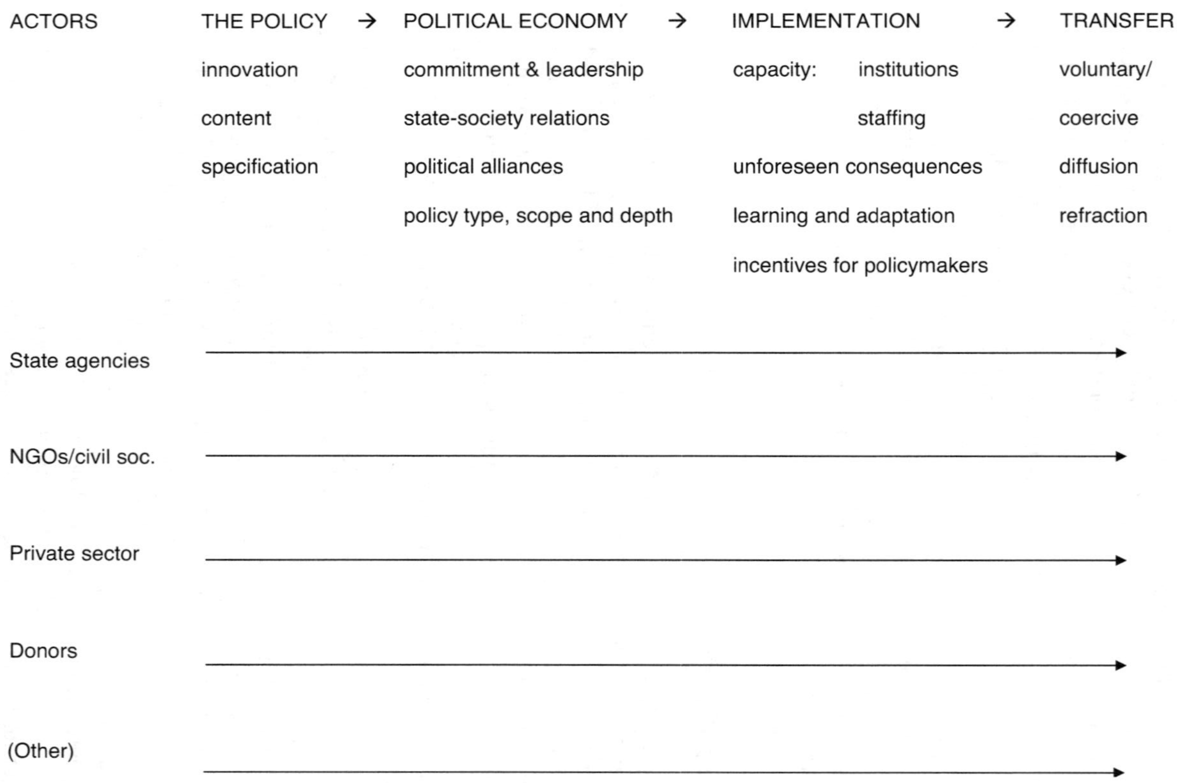

ACTORS	THE POLICY →	POLITICAL ECONOMY →	IMPLEMENTATION →	TRANSFER
	innovation	commitment & leadership	capacity: institutions	voluntary/
	content	state-society relations	staffing	coercive
	specification	political alliances	unforeseen consequences	diffusion
		policy type, scope and depth	learning and adaptation	refraction
			incentives for policymakers	

State agencies →

NGOs/civil soc. →

Private sector →

Donors →

(Other) →

Figure 1.3 A framework for understanding policy success

The experience of all but the original six members of the European Union that have had to adopt the *acquis communautaire*, tremendously onerous in the case of a small country like Malta, might suggest otherwise, yet the adoption was the consequence of freely choosing to join the European Union through a popular referendum vote.

A framework for understanding development success

We developed the framework shown as Figure 1.3 in the light of the above discussion, and at the start of the enquiry which has resulted in this edited collection. For clarity we have presented it as a linear model, so the usual qualifications about iteration and interaction between its elements need to be made (for example, the extent to which the separate policy actors constitute a coherent policy network). Apart from whatever intrinsic value it may have, we wanted to give our contributors a basis for reflecting on their cases. We knew that however fine the mesh of our net may be, it was very likely that some features of success, possibly the most interesting ones, would slip through it. Conversely, we also knew that there might be one or a small number of those features that would powerfully explain success, while others might be redundant. In our final chapter, therefore, we will revisit the framework to see how well it has survived the shock of contact with reality as represented by our seven cases, and in the hope that in the light of those cases we will be able to offer a better explanation of development success.

Cases of development success

Our case selection and its limitations

The case chapters were written in conversation with our framework. In the light of our research framework, we[6] looked for cases of success that would have the following features:

- They would target the enhancement of human capabilities, in particular for the people who have the greatest capability deficits.
- They should do so on a large scale: this might entail *scale-up* from an initial policy experiment.
- The policies would have been implemented over at least ten years, and preferably across at least one change of government: *policy duration* is important.

- They would preferably have succeeded *against the odds*; that is, at the point of inception a reasonable observer would have predicted that success was unlikely.

We also wished to see a spread of policy types and regions. In terms of policy type, our cases range from social service policies in education, health and housing (Grindle, Shankland and Cornwall, and Mitlin), through macroeconomic policies (Hofman *et al.* and Grindle again) and poverty reduction policies (via cash transfers – Melo – and micro-finance – Hulme and Moore) to governance reform policy (Jackson). In terms of geography, they span Africa, Asia and Latin America, though with a bias towards the latter.

We should perhaps make explicit a limitation which our approach to development success imposes, even if it is one that edited collections like ours usually skate over. In research design terms, we have an N=7 sample, one which is further limited by policy type (no case of rural development, for example) and geography (only one major case from Africa). Additionally, while all our authors had done primary research on their topics, it was not done specially for this study.

All those research design features were intentional. We wanted contributors to use their chapters as an opportunity to examine a single case in depth, looking again at their previous research through the development success 'lens'; and, while using hard data, to feel free to reflect and infer. But the limitation that these features impose will become evident in our final chapter, when we will draw out some tentative conclusions and recommendations.

Success at national and sub-national levels

The papers operate at two levels. Melo, Hofman *et al.* and Grindle analyse policies at a national level, a level at which questions of national political equilibria, leadership, synergies and sequencing arise. The remaining chapters engage with policy at a sub-national level, through an analysis of region-specific programmes (Hulme and Moore, Mitlin, Shankland and Cornwall, and Jackson), even if these can still be on a large scale, with some indeed evolving into national or even global initiatives. Engaging at this level leads to an emphasis on slightly different causal factors.

As readers make their way through our book, they will discover that our criteria for case selection did not survive unscathed. Just as we suspected (see our discussion of 'durability' above), success can indeed atrophy into entrenched failure, as Grindle will argue in her chapter on industrial and education policy in Latin America; and there can be less to success than meets the eye, as Mitlin will argue in relation to housing policy. But saying that pre-empts the cases themselves, which for the convenience of readers we now outline.

Success at national level

The first of the three national-level chapters is that of *Marcus Melo*. His concern is to explain the rise of cash transfer-based poverty reduction programmes during the 1990s in Brazil, and their continuance through to the present. He describes a process in which Brazil's steady democratization allowed for national mobilization around hunger and poverty and created an environment in which novel ideas on poverty reduction were able to emerge and – more importantly – to capture the attention of political leaders interested in getting elected. The first experiment with cash-transfer programmes in one large municipality thus prompted a second municipality controlled by another major political party to adopt the same instrument – and so the policy bandwagon began to roll.

Political ownership of the idea of conditional cash transfers, particularly once linked to education, became an arena of political competition. This competition led in turn to the programmes' diffusion and, in due course, adoption by the federal government under Fernando Henrique Cardoso. Furthermore, this national *Bolsa Escola* programme survived the transition to the Lula government in power at the time of writing. Indeed, although Lula's administration aimed to repackage and redesign the programme, the criticism (in particular from those groups that benefited from *Bolsa Escola*) was such that the new government's so-called *Bolsa Familia* programme retained many features of *Bolsa Escola*. Central to the success of both programmes has been the creation of a national Fund for Fighting Poverty, whose tax-based financing was secured through legislation.

In this history of policy diffusion, scaling up and durability, Melo argues that competition among political parties and leaders has played a central role, with all of them wanting to be associated with a very popular policy. While leadership, social mobilization and policy specification are all part of this success, for Melo political competition is key. One of the future challenges, however, will be that – because the policy has developed such a large interest group who are now concerned to sustain it – any future change to the policy will face stiff resistance, a problem that occupies an important part of each of the following two chapters.

Chapter 3, by *Bert Hofman, Ella R. Gudwin and Kian Wie Thee,* reviews Indonesia's development experience over the last 35 years. It explains the factors that led to the country's economic success in the three decades up to the late 1990s, but then explores how some of those factors also contributed to Indonesia's spectacular crisis in the late 1990s. The argument is that much of Indonesia's policy success was made possible by the same weak social and governance institutions which later on became the principal cause of the crisis.

Over 30 years between 1967 and 1997, Indonesia's GDP growth rate averaged a remarkable 7 percent. Rapid growth was accompanied by strong gains in human capital and poverty reduction, and a diversification of the economy away from agriculture. Growth was built on strong macroeconomic policies, supported by increasingly liberal trade and foreign investment and financial sector policies. These policies were by and large managed by a group of highly competent 'technocrats' isolated from the political sphere, who initiated structural reforms and created synergies between macroeconomic and sectoral policies. However, the country's core institutions did not keep pace with the reforms. Anaemic institutions made the country vulnerable to shocks, as a lack of appropriate controls and oversight had weakened the financial sector, and corruption increasingly undermined the political legitimacy of government and the credibility of its policies. When the Asian crisis hit in 1997, the weaknesses of the institutions, and notably of political mechanisms for building consensus on measures to fight the crisis and a judiciary to facilitate the restructuring of the economy, hampered crisis management and slowed Indonesia's recovery after the crisis. After the crisis, the country has taken on the difficult task of rebuilding its institutions.

So Hofman *et al.*'s is a story of good policies going bad over time, largely because institutional forms began to militate against flexible policy management, and because policies spawned an interest group in the form of the notorious 'crony capitalists' which resisted subsequent policy adaptation. In this sense their argument dovetails with the following chapter. Pointing out that 'new policies are not written on a tabula rasa', *Merilee Grindle* invites us to focus on the process through which a new policy dislodges an old one as an important component of policy success. She applies the Chapter 1 insight that success can atrophy into entrenched failure to the cases of industrial and education policy in Latin America. She shows that policies which had facilitated light consumer industry and increased basic access to education in the earlier period were not equal to the challenges of economic crisis in the early 1980s and of enhancing the quality as opposed to the quantity of education. However, even if the early policies had outlived their usefulness, they were difficult to dislodge because they had created interest groups in the form of industrialists and trade unions who had benefited from them and who resisted attempts to change them.

Yet unlike in Indonesia, the power of the interest groups was overcome. In Grindle's analysis, leadership was crucial. Having first become convinced of the need for change, presidents and executives deployed their power resources to drive change through. Where they were successful (they weren't always), it was by working from the top down, centralizing power and enhancing the role of agencies and institutions which favoured change, while neutralizing agencies and institutions (such as trade unions) which opposed it.

Were the new economic liberalization and quality-enhancing education policies successful? Interestingly, Grindle is agnostic on this point. Her concern is to insist that any new policy can only prevail if it succeeds in overcoming the vested interests that an established policy inevitably creates, and that the power of the executive will be crucial in order to achieve that.

Success at sub-national level

Where Melo, Hofman *et al.* and Grindle focus on national dynamics and institutions, the second set of chapters focuses on more localized policies, or on the ways in which national policies become locally successful. The first of these chapters traces the ascent of microfinance from a few localities and organizations in Bangladesh to a global scale; the second considers the conditions under which housing programmes for the poor succeed; the third looks at the embedding of Brazilian national health policies in local processes of citizenship formation, processes that have then helped secure the successful implementation of these policies; and the fourth explores the embedding of a provincial level planning model in Mozambique.

Microfinance is one of the most widely reported instances of successful policymaking. Revisiting earlier research, *David Hulme and Karen Moore* present evidence that, at least where Bangladesh is concerned, its success has been real. Roughly 11 million households, or around 80 percent of poor households, have had access to microfinance, leading to a positive impact on income growth and reduced vulnerability, and in turn to a decline in the poverty rate of the order of 2–5 percentage points. There is also evidence that it has increased women borrowers' economic independence, even if we seem to lack clear evidence that it has led to wider social or political empowerment.

Hulme and Moore's explanation of success invokes a number of our research framework elements, notably policy innovation and specification, implementation factors which include standardization and 'scaling up' of the distinctive Grameen borrower cell and group structure, effective human resource management, and policy transfer of the original Grameen Bank model to other Bangladeshi NGOs. Interestingly, government's role was mainly the passive one of not interfering with what the NGOs were doing.

Discussion of the importance of visionary leadership leads to a discussion of 'followership' in the form of the active participation of women borrowers themselves. Hulme and Moore suggest that we can best understand the latter as an instance of what Norman Uphoff, following Hirschman, has called 'social energy'.

Like Hulme and Moore, *Diana Mitlin* also discusses large-scale poverty reduction programmes in which nongovernmental actors play a significant role. Her particular interest is in housing programmes as poverty reduction instruments, and she uses the experience and evolution of four such programmes (in Chile, Mexico, Philippines and South Africa) as the basis for exploring the conditions under which housing programmes have been able to transfer substantial resources to poor people, on a large scale and over an extended period.

Central to Mitlin's argument is the notion that success in such programmes often has an inbuilt contradiction. In order to take poverty reduction programmes to scale – and thus engage in the types of redistribution that such a scaling up involves – it is very likely that state institutions will have to be involved, as was the case with Brazil's cash-transfer programmes. Likewise, large-scale delivery may require commercial private sector involvement. Of necessity, in other words, such programmes must be built on alliances. Yet incorporating such actors may pull programmes away from their core poverty reduction concerns. This happens for two reasons. First, political actors begin to see programmes as instruments of political benefit, and this can lead to changes in design and resource flows that reflect a compromise between poverty reduction and clientelism (in this sense Mitlin is less optimistic than Melo). Second, commercial actors are likely to push for programme designs that will maximize their earnings. In the case of housing programmes, this has meant favouring the provision of finished housing rather than self-provision, increasing unit costs and thus significantly reducing the number of households covered. The alliances underlying 'successful' programmes thus constitute a field of continuing socio-political interaction in which arguments about design are really larger arguments in disguise about the overall patterns of benefit distribution that will derive from programmes.

Thus, like Grindle, Mitlin notes that successful programmes create interest groups that can then become an obstacle to policy evolution. The future evolution of these programmes comes to depend on the balance of power among the different interest groups. In this sense, for Mitlin, a poverty reduction programme can only really be considered successful when it also builds political capacities among the poor, so that programmes serve poverty reduction rather than political or economic gain.

That conclusion is endorsed by *Andrea Cornwall and Alex Shankland's* study of citizen participation in Brazil's National Health System. This system, the *Sistema Única de Saúde* (SUS), encompassed not just the nuts and bolts of health care provision but also an array of institutions fostering citizen participation at municipal, state and national (federal) levels. At the core of Cornwall's and Shankland's interpretation of the longevity of the SUS is the notion that practices and institutions of citizenship embodied within the system have ensured not only its survival, but also the continuation of a set of radical principles that underlay its original design. In other words, while the SUS depends on alliances every bit as much as Mitlin's housing programmes do, the emphasis on empowerment has stopped other interest groups from watering down its key features.

The authors describe the SUS as an exception in Latin America, in the way that it has retained its identity as a rights-based and publicly funded programme. It survived neoliberal shocks, won increased tax-based funding under the Cardoso government of the 1990s and early 2000s, and continued to expand. While as usual, 'success' is not total (some observers point to service quality horror stories), in terms of our framework it has survived regime transition, gone to scale, been associated with significant health indicator gains and done all this against the political odds, given the dominance of neoliberal principles in Latin American social policy. Out of a variety of possible explanations (the model's origins in social movements; the alliances between health system, government bodies and the private sector; and the leadership capacity of certain ministers), Shankland and Cornwall highlight the inclusion of hundreds of thousands of citizens in the governance of the SUS through health councils and conferences deliberating on SUS policy and practice. These spaces of participation have also served as vehicles through which a range of other organizations, movements and cross-party groups have engaged in SUS governance, used the SUS and its underlying principles as a vehicle for promoting their own rights claims, and more generally come to identify with and defend the 'SUS project.'

Shankland and Cornwall's argument echoes Grindle's notion that policies create constituencies that proceed to defend the policies, as well as Mitlin's observation that those constituencies can have opposing interests. In this case, however, the emphasis is on processes of participation (rather than benefit distribution) as the vehicle through which constituencies are built.

Participation as a vehicle of constituency creation is also a theme of the final case chapter, which takes our enquiry into Africa. Beginning in 1995 a local planning, financing and governance model was introduced in Nampula province, northern Mozambique. Within five years it was being hailed as a success by Mozambique's Prime Minister, and donor and academic endorsement duly followed. *David Jackson* shows that while not fully embedded, by the time of writing the model was showing encouraging signs of durability, having put down some institutional roots and survived the replacement of key individuals who had sponsored it.

Jackson concentrates on the nature of the Nampula model and the evidence for its success. The model boils down to a series of District Development Plans which were implemented using a District Development Fund which the provincial administration made available to districts. He argues that although there is some evidence that this version of local planning has led to economic benefits, its principal value is political, in the contribution it has made to basic state legitimacy in the aftermath of civil war in a province neglected by both colonial and independent governments, where support for FRELIMO, the governing party, has been partial at best, and where freestanding donor-sponsored 'participative' projects have typically bypassed state structures. Jackson is careful to note the model's limitations. It is an exercise in deconcentration rather than full political decentralization; clear evidence of economic benefits is lacking; and attempts to replicate it elsewhere in Mozambique have had a patchy success. Yet unlike the policies discussed by Hofman and Grindle in this volume, the Nampula model has not outstayed its welcome, and Jackson therefore concludes with a plea for policymakers to be patient and to maintain their commitment.

An interesting feature of Jackson's chapter is his account of the operation of an informal policy coalition that has been crucial for policy ownership and success, but which has operated below the radar of formal government and donor reporting, partly because coalition members believed that they needed to be all things to all people and tell different stakeholders what they wanted to hear.

With these different experiences in mind, our final chapter draws lessons from the seven cases, whose main elements are summarized in Table 9.1. We review the evidence that the policies have had a large-scale human development and social and political impact that has been sustained over at least a decade, often against the odds. We go on to extract three key factors that have enabled success across the cases as a whole: power in the shape of organizations and coalitions, leadership and institutional design; and we incorporate them into an account of the stages of development success which we label 'institutionalized social energy' (Table 9.2). In this account, an upsurge of 'social energy' generates a policy idea (or highlights an existing idea) around which a coalition assembles, which in turn throws up a leader who gets the idea on the policy agenda and overcomes opposition from supporters of the old dispensation. The coalition is then institutionalized, empowering beneficiaries and deflecting patrons and rent seekers, and the policy is consolidated through feedback to adapt it to changing circumstances. After some suggestions for further research and some tentative recommendations to policymakers, we close by inviting readers to join us in celebrating and drawing inspiration from the cases of development success which our collection has presented.

Notes

1 Simon (1973). Copyright restrictions prevent us from quoting Simon's pretty and witty words, but at the time of writing they were easily available via a well-known Internet search engine.
2 Cowen and Shenton (1998, 1996) distinguish between development as an immanent, unintentional process – as in the development of capitalism; and development as an intentional process, as in development policy and programmes.
3 Readers will note the multidimensional notion of poverty associated with livelihood and well-being approaches underlying this notion of assets. See, for instance, Bebbington (1999), Gough and McGregor (2007), Moser (1998), and World Bank (2000).
4 The notion of leadership on the part of both politicians and bureaucrats is often seen as an element in both capacity and political will. We discuss it below in the context of political economy factors.
5 See also the special issue of *World Development* on implementation: vol. 24, issue 9.
6 We wish to record again our gratitude to colleagues at our partner institutes, who identified several of the cases: Anne-Marie Goetz of IDS, Sussex for Chapters 2 and 7 and Michael Hubbard of IDD, Birmingham for Chapter 8.

2

Political Competition Can Be Positive: Embedding Cash Transfer Programmes in Brazil

Marcus André Melo

Introduction: political competition and development success

This chapter argues that political competition in new democracies can play an important role in the formation, implementation and sustainability of anti-poverty programmes. Much of the current literature on the determinants of policy success stresses that politics matters. However, politics in this context is usually discussed with reference to hard-to-specify concepts (such as political leadership), to the indirect effects of democracy (such as transparency and the increased flow of public information) or to increased civic engagement and popular participation. While I recognize that in some contexts these factors do play a role in explaining development success and institutional change, public policy decisions are primarily made by political actors in formal political institutions who are driven by concerns with political survival. In democracies this essentially means the ability to win elections. This statement is a truism for established industrial democracies, but is a neglected dimension in current analyses of public policy in developing countries. Most authors who focus on domestic politics in new democracies have focused on how the electoral process is governed by a clientelistic logic that undermines efforts at reforming existing programmes or introducing new programmes (for Brazil see Samuels, 2003). Political competition is seldom viewed in a positive light.

To advance these arguments, the chapter discusses a case of policy success in which political competition played a crucial role. The case in question is the *Bolsa Escola* programme in Brazil, a poverty reduction programme introduced under the government of Fernando Henrique

Cardoso (1994–2002) and continuing to the present. This widely acclaimed conditional cash-transfer programme, which according to the World Bank 'became a well known trade mark and export of Brazilian social policy',[1] illustrates how political competition has generated policy emulation in sub-national governments that in turn has influenced policy at the national level. Thus political competition engendered policy emulation and policy transfer and led ultimately to the scaling up of local initiatives.

The chapter is organized as follows. The first section briefly reviews arguments found in the current literature on policy reforms. The second section discusses the issue of policy diffusion and explores its link with political competition. The two subsequent sections describe the political and social context of the Cardoso government in Brazil, and go on to analyze the emergence and evolution of the *Bolsa Escola* programme as a case of policy success which is partly explained by that context. The *Bolsa Escola* programme has been scaled up and survived a major shift in government when the Lula government was elected in 2002, and thus has passed the test of *durability* (McCourt and Bebbington, Chapter 1, this volume). Starting at the municipal level, in 1994, through a number of experiments by mayors, the programme has been scaled up through various steps and is now universal in coverage, having in its current model, the *Bolsa Família,* 10 million recipients as of mid-2006. Its impact on schooling and nutrition is also significant (Bourguignon *et al.*, 2003).

Explaining policy success: the political survival imperative

The limitations of the policy reform literature

Governance institutions and domestic politics have attracted a lot of attention in the development and public policy literature in the 1980s and 1990s. That institutions and politics matter is now the conventional wisdom. Even the traditionally cautious multilateral institutions have abandoned their earlier naïvety – at least in their position papers and public statements – and now recognize that political elites are key actors in the policy process (Nelson, 2000). However, the existing literature on policy reform and policy success tends to subsume politics in terms of difficult-to-specify concepts such as political will, political leadership or political commitment. It also usually cites lack of institutional endowments and capacity as the reason why programmes fail. But political will can be a scapegoat that multilateral institutions use for programmes that have failed for other reasons (Chapter 1, this volume). In turn, 'institutional capacity' is a conceptual procrustean bed, and is not very useful for explaining differences in the performance of programmes within a single country.

Where political leadership is concerned, it is difficult if not impossible to pin that concept down without conceptual tools drawn from psychology which political scientists and policy analysts are ill-equipped to use. More fundamentally, we lack an understanding of how much weight we should give to agency and how much to political, social and institutional structure (Chapter 1, this volume).

Leaders' survival requires followers' support

Fiorina and Shepsle (1989) have argued that in democratic contexts political leadership is better conceptualized with reference to the leader's ability to induce followers to cooperate and sustain him or her as a leader. If the leader fails to secure a majority, his or her leadership position is jeopardized. In this view, the traditional perspective on leadership is reversed. Rather than followers depending on leaders for protection or patronage, it is leaders that need the support of followers. When countries move to democracy, old types of leadership give way to modern, or at least more 'democratic', types of political leadership based on the ability to secure majorities. In the context of new democracies such as those of the Southern Cone in Latin America this means that self-governing groups and institutions – parties and other representative institutions such as Assemblies – and elected officials have to secure the support of their constituencies and their members in order to guarantee the majority required to retain leadership. Even when a charismatic mode of domination (to use Weberian language) plays an important part in the explanation, support has to be established through electoral competition. This sets in motion an interesting strategic dynamic dictated by political survival.

In addition to the focus on leadership, the current literature on policy reform has also drawn attention to the governance-enhancing effects of democratization. These effects include the fact that because new actors enter the policy arena, there is more feedback from stakeholders, which improves the quality of decisions. In addition, democratization is considered likely to improve policy implementation because problems of implementation can be more promptly detected and corrected. Participation and democratic deliberation also contribute to enhanced legitimacy. The growing literature on deliberative styles of policymaking has documented the value of civic engagement in democratic contexts and has mapped out innovative institutional designs that foster it (Bohman and Rehg, 1997).

Other factors in explaining development success

However, there has been much less emphasis on the role of formal political institutions and the political survival imperative as part of the explanation of successful policy reform. Studies of political institutions, electoral processes and political competition in the new democracies have insisted that clientelism is a basic trait of policy formation and an almost insurmountable obstacle to change (for Brazil in comparative perspective see Ames, 2001; Mainwaring, 1999; Samuels, 2003). This strand of the literature is largely negative. So also is the broader literature on policy reform, which has listed the very many factors that undermine reforms, and explained why they fail (see Ames, 2001 on Brazil). However, failure is not universal: rather, it is analysts who have been unable to detect successes (Chapter 1, this volume; see also Tendler, 1997). In this regard, political competition and formal political institutions are a neglected part of the story as the case of the *Bolsa Escola* shows.

Certainly some authors have extended our knowledge of the factors influencing the success of reforms and innovations. In Latin America in particular, the reform of the social sectors has attracted a great deal of research (Grindle, 2004; Kaufman and Nelson, 2004). Factors such as the timing, sequencing and packaging of reforms, all of which are associated with policy entrepreneurship and political leadership, are crucial in shaping the incentives that actors have during the reform process (Grindle, 2004). They are particularly important in areas where reform implies costs to key actors, as do most so-called second-generation reforms (Graham and Naím, 1999). Unlike first-generation reforms, which focused on macroeconomics, privatization and fiscal matters, the second-generation reforms entail institutional change.[2] They are administratively more complex, and they require the cooperation of many actors including, for instance, teachers, health workers and other service providers. The reform beneficiaries are usually large and diffuse sections of the population, while reform costs are concentrated in a small number of often highly organized and vocal groups. The implementation of transfer schemes such as the *Bolsa Escola*, for instance, while not imposing costs on service providers, does imply costs for political elites that control old-style poverty programmes, and for taxpayers.[3] They also have some of the features already mentioned, such as complexity and the need for actors to cooperate.

Nelson (2000) suggests that reforms of social programmes lack clear models that should be followed, in contrast with the well-known recipes for monetary stabilization. This is only partly true, since many models have been proposed as recipes, such as social funds, participatory budgeting and, most importantly for our purposes in this paper, conditional cash transfers such as *Bolsa Escola*. However, the number and variety of recipes for social programmes are greater, and their effectiveness is not well established, as policy outcomes are difficult to quantify. Whether such programmes are the result of policy transfer, in which case their diffusion depends on the conditions that make imported models work (Dolowitz and Marsh, 1996), or of indigenous experimentation, they do not take place in a political vacuum. Elected officials, who in federal systems are located in the different tiers of government, are the key actors.

The diffusion of policy models and the politics of policy emulation

Policy 'bandwagoning': emulation as strategic political behaviour

In the special but increasingly prevalent case of policy innovation resulting from policy transfer, attention has been given to the extent to which political leaders and policy elites are aware of potential policy lessons and the extent to which these experiences have been utilized in policy reforms (Dolowitz and Marsh, 1996). In this connection, a useful distinction was made by Ikenberry (1990) between processes of social learning (associated with the problem-solving behaviour of epistemic communities and transnational policy networks), coercion (through threats and conditionalities imposed by external actors) and policy 'bandwagoning' (active emulation by bureaucracies and elites of other experiences).

However, the question of *whose* experience is to be emulated and *when* a policy model is to be copied is key. Diffusion is not a smooth semi-automatic mechanism, mediated by language, culture or colonial legacy, culminating in organizational isomorphism, as part of the literature seems to argue. It is frequently conflict-ridden and intertwined with redistributive issues. In DiMaggio and Powell's (1983) 'organizational isomorphism' model, actors act purposefully: they consciously imitate the institutional forms of the organizations they compete with or depend upon. Mimetism, in this perspective, is seen not as an automatic mechanism, as in many diffusion studies, but as a choice. Likewise, political leaders and policy elites in diffusion processes actively pursue policy models and use external actors strategically. In many cases, as argued by Ikenberry (1990), they actively pursue external pressure because it helps them implement the policies they already want. International organizations and other external actors provide information and resources that serve to create or strengthen reform coalitions.

What may appear, then, as external coercive pressures may represent strategic behaviour rather than passive imitation. External pressure may actually be welcomed and manipulated by reform elites so as to strengthen their domestic political position – it 'strengthens the domestic hand of the state' (Ikenberry, 1990) – or, less nobly, to save their political skin. In other words, in democracies – even in imperfect democracies where the political market is plagued by information asymmetries between citizens and politicians – politicians will favour innovations that they think will produce tangible benefits for their political constituencies. They will act as policy entrepreneurs, introducing new policy ideas that mobilize support or bring about realignments that bolster their position.[4]

The literature on policy transfer usually discusses the processes of policy 'bandwagoning' on an international scale by focusing on the many cases where international institutions play an active role in the dissemination of a policy model or programme (using technical assistance, donations and loans). Other cases examine how 'implants' are transferred from one country to another, though the active roles played by certain policy elites, NGO groups and other actors, and in the absence of international multilateral institutions. Much less emphasis is put on domestic processes of policy diffusion and on the incentives politicians have to pursue certain policy models. How do these processes take place *within* a country? What are the political factors that govern the scaling up of programmes? This chapter helps fill this gap through an analysis of Brazil's *Bolsa Escola* programme.

Policy 'lock-in'

A final conceptual point should be made before we proceed. Once in place, a programme creates its own constituency. Public policy is path-dependent: the current portfolio of policies depends very much on the policies of the past. Those policies' beneficiaries, such as bureaucracies and advocacy groups, are the obvious constituencies. This has been highlighted in a number of studies of social policy (see for example Pierson, 1994).

The basic implication for the process of policy diffusion in social policy is that diffusion is not linear. The accompanying 'politics of expansion' is characterized by increasing programme legitimacy and growing support. The resulting political equilibrium can only be transformed by a (frequently exogenous) shock. Once a certain threshold is reached, programme sustainability is somewhat inbuilt in the programme, for better or for worse, just as Merilee Grindle has argued (Chapter 4, this volume).

Background: democracy and antipoverty policies in Brazil

Post-dictatorship Brazil: centripetal and centrifugal forces

Some preliminary information on the context in which antipoverty programmes emerged in Brazil may be helpful. Brazil returned to democracy in 1985 after 20 years of military rule, following a protracted liberalization process that started in the mid-1970s. Unlike other similar regimes in Latin America, the military regime in Brazil did not close Congress, and elections continued to be held at all three levels of government (federal, state and municipal). Thus some electoral competition was allowed within the constraints posed by the purging of political parties and individual politicians' opposition to the regime. The main opposition party, the Party of The Brazilian Democratic Movement (PMDB), was the umbrella organization within which those opposing the military gathered such as president-to-be Fernando Henrique Cardoso. In the late 1970s the PMDB was able to amass critical electoral support and, in conjunction with civil society associations, to negotiate the transition to democracy in the early 1980s through 'transition by transaction'. This culminated in the impressive popular campaign for direct elections in 1984, and the coming into power of a civilian opposition Senator as President in 1985. Following changes in the legislation that allowed the setting up of new political parties, other organizations emerged within the left that were to be critical in the 1990s, such as the Workers' Party (PT)[5] and the Brazilian Social Democratic Party (PSDB), founded by dissidents within the PMDB, including Cardoso himself.

A key episode in the transition to democracy was the drafting of the new Constitution in 1987 and 1988. It encompassed the redesign of many political institutions, and also new social and political rights. In addition, it mandated further decentralization within an already fairly decentralized political system. The basic elements of the political system as it existed before the Military period – the federal structure, presidentialism, bicameralism and electoral institutions – remained intact.

The emerging political system is decentralized and fragmented (Ames, 2001; Samuels, 2003): Brazil's federalism is both robust and unbalanced. The states enjoy great fiscal and political autonomy. Almost half of total public revenue is in the hands of the states and the 5600 municipalities;[6] one third is collected directly by sub-national governments. As a consequence, governors – particularly those of the larger states – are key political players.

After the move to democracy in 1985, the two-party system that operated under military rule gave way to a multiparty system with a very large number of parties. Proportional representation is not the only reason for the fragmented party system. Political parties have not been able to develop strong identities and are not deeply rooted. With a few exceptions, notably the PT, party affiliations are loose. Presidents, governors and mayors are elected by direct vote and have been supported by large coalitions. Under Cardoso, none of the three largest parties held more than 20 percent of the seats in the Chamber of Deputies – not even his own. On the other hand, presidents have strong prerogatives that help them overcome party fragmentation and implement their agendas (Mainwaring, 1999).

In sum, there are both centrifugal and centripetal forces in the Brazilian political system. The centrifugal forces include the electoral laws, sub-national fiscal autonomy, regionalism and regionally based factionalism, weak parties and a fragmented party system. The centripetal forces are the President's constitutional powers and the vast resources available to him or her, and also the internal organization of Congress. The centrifugal forces constrain the ability of Presidents to do what they want, but not quite to the extent of stalemate or gridlock (Melo, 2003).

Electoral competition and political rewards

Coalitional presidentialism in Brazil has an important consequence for political accountability: it blurs the responsibilities of the executives at the three tiers of government and of the partners of the coalitions. Municipalities, state governments and the federal government can all initiate their own policies, although sub-national governments are required to defer to federal initiatives. Thus the federal government may offer funding conditional on the state governments or the municipalities approving the federal rules. When different political forces control different levels of government, there is jockeying over who will get the political reward from a new programme. Thus there is intense competition to be seen as the instigator of popular programmes, as with the cash-transfer schemes.

The 1988 constitution and its effect on policymaking

Understanding policymaking in the area of social policy and poverty alleviation requires an understanding of the 1988 Constitution. It reflects the agenda overload of the new democratic regime, and the dissatisfaction with the way that policy was made centrally and undemocratically under military rule. Thus it devolved administrative autonomy to sub-national governments and conferred new tax powers on the states and municipalities, which also received a larger share of federal tax revenues (10 percent and 15 percent respectively), sometimes in the form of automatic transfers.

The municipalities acquired federal status; Brazil is the only country in the world where this is so. Along with the states, municipalities have become autonomous constituent units of the federation. The constitution also mandated the decentralization of social policy ranging from health through education to social assistance.[7] Furthermore, the Constitution mandated participatory arrangements, with a view to promoting popular control of government (see Cornwall and Shankland, this volume).

The Constitution also stipulates a poverty alleviation role for the state. According to Article 23, poverty alleviation is the joint mandate of the Federal Government, the states and the municipal governments. There are a number of specific provisions of a redistributive nature, including the equalization of rural and urban social security benefits.

However, Brazil's social indicators contrast sharply with the broad reach of its social programmes (Draibe, 2002a; 2002b). Brazil spends some 22 percent of GDP in the social sector – a total of $120 billion at the time of writing, equivalent to a per capita social spending of more than US$1000. Two thirds of that amount goes on pensions, much of it to the better-off. The income transfer programmes are very large by developing country standards and cost 2.5 percent of GDP. The anti-poverty programmes, many of which preceded the Cardoso years, and even the Constitution of 1998 are complex and quite effective. Because of the autonomy enjoyed by municipalities and states, there is intense sub-national experimentation. This also explains a great deal of the complexity of intergovernmental relations in the social sector.

Social policy in the new democracy

Cardoso's political inheritance

The social policies implemented by the Cardoso government have to be viewed against the backdrop of the political agenda it inherited, which had four key elements. The first was the continuation of the Real Plan,[8] whose success had propelled him into the Presidency, and also brought other members of his party into governorships on Cardoso's coattails. The failure of earlier stabilization plans had caused real hardship as well as destabilized the economy. Fiscal matters became if anything ever more important in Cardoso's second term. The run against the Real in late 1998, prompted by the Russian crisis, led to the devaluation of the currency. Thus Cardoso had to reconcile fiscal policy and poverty alleviation.[9]

The second element in Cardoso's political inheritance was the social reform agenda. It included reforms targeted at redeeming what became known as the country's 'social debt'. Redistributive issues and pro-poor policies were prominent, but the agenda also included decentralization, participation and social control. These were encapsulated in the Constitution and in the enabling legislation that accompanied it. They led to the setting up of thousands of sector-specific municipal councils in the 1990s, running the gamut of health care, education, social assistance, urban development, employment and children's rights (the list is not exhaustive) to ensure that the beneficiaries of programmes participated in policymaking.

The third element was the poverty issue, which had galvanized public opinion. The climate of civil solidarity created by the successful campaign for the impeachment of former President Collor spawned a popular mobilization against hunger. Civil society organizations, including religious groups, NGOs and the professional bodies which had participated in the Movement for Ethics in Politics all participated. IBASE, one of Brazil's largest advocacy NGOs[10] which had played a role in the impeachment campaign, led a countrywide campaign to distribute food. This led in turn to the setting up of thousands of local committees for food distribution. Politicians, mainly from the PT, established a Parliamentary Front for Action for Citizenship. IPEA, the Planning Ministry's economic think tank, prepared a 'map of hunger'. The publicity that greeted the map, and the revelation that 32 million people were living in extreme poverty, led the government to declare that the country was in a 'state of social calamity'. A commission was set up to draft a 'national plan for fighting poverty and misery', with members drawn from both government and civil society.

The fourth element was the policy agenda of Cardoso's political competitors, particularly at the sub-national levels, and more particularly still in the municipalities controlled by opposition parties such as the PT and the PSB. Cardoso also had to contend with popular discontent over rising unemployment which the PT exploited, especially during his second term.

Because of these four elements, Cardoso was in no position to make radically new proposals in the social area. Instead, he moved to deepen the processes that were already in motion, introducing limited measures consistent with the broader prevailing line. This is not to say that there was no space for important innovations, as our analysis of the *Bolsa Escola* will show, but that Cardoso was operating in an environment favourable to pro-poor policies and where substantial innovations were already being implemented at both national and sub-national levels.

The *Bolsa Escola*

As we shall see, the *Bolsa Escola* was the outcome of intense of policy competition and emulation between Cardoso and the PT. Both it and the *Bolsa Familia* which succeeded it have been flagship programmes (World Bank, 2004b: 15), with the *Bolsa Familia* seen as a crucial plank in the Lula government's platform for the 2006 presidential election.

Origins and implementation

The *Bolsa Escola* was established by the Cardoso government in 1997. By 2002 it was costing some US$0.8 billion dollars annually and benefiting the 11 million children of five million families, or one in three children between the ages of 7 and 14. The Lula government which came to power in 2003 has built on *Bolsa Escola* by expanding it and fusing it with two other cash-transfer programmes to create the *Bolsa Familia* in 2004.[11] By December 2005, the programme had reached 8.7 million families, benefiting 34 million family members, and the cost had risen to an annual US$2.2 billion.

Despite its flagship status for Cardoso's government, the *Bolsa Escola* was the brainchild of a PT senator, Eduardo Suplicy. Suplicy had presented preliminary proposals for a universal basic income in the late 1980s when he was a Federal Deputy for the state of São Paulo. He was influenced by the ideas of negative income taxation proposed by the

US economist Milton Friedman, as well as similar proposals that were being discussed in a number of countries and by a few individuals in Brazil. His contacts with the Basic Income European Network were particularly influential. Established in 1986, this network had organized seminars on citizens' income as a solution to high unemployment.[12]

When Suplicy was elected Senator he tabled a bill creating a Minimum Income Guarantee Programme. The bill proposed that individuals whose earnings fell below two and a half times the minimum monthly wage would be entitled to a negative income tax. For people in employment, the tax would be equivalent to half the difference between that income threshold and their actual income; for the unemployed it would be equivalent to 30 percent of the difference.

When the bill was discussed in the Senate Committee for Economic Affairs, it was watered down somewhat. It was decided that the 30 percent figure would apply to everyone, and would rise to 50 percent only when the fiscal situation permitted. The programme would also be phased in over a period of eight years. In the first year it would apply only to people over 64 years, in the following year to people over 55, and would only extend to the entire population over 25 in 2000. This dilution allowed the Committee to approve the bill by 77 votes to zero, with four abstentions. All the party leaders praised the bill. Even Cardoso as the leader of the PSDB supported it despite some misgivings, dubbing it a 'realistic utopia'. There was therefore no need to put the bill to a vote in the Chamber of Deputies.

Between 1991 and 1994, the issue of a minimum income began to be discussed in the press and among economists. At a 1991 meeting of economists linked to the PT, a leading poverty economist called José Márcio Camargo argued that a basic income by itself would have a purely short-term distributive effect, but no impact on productivity or intergenerational poverty. He therefore proposed making it conditional on school attendance, even though this would mean the exclusion of poor families who were childless. During the presidential campaign of 1994, Suplicy, who was close to the PT economists' group, managed to get the proposal added in this modified form to the Workers' Party Action Plan. By 1998 it had gathered sufficient momentum to be included in the Party Platform.[13]

At the outset, Suplicy's crusade, conducted with his characteristic panache, was seen as eccentric and utopian. With the link to education and the economists' blessing, however, policymakers began to take it seriously. In the new democratic climate, the potential political dividend could not be ignored. The modified and phased *Bolsa Escola* proposal passed into law in 1997, with a further modification in 2001.

Income-transfer programmes at municipal level

Campinas had been the first municipality to implement a basic income programme, as early as 1994. Campinas became the laboratory for many experiments which the Cardoso government subsequently extended to the federal level, and many of its officials were later appointed to key positions in the federal *Bolsa Escola* and other related programmes. The Mayor, Magalhães Teixeira (alias Grama), formerly a federal deputy and co-founder of PSDB with Cardoso, called on his aides to set up this programme. His former Coordinator for Social Policy recalls:

> Grama called me on a Saturday in August 1994 and said, 'Come to my house because Senator Suplicy is coming to visit me and we are going to implement his proposal for minimum income here. Campinas is going to be the first city to have this kind of programme.'[14]

The Mayor asked his advisors to prepare a bill providing for 1 percent of the Municipality's revenue to be earmarked for a Minimum Income Guarantee Scheme. The bill reached the Municipal Chamber on a Monday and was approved three days later. PT councillors opposed the bill in the first vote, but swayed by Suplicy's endorsement they supported it in the second vote.[15] The bill established the principle that every family with an income below half the minimum wage and with children under 14 at school would have the right to a monthly income supplement equivalent to 50 percent of the minimum wage, subject to prior residence in Campinas of at least two years (because the cost of extending the scheme to all of the 3700 families who would otherwise have qualified would have far outstripped the magic 1 percent figure).[16]

At the same time that the programme was being established in Campinas, the PT governor of Brasília, Cristovão Buarque, created a similar scheme. During the electoral campaign in 1994, he had promised to implement a minimum income scheme if he won the election. It was duly launched in January 1995, and immediately attracted more attention than it had in Campinas. Brasilia is the capital, and the governor himself was a prominent political figure and intellectual. In Brasilia, the residence requirement was five years and the age range covered was from 7 to 14. The programme reached 50,000 children at its peak. Other mid-sized cities followed suit, and so did large metropolises such as Belo Horizonte. By the end of the first Cardoso government in 1998, 60 Brazilian municipalities and four states were implementing minimum income programmes conditional on school attendance.[17]

Income transfers at federal level: policy competition as a driving force

Meanwhile at federal level, six proposals for conditional income transfers were tabled in Congress in 1995 and 1996. In the atmosphere of intense political competition which led up to the general elections of November 1998, Cardoso grew convinced that his government had to respond, and his party tabled a bill of its own, which became Law 9.533 in December 1997. It authorized the Federal Government to transfer funds to municipalities whose tax revenue and per capita family incomes were both below the average for the states in which they were located. Families with per capita monthly income below 50 percent of the minimum wage and with children under 14 attending school would be entitled to a fixed stipend. The measure was to be phased in over five years. In the first year, only 20 percent of the municipalities with the worst indicators would be covered; in the next, an additional 20 percent would qualify; and so on until every municipality was covered.

The very day after Cardoso sanctioned Law 9.533, Suplicy submitted a bill increasing the value of the benefit. Once again, the timing reflects the intense political competition around the issue. The Senate approved the bill, but before the Chamber could discuss it, Cardoso submitted his own bill extending the benefits to all Brazilian municipalities, and when it was enacted he called it the 'Law Magalhães Teixeira' in honour of 'Grama', the by now deceased Mayor and income-transfer pioneer who was also a prominent PSDB member.

Thus we see the importance of policy competition driven by a combination of electoral incentives and genuine commitment to alleviating poverty. There was competition at every level, with governors and mayors all claiming to be the first to introduce the scheme, and with municipalities and states, particularly those governed by opposition parties, ratcheting its value upwards. At state level, Rio de Janeiro was followed in quick succession by Amapá, Goiás and Ceará. Indeed the political momentum became unstoppable. By 2002, 95 percent of municipalities had an income transfer scheme, from which 4.5 million families, or almost 30 million people, were benefiting at a cost of

1.7 billion reais. By 2004, just before the incoming Lula administration launched the *Bolsa Familia*, there were only 48 out of Brazil's 5512 municipalities which did not have a scheme.

Direct transfer as an innovative element

Perhaps the scheme's most innovative aspect of the programme was the way it operated. Mothers (or fathers in the absence of a mother) were given a bank card from the state-owned National Savings Bank which they could use to withdraw money as long as they could provide evidence that their children had an 85 percent school attendance. The age bracket was extended to children aged 6 to 15. Families with children in the new age bracket and with per capita income falling below half the minimum wage would be entitled to R$15, 30 or 45 per month, depending on the number of children.

Because there were no intermediaries, the likelihood of the money actually reaching the families was high. In the scheme introduced in 1997, the money had been allocated to the municipalities, creating the possibility of misappropriation or diversion: local elites have in fact often favoured social programmes because they were able to benefit corruptly from them. This innovation reduced their ability to do that (although it did not remove it altogether: the scheme has still suffered from some local manipulation).

Cash-transfer programmes in other sectors

The implementation of the federal *Bolsa Escola* by the Ministry of Education also prompted the setting up of similar programmes in other sectors. The most important of them was the *Bolsa Alimentação* in the Ministry of Health. We have seen that the *Bolsa Escola* was restricted to families with children between 7 and 14. The *Bolsa Alimentação* ('nutrition scholarship') was designed to reduce nutritional deficiencies in younger children and infant mortality among the poorest households. It provided for money transfers to very low income families from initial pregnancy up to the age of 6. Once again the cash transfer was conditional, this time on women committing themselves to a 'Charter of Responsibilities' which included regular attendance at prenatal care clinics, growth monitoring, compliance with vaccination schedules and health education. It was hoped that this would increase poor families' use of local health services.

Once again also, the creation of the *Bolsa Alimentação* was marked by political competition, this time between the Education and Health ministers, Paulo Renato and José Serra, who were vying to become the presidential candidate of Cardoso's coalition in the presidential election of 2002 (since the Constitution did not allow Cardoso to run for office for a third time). In fact, key informants believed that Serra's *Bolsa Alimentação* was his direct response to the potential threat posed by Renato's huge success with the *Bolsa Escola*.[18]

Cash transfers under Lula

As already mentioned, the *Bolsa Escola* survived the transition to the Lula government. The cash-transfer programmes were much debated during the presidential campaign. In fact, the centerpiece of Lula's platform was his plan to eliminate hunger in the country while maintaining fiscal stability, which he advertised in various ways, including a Letter to the Brazilian People during the election campaign and by holding his first ministerial meeting in a small town in one of Brazil's poorest areas.

More concretely, upon taking office he announced the creation of a new *Ministério Extraordinário para a Segurança Alimentar e Combate a Fome*, or *MESA* (Special Ministry for Food Security and the Fight Against Hunger). The showpiece of this flagship policy was the *Fome Zero* programme. In it, municipalities with very low Human Development Index ratings were to be selected as priorities, and households with per capita income of less than half the minimum wage would receive a food bonus of equivalent to US$18 through the medium of a *Cartão Alimentação*, a debit card that they could use in registered shops.

But ten months after its announcement, the programme had not been properly implemented, in the face of criticisms from policy experts, NGOs and others. It was stigmatized as *'assistencialista'* (paternalist), modeled on failed food coupons schemes in the US: poor people were not free to decide how to use their money. There were also technical flaws. The requirement for families to produce evidence that they had used the money to buy food from registered shops was very difficult to implement. Moreover, there was the potential for fraud, and for the development of a market for the food cards.

Faced with this overwhelming criticism, the government dismissed the *Fome Zero* mentor José Graziano and created a new 'super ministry' for the social sectors – the *Ministério para o Desenvolvimento Social e Combate à Fome* (Ministry for Social Development and the Fight Against Hunger). At the same time, the government decided to introduce a single card, the *Cartão Família,* bringing together food benefit and three other conditional income transfers. Yet again these benefits were to be conditional on evidence of vaccination, school attendance etc.

Thus the government abandoned its piecemeal initiatives and moved to consolidate the cash-transfer programmes inherited from Cardoso. Those programmes had been fragmented, with the *Bolsa Escola* in the Ministry of Education, the *Bolsa Alimentação* under the Health Ministry and a gas benefit which came under the Ministry of Energy. The idea of a single card or *Bolsa* wasn't new: in 2001, the Cardoso government was already developing a *Caixa Econômica Federal* (National Savings Bank) as the operational arm for its cash transfers, and was working on a unified Registry of social programmes (*Cadastro Único*) (FAO, World Bank and IDB, 2002).

Taxing for the poor

The success of both the *Bolsa Escola* and the *Bolsa Familia* depended on the existence of the *Fundo de Combate à Pobreza* (Fund for Fighting Poverty). Following the intense mobilization around poverty alleviation in the early- and mid-1990s, no fewer than 98 related legislative proposals were tabled in the Chamber and the Senate. In line with the pattern we have seen already in this chapter, Conservative and opposition politicians fought fiercely for the authorship of the proposals, using the Special Committee set up by Congress to examine the issue of poverty alleviation as their battleground. (The Committee also became a forum for opposition politicians to criticize Cardoso's policies in general, and his macroeconomic policy in particular.) It was this committee which prepared the constitutional amendment that created the Fund for Fighting Poverty.

The draft amendment had contained a provision for taxing individual wealth and assets, originally proposed by Cardoso while he was still a senator. What became Constitutional Amendment 31, however, was a compromise in which the absence of the provision was justified by reference to parallel discussion of a separate tax reform proposal, which envisaged raising the rate of an existing tax such as the tax on financial transactions. That tax had been introduced in 1993 by a 'sunset clause' in the constitution which was to operate for only two years. The government proposed to extend it for three more years. When the extension was put to a vote again in 1999, the government used the opportunity to find money for its new Poverty Fund. The compromise solution, therefore, was that the government agreed to endorse the Fund bill as long as the tax on financial transactions was renewed. The government then supported the Special Committee's proposal and accepted that an increase in the tax rate would be earmarked for the fund.

Constitutional amendment 12/1996 created a new version of the tax on financial transactions, at a rate of 0.25 percent. Initially valid for two years, Constitutional Amendment 21 extended it for three more years. The rate was raised to 0.38 percent, with a provision that if the annual proceeds did not reach 4 billion reais, the national government would make up the difference from general tax revenue. As it was the President of the Senate, Antônio Carlos Magalhães, who submitted the final proposal (approved as Constitutional Amendment 31), it was his party, the PFL, that got most of the political credit, even though the Amendment was the fruit of the Committee's joint work.

It should be noted that nothing resembling all this appeared in Magalhães's original proposal. The Cardoso government approved the constitutional amendment and extended the duration of the tax by an additional two years. Because the fund would now last for ten years, further extensions would be locked in. This attempt to cement the budget for poverty alleviation should be understood as part of the logrolling or trade-off between the executive and legislative branches. The executive maintained fiscal stability by increasing taxes and, in return, Congress received some poverty alleviation programmes protected from discretionary executive budget cuts.[19]

To fully understand Cardoso's tactics we need to emphasize how Cardoso used the PFL party's pressure to create the fund. Politicians wanted to be associated with the proposal because of its obvious electoral dividends, Cardoso no less than anyone else. But Cardoso faced resistance from his financial and planning advisors, as well as the fiscal constraints imposed by the agreement with the IMF which was then in force. His solution was to let his coalition have the authorship of the proposal while at the same time blaming his partners for making him do it. As Maria Helena Castro, a top social policy advisor with the Government, observed:

> (Cardoso)'s astuteness as a political negotiator was that he threw (the proposal for the fund) at the PFL as a message for the economic policy-makers. He wanted the fund, but the economic policy group did not. So in order not to create a conflict, and to placate the animosities, he became the trapeze artist and the manager of a political game in which he himself ... was in favour of one solution.

> He knew that it was the only way to do a lot of things ...The Fund for Fighting Poverty was strategic for (Cardoso). He was in his second term, and the economic restrictions on him were very severe. He started in the middle of a crisis, which led to a second crisis, and so on and so forth. The only way he could do something for the future different from the Real Plan – which was a great achievement of his presidency – was to find some new money. And where could he go for that? Thus I am convinced that all this was his personal political calculation.[20]

In short, pressures from Cardoso's coalition partner, the PFL, from sub-national interests linked to the governing coalition and from the coalition's political rival, the PT, all combined to prompt the government to create a funding mechanism for the scaling up of the municipal programmes.

The successful diffusion and scaling up of *Bolsa Escola*

Five factors explain the successful diffusion of *Bolsa Escola*. The first is the imperative for politicians at every level to claim the credit for it. It was incessantly cited by the PT and the PSDB as a key solidarity element in their party platforms, and the parties trumpeted the number of municipalities which they governed which were implementing it. In many municipalities, such as Sao Paulo and Belo Horizonte, the mayor refused the Federal Government aid for the programme, claiming that the administration could afford a more generous benefit. It is hard to see how the programme could have been scaled up in the way it was in the absence of such intense policy competition. If the ability to articulate the preferences of a majority is a crucial part of political leadership, as we argued at the outset that it is, then it can be argued that while Suplicy, drawing from the international marketplace of innovative ideas, was the instigator of the cash-transfer schemes, his success still depended on an already existing consensus on the need to combat poverty.

It is in keeping with our argument that the experience of other programmes of conditional cash transfer such as Mexico's 'Oportunidades' (formerly called 'Progresa'), the world's first large-scale cash-transfer programme introduced in 1997, do not seem to have influenced the creation of the *Bolsa Escola*. Unlike 'Progresa', which was the brainchild of an economics professor from Boston University and was taken up by the Zedillo administration, *Bolsa Escola* was the result of a bottom-up process of policy formation driven by political competition and policy emulation rather than a top-down proposal from national policy elites.

Second, the policy diffusion did not come from outside. As a programme that was scaled up from experiments at the municipal and state levels, it was not influenced by external actors such as the multilateral institutions. The Word Bank provided loans for the programme, but only when it was already established and had a stable source of funding.[21]

Third, a condition for the success of conditional cash-transfer schemes is that there has to be a consensus on their desirability. This was achieved in Brazil by the intense popular mobilization around the issue of poverty. The Action for Combating Hunger provided its point of departure. The consensus was also part of the broader process of democratization, a process in which the 'social debt' of the country was widely debated. That debate in turn created a market for ideas for combating poverty which came to be dominated by the initiatives of the two modern political forces, the PT and the PSDB. In this context, populist and traditional clientelistic schemes lost their appeal. An example of this is the gubernatorial race in the impoverished state of Piaui when, in a highly publicized episode, the PFL candidate registered in a public notary his pledge to maintain the *Bolsa Escola* that had been implemented by his opponent. Further evidence of the consensus comes in the number of editorials that appeared in 1999 in the country's most important newspapers, even those that supported the government, condemning the newly elected governor of Brasilia for discontinuing the programme in the nation's capital.

Fourth, federal involvement was a result not only of the identification of sub-national initiatives with the PT and PSDB, but also of the strategic interaction of municipalities in the 'policy emulation game'. This competition generated externalities in the form of the welfare 'magnet effect' identified by Peterson and Rom (1990) in the US. Successful programmes attracted a lot of attention and created the need to introduce barriers to entry such as residence requirements for potential beneficiaries. These barriers represented a political cost, since they ran counter to the programmes' inclusive philosophy. These welfare 'magnets' also faced tremendous fiscal problems, which only the participation of the federal government allowed the municipalities to overcome.

Fifth, once in place, the *Bolsa Escola* created its own constituency. As suggested by Pierson (1994) and Grindle (Chapter 4, this volume), in programmes like these beneficiaries tend to use their political influence to lock the benefits in place, or even extend them if they can. In Brazil's competitive electoral environment described in this chapter, beneficiaries used elections to do this. The backlash against *Fome Zero* can be explained by the pressures from its beneficiaries and from the policy elites and bureaucracies associated with it.

Conclusion: political competition can be positive

Although the successful diffusion and scaling up of the *Bolsa Escola* cannot be attributed solely to the political competition between the two leading political forces and their coalitions' allies, this chapter has shown that it was the main driving force behind the 'bandwagoning' of a successful policy model, with the public consensus on the need to fight poverty as an important precondition.[22] Contrary to the received wisdom about electoral politics in new democracies, electoral incentives encouraged politicians to offer inclusive programmes with the characteristics of public goods. The public consensus also reduced the political cost of funding the programme, of ensuring cooperation from stakeholders and overcoming resistance from traditional elites. The backlash at the beginning of the Lula government against the planned change in the *Bolsa Escola* model and its replacement by a food coupon scheme, and the subsequent expansion and continuation of the programme under the *Bolsa Familia* label suggest that the programme has generated a large and stable political support base.

To what extent are these specific findings generalizable to other countries? We must be cautious here. They are probably most relevant to understanding policy processes in new federal democracies where there is intense political competition. More research is needed to establish their validity in increasingly decentralized political systems elsewhere in the world. Nonetheless, the general claim which we made in the introduction to this chapter, that the political survival imperative drives public policy decisions, is of a more universal nature. We hope that our analysis has given some substance to that claim.

Notes

1 Cf. World Bank (2004b: 26). *Bolsa Escola* has become the flagship programme of both the Cardoso (1995–2002) and Lula (2003–) governments, in the latter case through its successor, the *Bolsa Familia*.

2 That said, some merely involve the expansion of coverage, creating a win-win situation, a process described by Nelson (2000) as the 'politics of expansion'.

3 Because taxpayers tend not to mobilize against escalating taxation, the resistance usually comes from the financial and planning ministries as well as the central bank.
4 A strategy that Riker (1986) calls *herestethics*.
5 Other small leftist parties included the Communist Parties (PCB and PC do B) and the socialists (PSB).
6 Municipalities in Brazil cover both urban and rural territories.
7 Cf. Melo and Rezende (2004). See also the essays in Coelho *et al.* (2005).
8 Cardoso proposed the Real Plan in July 1994 while holding the post of finance minister in the Franco government. The Plan was the only one out of several attempts in the late 80s and early 90s to eradicate hyperinflation.
9 Although the World Bank and IADB have extensive lending operations in Brazil which are highly diversified across the social sectors, Brazil is not dependent on financing from these institutions because of the extensive funding mechanisms set up for the social sectors. 80 percent of the Brazilian budget is earmarked for the social sectors, mostly in the form of pensions. About half of the federal revenue comes from the so-called 'social contributions': payroll taxes collected from employers and employees, turnover tax and profit taxes paid by firms (Cofins and CSLL) and a tax on financial transactions.
10 The leader of IBASE, Betinho, hit the international headlines because of his campaign against hunger. The campaign led to the establishment of Hunger committees throughout the country.
11 The *Bolsa Familia* at the time of writing was an overarching welfare reform programme that will consolidate numerous smaller programmes to become the largest cash-transfer programme internationally, both in terms of coverage and financing (Rawlings, 2004).
12 Suplicy attributes the original idea to a colleague from the Getulio Vargas Foundation Economic Department, Antonio Maria da Silveira.
13 Suplicy (2002: 130). A radical wing within the Party opposed the motion.
14 Maria Helena Guimarães de Castro (interview with the author, 2003).
15 For Suplicy's account of these developments, see Suplicy (2002: 125–6).
16 Maria Helena Guimarães de Castro (interview).
17 World Bank Brazil (2001). The states were Amapá. Amazonas, Tocantins and Distrito Federal.
18 Interviews with Sergio Tiezzi, Maria Helena Castro and Gilda Portugal, and with Gildea Gouvea.
19 The amendment prohibits the *desvinculação* (withdrawal of earmarking) of the fund's resources.
20 This interpretation was also endorsed in our interviews by other key players, namely Vilmar Faria, Gilda Portugal and Maria Helena Castro.
21 The World Bank provided a loan of U$512 million in 2004, which was estimated to account for 10 percent of the expected expenditures of the project. In turn, IADB provided US$1 billion, also in 2004.
22 Thus 'bandwagoning' may help explain why, in the words of the saying and at least where development policy is concerned, 'success has many fathers but failure is an orphan.'

3
Managing the Indonesian Economy: Good Policies, Weak Institutions

Bert Hofman, Ella R. Gudwin and Kian Wie Thee[1]

> *The tragedy of...the New Order is that political and institutional developments were not tackled while there were the opportunity and resources to do so.* (Dick, 2002: 214)

Introduction

Soeharto's *New Order* government produced a remarkable three decades of rapid growth. From 1967 to 1997, Indonesia's GDP grew by an average of 7 percent per annum and by 1995 Indonesia's per capita income had grown to over four times the 1967 level, reaching $1100 (Booth, 2002). The number of people living in poverty declined from over 60 percent of the population in 1965 to 11 percent in 1996, while social indicators demonstrated impressive gains. Indonesia was, in short, a dramatic development success in all the senses outlined in Chapter 1: policies achieved their desired goals; enhanced human capabilities along the way; were (in its earlier decades at least) the products of a state deemed legitimate in many eyes; and produced sustained effects over the years. Indonesia's economic success resulted from a pragmatic approach to economic management, with a group of technocrats shaping macroeconomic policies that coalesced with specific strategies for other sectors. In 1993, the World Bank (1993a) named Indonesia among the High Performing Asian Economies (HPAEs). Although critics pointed to the weak financial sector, lack of rule of law and rising corruption as factors that could undermine the country's success, it was, as one observer remarked, 'hard to argue with 7 percent growth.'[2]

The widespread praise for Indonesia's success made the shock of the country's economic crisis all the larger. In July 1997, contagion from the Thai Baht triggered a currency crisis in Indonesia, which rapidly turned into a financial crisis, an economic crisis and then a political crisis. GDP plunged by 14 percent, poverty doubled to almost 28 percent of the population at the height of the crisis, inflation peaked at 80 percent, and much of the banking system and corporate Indonesia fell into bankruptcy. In May mass demonstrations calling for *reformasi* (reform) forced President Soeharto to resign. In 1999, his successor, Vice President BJ Habibbie, gave way to the first democratically elected president, Megawati Soekarnoputri. It took Indonesia seven years to regain pre-crisis levels of GDP. By 2004, GDP per capita still hovered below 1997 levels, while the 50 percent of GDP in government debt needed to recapitalize the banking system will be a fiscal burden for the foreseeable future. At the end of 2003, more than six years after the onset of the Asian Crisis, Indonesia was the last of the former crisis countries to graduate from the IMF supported stabilization programme.

Since the 1997 Asian Economic Crisis, political scientists and economists have commented on the ways in which weak institutions – economic, political and legal – contributed to the collapse of Indonesia's miracle growth and underpinned its haphazard recovery. A common refrain is that the economic crisis revealed weaknesses in Indonesia's institutions that had been disguised by, or ignored in light of, rapid rates of growth. While studies of cross panel data demonstrate that institutions dominate everything else in explaining growth (Rodrik *et al.*, 2004),[3] this finding does not seem to fit the Indonesian experience. In contrast, Indonesia demonstrated high rates of growth for decades, despite its weak institutions. Additionally, the Indonesian experience only partially correlates with Rodrik's (1999) conclusion that countries with weak institutions (and ethnically diverse population and relatively unequal income distribution) do not manage economic crisis as well as those with strong ones. Soeharto's administration adeptly managed several other crises in years prior again, despite its weak institutions, or some would argue because of them. The economic crisis of the mid-1960s, the 1975 Pertamina crisis and the economic crises in the early 1980s after the oil price collapse were managed in an exemplary manner, with the implementation of swift measures to restore macroeconomic balance and structural reforms to rekindle growth. The absence of organized political opposition, concentration of powers in the hands of the president, a weak civil service unable to defend its vested interests and a business community closely aligned with political powers all enabled swift implementation of good policies. The absence of an ideological debate and the dire economic conditions after Soekarno left office in 1966 may also have contributed to the pragmatic economic policies implemented in the Soeharto era.[4]

What had changed by the 1990s were the complexity of the economy, the external environment and the nature of the Soeharto regime. The reforms of the 1980s had made Indonesia a much more diversified, private-sector-led economy with a rapidly developing financial sector. These required a stronger legal system and new supervisory institutions both of which were lacking. A surge in international capital flows had rendered two cornerstones of Indonesia's macroeconomic policy inappropriate for maintaining economic stability. The managed exchange rate (a soft peg to the US dollar) combined with an extremely open capital account encouraged firms to borrow abroad, and left the currency vulnerable to speculative attacks. But perhaps most important was the change in the nature of the regime, which had become increasingly prone to corruption, undermining the legitimacy of the regime and the credibility of its policies, a feature of paramount importance in the 'modern' capital account crises of the 1990s. Indeed the issue of governance coloured the perception of how Indonesia would manage the crisis, and the lack of confidence that this created appears to account for why Indonesia was hit hardest among all the other countries affected by the Asian financial crisis (World Bank, 1998b: 1.10 and 1.11).

Indonesia's institutions are not solely an artifact of the New Order period – weaknesses date back to colonial and even pre-colonial times. Before Soeharto, President Soekarno had already started to undermine the political institutions and the judiciary at a time when these had only just emerged from the Dutch colonial regime. The colonial regime itself had stymied political development, built little in terms of an indigenous civil service[5] and left large parts of judicial administration to traditional leaders rather than courts. Furthermore, corruption in both the Dutch and indigenous civil service had been a permanent fixture during the colonial administration, and is argued by many to have led to the collapse of the once-ruling Dutch East India Company at the end of the 18th century. Increasingly, these deep roots of institutions – including population density in colonies and land distribution at early statehood – are recognized as being important, if not decisive for development trajectories (see Hoff, 2003: 205ff. for a recent survey).

This chapter proceeds as follows. After a brief description of Indonesia's 'growth miracle' – it explores characteristics of the economic policies and institutions that underwrote this 'miracle'. It then examines the institutional and political trends that began to undermine this success and ultimately underpinned the 1997 crisis. It concludes by drawing out lessons regarding the processes through which development success can be sustained over time. These lessons complement several of those in both the introductory chapter and Grindle's discussion of good policies that turn bad.

Indonesia's growth miracle

Soeharto's *New Order* government, which took over from Soekarno in 1966 after the abortive September 30th 1965 coup, inherited an economy in crisis. Soekarno's *Guided Democracy and Guided Economy* had focused on political development, nationalized the extensive remaining Dutch economic interests in 1958 and spent an unsustainable sum on military conflicts. Consequently, chronic budget deficits financed by the central bank had driven inflation up to over 600 percent by the mid-1960s, the black market premium on the Rupiah had skyrocketed to 800 percent, the country had defaulted on its international debt and growth had come to a halt.

From these ruins, Soeharto's reign built an Indonesia that grew on average to 7 percent per year over the next 30 years. The level as well as the quality of Indonesia's growth was impressive. A considerable part of this growth can be explained by increases in productivity (Table 3.1),[6] as the country moved from a predominantly agricultural to a more industrialized production base. The wealth of the oil boom was in part invested in a vast expansion of the education and health system during the 1970s and 1980s and the resulting increase in years of schooling in the labour force further contributed to growth.

The structure of the economy experienced rapid change. Although agriculture, services and manufacturing all showed steady growth, that of manufacturing far outpaced the others. The share of agriculture declined from an estimated 51 percent in 1960 to 17 percent by 1997, whereas the share of industry rose from 28 to 42 percent.

Growth benefited a broad range of the population. Per capita income grew from $817 to $3346 in PPP dollars from 1965 to 1995 – an annual average growth rate of 4.4 percent. Poverty, which had affected the majority of the population in the mid-1960s, fell to 11 percent by 1996 (Figure 3.1), and a wide range of human development indicators saw impressive progress. The income of the bottom 20 percent income earners by and large grew at the same pace as overall income (Timmer, 2004) making Indonesia's growth highly pro-poor. Even during the high growth years Indonesia's (expenditure) Gini Index rose only slightly from 0.32 in 1987 to 0.36 in 1996,[7] indicating that by international standards, Indonesia's income distribution was and remained moderately equal (although there is significant doubt about these income distribution numbers, which come from Indonesia's Central Bureau of Statistics). In the mid-1990s Indonesia's per capita income level reached $1100 and in 1995 the number of inhabitants living on $1 a day had declined to 21.9 million from 87.2 million in 1970. In 1996 15.7 percent of the population fell below the poverty line, down from an estimated 40.4 percent in 1976 and a probable over 70 percent in the mid-1960s (Booth, 1998: 128).

Table 3.1 Indonesia growth accounting

	1961–2000	1961–1970	1971–1980	1981–1990	1990–1997
GDP growth	5.5	4.0	7.6	6.2	7.4
Capital stock	1.2	–1.9	2.0	2.7	2.9
Labour force	1.8	1.4	1.9	2.0	1.9
Years of schooling	0.6	0.9	0.6	0.2	0.6
TFP	1.9	3.6	3.2	1.2	2.0

Source: World Bank staff estimates based on Summers and Heston, GDP Data, and Barro.

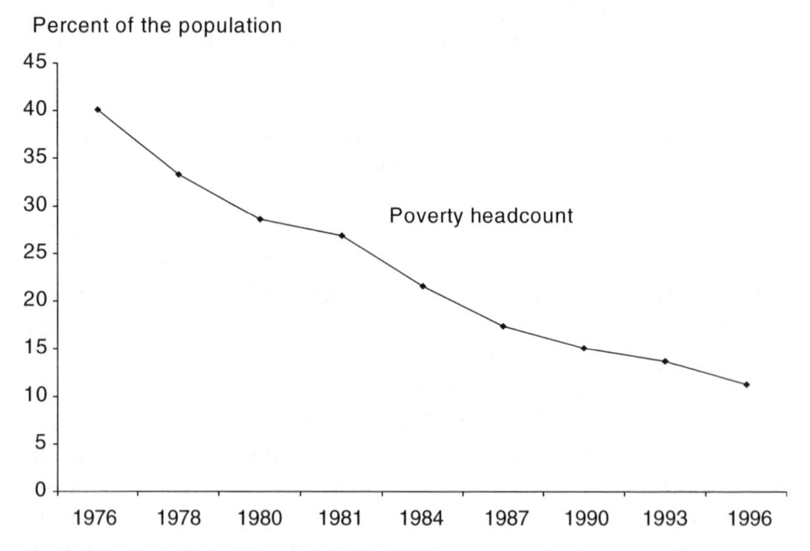

Figure 3.1 Poverty headcount, 1976–1996
Source: World Development Indicators.

Table 3.2 Indonesia social indicators

	1970	1980	1990	2000
Adult literacy	57	70	80	87
Primary school enrolment	80	107	112	110
Secondary school enrolment	16.1	29.1	44.0	57
Life expectancy	47.9	54.8	61.7	66
Infant mortality (per 000 births)	118.0	90.0	60.0	40.9
Population growth rate	2.1	2.0	1.8	1.4

Indonesia's social development was almost as impressive as the country's growth record (Table 3.2). Booming oil revenues in the 1970s financed large increase in government expenditures on new health and education systems, with substantial gains in infant mortality and primary school enrollment levels. While some social indicators, notably maternal mortality were lagging, and increasingly the quality of education became an issue in the 1990s (World Bank, 2003a), these indicators remain impressive.

Economic policies and institutions

Indonesia's success was built on a combination of policies that set the macroeconomic and structural conditions for rapid growth, while linking the poor rural population with that rapid growth by investment in infrastructure, agriculture, education and health (Hofman *et al.*, 2004; Timmer, 2004). While the core macroeconomic policies were by and large 'orthodox' these were supported by agricultural policies and industrial policies that were far less so. In times of macroeconomic difficulties, the microeconomic policies pursued were by and large aimed at liberalization – which was duly rewarded with renewed growth. But microeconomic policies deteriorated in times of relative macroeconomic stability, and by the 1990s increasingly fell victim to the crony capitalism of the first family and their affiliates.

The policies that created the New Order economic miracle were in large parts designed by a select group of economists from the University of Indonesia that became known as the 'technocrats.'[8] Throughout the New Order, with ebbs and flows, this group of people and their affiliates were able to determine key features of economic policy in relative isolation from day-to-day politics. They earned their reputation from the first years of the Soeharto presidency, as their '3 October' 1966 plan rapidly stabilized the economy and delivered growth.[9] All this is in keeping with the role played by their regional counterparts:

> Each (of the HPAEs) boasts at least a small ideologically consistent technocratic core that answers directly to the top leaders and therefore has some independence from the legislature and other sources of political pressures. (World Bank, 1993a: 170)

A key vehicle for the technocrats was the strong planning agency, Badan Perencanaan Nasional, or *Bappenas*. Key tools, notably the 25-year plan, the five-year plan and the annual budget – legitimized by the *GBHM* or 'Broad Guidelines on Government Policies' issued by the MPR, the highest constitutional body – provided a strong framework for development planning and finance. And through a Monetary Board fiscal, monetary and external borrowing policies were coordinated, and targeted at development. All these institutions were dominated by the technocrats for most of Soeharto's reign.

The influence of the technocrats was, however, repeatedly undermined by others, including the 'technologists' who saw aggressive industrial policy based on increasingly high technology projects as the best way to develop Indonesia, army generals who provided the political backbone of the Soeharto regime and who were long accustomed to arbitrary rent-seeking behavior in their business dealings (Elson, 2001: 151) and the 'cronies' who increasingly used the state for personal gains. 'In times of economic distress ... [the technocrats] have enjoyed a broad mandate to determine policies. At other times, their influence has been more restricted' (Schwarz, 1994: 52), although the technocrats did hold influential economic policy posts since the early days of the New Order – and some remained economic advisors to President Wahid and President Megawati Soekarnoputri.

Macroeconomic policies

Given the hyperinflation during the latter days of Soekarno, New Order economic policies focused on restoring and maintaining macroeconomic stability. During the 1967–1970 stabilization period, several core institutions of economic management were to be established that lasted throughout the New Order, including an open capital account, a competitive exchange rate and a balanced budget rule.

A key institution of fiscal restraint was the Balanced Budget rule. This was announced in December 1966 with the statement that the government's expenditures would be limited by the state's revenues, so that the deficit could be eliminated 'as much as possible' (Prawiro, 1998: 17 and 23–34). This rule effectively limited deficits to those that could be financed by foreign borrowing from the IGGI donors. Donor financing was substantial, accounting for over 30 percent of government expenditures in 1967, and gradually declining to 24 percent by 1970 (Woo *et al.*, 1994: 47). Throughout the Soeharto years the government was careful to demonstrate compliance with the balanced budget rule. However, over the years the practice of off-budget spending became increasingly prominent as a means of covertly circumventing the constraints of a balanced budget without tripping alarms (Macintyre, 2002: 159; Nasution, 1995: 4–5).

A further strong restraint on government macroeconomic policies came from its external policies. Over the course of 1967–71, Indonesia moved to a unified, fully convertible fixed exchange rate, with only limited capital controls – a first in the developing world (Cole and Slade, 1996; Prawiro, 1998; World Bank, 1968). This exchange arrangement not only assured foreign investors that they would be able to repatriate their earnings, but also became a disciplining device on the government's macroeconomic policies: policy mistakes would (and sometimes did) trigger capital outflow, and therefore urged for a correction. Abolition of exchange controls also gave a strong boost to exports, which showed growth of about 10 percent per year during the stabilization years 1966–1970, and grew more rapidly than GDP for most of the New Order period.

A final tool in macroeconomic management was the exchange rate. Unlike other countries that held off devaluations until considerable loss of foreign reserves had occurred, Indonesia used this tool in a timely manner, and even preventively. Regular exchange rate adjustments also prevented Indonesia – unlike other oil producers – from falling victim to the 'Dutch Disease,' where large natural resource receipts make a country's tradable sector uncompetitive. Between 1986 and 1997 Indonesia followed a crawling peg regime that by and large neutralized the effects of domestic inflation on the country's competitive position. Given the importance of the tradable goods sector in Indonesia's economy and the fact that devaluation benefits this sector, these policies encountered little opposition. Furthermore, the distribution of tradable goods producers – notably farmers and natural resource producers – in rural areas and Indonesia's outer islands, also helped maintain regional and urban/rural balance in the distribution of growth benefits.

Agricultural policies

Agricultural (in particular rice) policies of the New Order government were central to poverty alleviation and political stabilization. Far from being orthodox, these policies relied on subsidies for rice production, market intervention and investment in agricultural infrastructure that linked the rural hinterland with a rapidly growing modern economy. As rice is the staple for most Indonesians, its price and availability were vital in maintaining overall price stability as well as political stability, particularly in a context in which the New Order government's hold on power remained fragile (Hill, 1996: 123, 128), and support for the communist party in the countryside had been significant.

Policies combined agricultural intensification and interventions in both the rice and inputs markets. *Bulog* (the Food Logistics Agency) defended producer rice prices through government purchases, and consumer rice prices through injecting stored or imported rice supplies into domestic markets when shortages caused the price of rice to rise excessively. This required large and ongoing subsidies from the government budget and through the credit system, but in general Bulog was successful in maintaining appropriate rice prices (Pearson and Monke, 1991: 2–3). Rice policy was also closely related to the government's efforts at fostering production increases through provision of subsidized inputs (High Yield Varieties, fertilizer and pesticides), credits and information. Fertilizer distribution was partially turned over to the private sector, which was obliged to sell at a stipulated ceiling price (Timmer, 1981: 38). By setting a national fertilizer price ceiling, it became possible to set a national floor price for rice (Timmer, 1981: 38).

During the first half of the 1980s rice output grew rapidly (Figure 3.2) as a result of good weather and the rapid spread of 'green revolution' technology. Between 1975 and 1985 the share of farmers using new High Yield Varieties rose from 50 to 85 percent. Indeed, yield increases accounted for 71 percent of output growth in irrigated rice fields in Indonesia during the period 1971/75 through 1981/85 (Booth, 1988: 39–41). Extensive government investment in irrigation, made possible by vastly increased oil revenues, facilitated area expansion and rice intensification. The oil boom of the 1970s also enabled the government to make large investments in the improvement and expansion of infrastructure, including roads, transport and communications facilities, grain storage facilities and fertilizer plants (Tabor, 1992: 172–3). These investments allowed for increases in the farm gate prices without undue increases in the consumer price. Investment in physical infrastructure

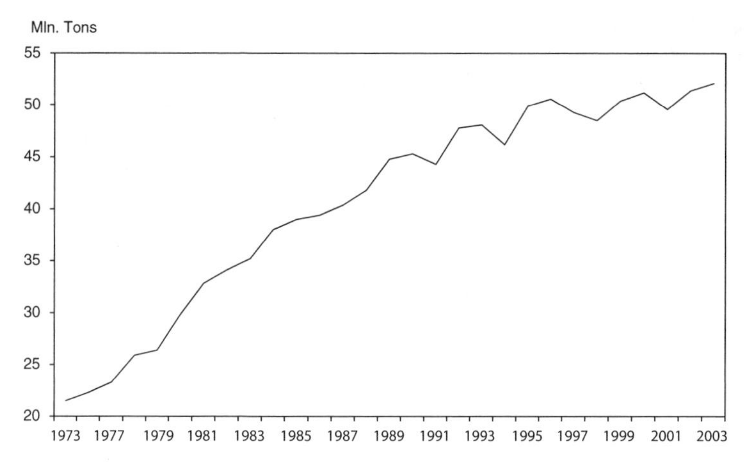

Figure 3.2 Production of dry, unmilled rice (paddy), 1973–2003 (millions of tons)
Source: Badan Pusat Statistik: Statistical Yearbook of Indonesia, successive issues.

was complemented by development of public sector institutions that provided the rice economy with financial, marketing and extension services. These institutional innovations served as an important link between expanding production possibilities and improved physical infrastructure by providing the financial and educational prerequisites for technological innovation (Tabor, 1992: 173–4). Thus, as the education level of the rural population increased, a more sophisticated rice policy was gradually introduced.

Industrial and trade policies

During the three decades before Indonesia was hit by the Asian economic crisis, the country experienced an unprecedented economic and industrial transformation. When the New Order government assumed power in 1966, Indonesia's manufacturing sector was miniscule, and in 1965 Indonesia was the least industrialized among the five original ASEAN countries if measured by the percentage share of manufacturing in GDP. However, by 1993 Indonesia, along with Malaysia and Thailand, was named one of the three 'newly industrializing economies' (NIEs) of Southeast Asia in the World Bank's 'East Asian Miracle' study (World Bank, 1993a: 1; Table 3.3). While in 1965 Indonesia's manufacturing sector generated just 8 percent of GDP, by 1998 it generated more than a quarter. Indonesia had become a 'semi-industrial' country and exporter of

Table 3.3 Indonesia's industrial transformation in ASEAN perspectives, 1975–1998

	Manufacturing value added (US$ millions)		**Manufacturing (% of GDP)**		**Manufacturing exports (As % of total exports)**	
	1970	**1996**	**1965**	**1998**	**1980**	**1997**
Indonesia	994	58,244	8	26	2	42
Malaysia	500	34,030	9	34	19	76
Philippines	1622	18,908	20	22	21	45
Thailand	1130	51,525	14	29	25	71

Source: World Bank: World Development Indicators, successive issues.

manufactured products: in 1980 manufactured exports only accounted for 2 percent of total exports, while in 1997 their contribution had risen to no less than 42 percent.

Industrial and trade policies by no means followed a straight path: liberalization of the 1960s was followed by a more protectionist stance in the 1970s, which again was succeeded by a more liberal stance during the 1980s. Indeed, trade and industry policies were the main battleground of policy direction, their control dispersed over numerous line ministries. Moreover, implementation of trade policies was to a large extent in the hands of the customs service, an organization that has had a history of corruption, making the effective tariffs very different from the stated ones.

While the oil boom lasted, industrial strategy constituted 'a massive exercise in import-substitution' (Gray, 1982: 41–2), with a public sector dominated economic strategy emphasizing public financing of highly capital-intensive projects. Effective tariff protection went up, especially in import-substituting industries. The share of government development expenditures in total domestic investment increased from 28 percent for the years 1968–1974, to approximately 60 percent in the years 1974–1979. However, once the oil boom had ended in 1982, the Indonesian government could no longer afford to pursue this import-substituting pattern of industrializing, and had to pursue a more outward-looking, export-promoting industrialization strategy (Thee, 1989: 150), albeit initially with some hesitation. After an even steeper rise in the price of oil in early 1986, the government finally made a determined effort at export promotion, including the introduction of a series of deregulation measures to improve the investment climate for private business, domestic or foreign.

Two institutional innovations helped the technocrats regain control over policy in this area: the Tariff Team (*Tim Tarif*) and the outsourcing of the customs service. Tim Tarif, set up in 1985, centralized controls over the tariff setting process. Composed of representatives of a number of ministries, the team was to advise the Minister of Finance on tariffs, and it ensured that all perspectives on any tariff proposal were heard, rather than only the views of one Ministry. The most controversial and strikingly effective measure was the reform of the notoriously corrupt Directorate-General of Customs. The investigation and clearance of import consignments worth more than $5000 was transferred to a Swiss firm and custom controls over exports and inter-island trade were abolished altogether (Nasution, 1985: 11). Some estimate that clearance costs dropped immediately to one-fifth of their former level (Dick, 1985: 10), giving a strong boost to trade and tariff revenues alike. These measures led to a surge of manufactured exports and from 1987 to 1992 manufactured exports increased at an average annual rate of 27 percent (HIID, 1995: 1).

Financial sector policies

Financial sector liberalization was a latecomer among Indonesia's reforms. Soekarno had monopolized the banking system, centralizing it into one body that performed both central bank and commercial bank functions. Soeharto retained a state-dominated system until well into the 1980s. When liberalization finally occurred in earnest, it was too rapid and not coupled with the development of an independent, strong supervisory capacity. Consequently, the sector became the center of the economic crisis after 1997.

After initial reforms in 1983, 1988 marked the second major package for bank deregulation. Known as the *PAKTO* Reforms, their main goal was to enhance financial sector efficiency by encouraging competition and increasing the availability of long-term finance by promoting the development of a capital market. Just four months later licenses had been approved for seven new national commercial banks, three joint ventures with foreign banks and 47 secondary banks (World Bank, 1989: 79). The package also included a reduction in the required reserve ratios from an average 11 percent to a uniform level of 2 percent of all third-party liabilities. This very low capital requirement reduced the intermediation costs for banks and increased the potential monetary expansion from any given increase in reserves (Cole and Slade, 1996: 23). This and subsequent reforms contributed to a burst of financial system activity. Domestic credit jumped from Rp.3.9 trillion in 1988 to 6.2 trillion in 1989 and 9.3 trillion in 1990 (up from just Rp.1 billion in 1984), and the number of banks increased from 111 in 1988 to 171 in 1990 and 240 in 1994 (Sitorus and Srinivas, 2004: Table 1a).

These extensive banking liberalization measures required new regulatory measures yet many of these issues had not been addressed when the crisis broke (indeed the government resisted World Bank pressure for reforms), and it is no surprise that banking trouble was already rife well before the crisis. 'Without doubt the financial deregulation drive since 1983 has been an important factor behind Indonesia's excellent growth performance of recent years. But the pace of change (and the weakness of the starting point) has raised doubts about the fundamental health of the sector. In particular, there is a concern that – in a worse case scenario – the sector would magnify any serious disturbance, spreading shockwaves throughout the economy, with destabilizing feedback effects on the macro economy.' (World Bank, 1996, quoted in Kenward, 2002).

Crony capitalism rising

The 1990s saw a growing perception among Indonesians that deregulation and economic growth were benefiting only a small percentage of the population. Deregulation seemed to reduce bureaucratic hurdles for big companies but not for small firms (Schwarz borrowing from Rizal Ramli, 1994: 79). In addition, technocrats had designed the banking deregulations in consultation with international experts, and viewed new laws on a par with international standards as important building blocks for improving Indonesia's competitiveness in the world economy. Thus, some nationalistic groups accused the government of creating a business environment that benefited international investors rather than indigenous Indonesians.[10] The 1990s also saw a declining influence of the technocrats in the Soeharto government. They had been given room to improve Indonesia's growth and investment climate by opening up the financial sector, lowering import tariffs and removing some non-trade barriers. However, Soeharto gave the technocrats only a limited mandate to carry out economic reforms, which resulted in a lack of cooperation and coordination between the economic ministries and other cabinet branches that ultimately undermined the technocrats' policies.

Animosities grew towards those ethnic Chinese in the merchant and trade industries who appeared to be benefiting from liberalization more than indigenous Indonesian *pribumi* entrepreneurs. Soeharto's family had also entered businesses in a major way, and increasingly foreign and domestic investors alike found it necessary to invite a family member as shareholder into their venture, in order to receive the right approvals and policies for their venture to succeed. Soeharto family members landed a clove monopoly, a plastic monopoly, exemptions from the restrictions on foreign borrowing and protective tariffs, and it also ventured into TV stations, toll roads, banking, power stations, a 'national car' project, and even a 'national shoe project' which, if implemented, would have forced every school child to buy shoes from a company owned by a Soeharto grandson.

Institutional underpinnings

In contrast to the successes in economic policy, Indonesia's institutions – with the exception of the Presidency and the Military – suffered decline during the New Order era. Soeharto saw social and political order and economic development as two sides of the same coin (Schwarz, 1994: 24–39), and he shaped Indonesia's institutions accordingly. The New Order administration asserted that a strong state, with the capability of suppressing (as opposed to diffusing) antagonisms based on ethnicity, religion, or geography, was a pre-condition for industrialization. The military became the key instrument for eradicating subversive and 'destabilizing' forces within society and the administration severely limited popular participation in politics.[11] The latter would be achieved not by disbanding all civilian political activity,[12] but by restructuring the political system in such a way that it could no longer compete with the executive office for power. The forms of government would stay, but those outside the executive branch would be steadily drained of influence (Schwarz, 1994: 30).

Indonesia's political debate became increasingly subdued and often actively suppressed under the New Order. After the violent suppression of actual and alleged communists during 1965–1966, Golkar increasingly dominated the political landscape. Parties were 'simplified' in the 1970s and limited to three. Limitations on press freedom and on civil society, combined with *Pancasila*, the country's state philosophy, stifled political debate, making it ever less free (Figure 3.3), in contrast to that of the other HPAEs, which gradually eased political restrictions. It is in this sense that we talk of Indonesia's economic policies being accompanied by weak institutions. We note five dimensions of this weakness.

First, the regime drastically 'simplified' the political party landscape and curtailed electoral democracy. Central to this political landscape was Golkar, an army-organized alliance of anti-communist groups that had been set up in 1964 in the late Soekarno period. Golkar was designed as an umbrella organization for hundreds of functional groups (*Golongan Karya* – shortened to *Golkar*) of peasants, workers, students, women, small-scale entrepreneurs and others, though these individual associations soon lost their identities. Golkar was Soeharto's political vehicle from the outset, and it dominated the Indonesian political scene until the 1999 election. At the same time, Golkar guaranteed the military a sizeable bloc of seats in parliament,[13] as well as access to high-level civil service jobs in both Jakarta and the provinces (Vatikiotis, 1993: 70–1). This helped to ensure political stability, and thereby create favourable economic conditions, by neutralizing the threat of a military takeover. But it was at the expense of hindering the development of a strong civilian bureaucracy.

The flip side of Golkar's hegemony was the systematic weakening of other forms of political organization and participation. Not only did the armed forces wage an intensive campaign against suspected members of PKI (the Indonesian Communist Party), they also restricted organized Islamic groups, some of which had separatist agendas, but

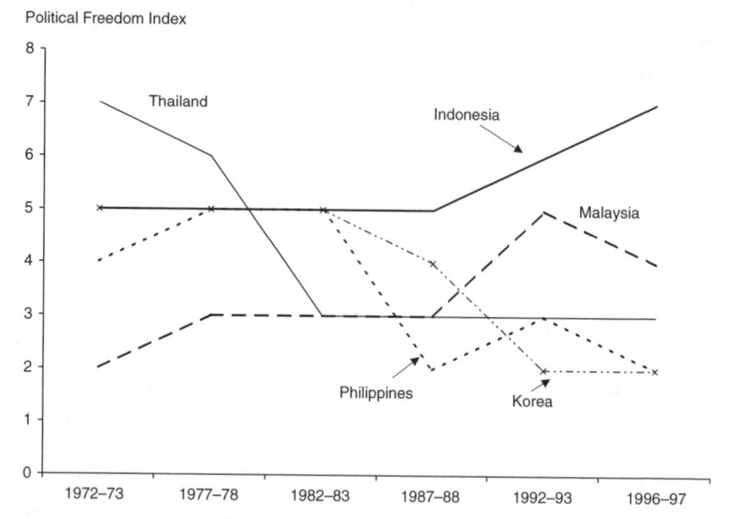

Figure 3.3 Declining political freedom (political freedom index, selected countries)
Note: Political Freedom Index ranges from 1 (free) to 7 (not free).
Source: Freedom House.

most of which were feared simply because of their ability to mobilize large numbers of people. In the name of development (*'Politik tidak, Pembangunan ya'*, 'Politics no, Development yes'), the regime also constrained political participation. After the 1971 elections, people were allowed to vote every five years, but apart from a brief campaign period prior to elections, political activities would otherwise be banned. This effectively 'depoliticized the Indonesian population' (Leo Suryadinata, 1979: 70), but just to be sure, the regime also reduced the number of political parties to three, Golkar and two others. The four Islamic parties that had contested the 1971 election were forced to amalgamate as one (the PPP), while the five secular parties were crushed together to form the Indonesian Democratic Party (PDI). This exercise effectively subverted democracy and undermined political opposition.

This weakening of political society was accompanied by suppression of civil society. In January 1974, thousands of students in Jakarta staged demonstrations during a visit by the Japanese Prime Minister Tanaka. Alarmed, the government clamped down on free speech, closing 12 newspapers and magazines and placing restrictions on public meetings. The students continued their protests until the government eventually responded by issuing the 1978 *Campus Normalization Law*, which essentially put a stop to all political activity within the student community (Schwarz, 1994: 33–6). This pattern of press restriction continued during the remainder of the regime. In the five decades following independence, the government issued only 289 publishing licenses. In only the 12 months following Soeharto's resignation it issued 718 licenses (Tesoro, 2000). A public sphere in which policy could be framed, debated and reworked was simply not allowed to exist.

Third, while the New Order government sought to control the national political system, it also had designs at the grassroots level. In the name of national unity and the acceleration of development, the government implemented Law no. 5/1979 on Village Governance, which imposed a uniform Javanese model of administration on 63,000 villages throughout the country. This law redesignated each village as a *desa*, the Javanese structure of village organization, and removed existing traditional *adat* systems of administration and decision-making both in the name of development and in order to exert central political control over the villages to promote national security and economic development. Indeed, the Village Law was at once a means of fostering simplification at the grassroots level and of facilitating the delivery of development services. For instance, the *Inpres Desa* (village grant) gave birth to a special programme for underdeveloped villages (*Inpres Desa Tertinggal)* and later the *Village Improvement Programme*, which in turn became the inspiration for the *Kecamatan Development Programme* which is now the largest community development programme in Indonesia, operating in 27,000 villages (Guggenheim, 2006). Village development came at a price, however. Anecdotally, villages that supported *Golkar* in the elections were rewarded with development programmes. In addition, it was common practice for Golkar to give village heads (*lurah* or *kepala desa*) incentives in the form of cash or, more often, land or agricultural produce to ensure that everyone in their communities voted for Golkar.

Not only were civil and political society institutions weakened and distorted – so also were institutions of the state, in particular the judiciary and the civil service. The judiciary had entered decline well before the New Order government took office, and any pretence of an independent judiciary was abandoned under 'Guided Democracy,' the political system put in place by Soekarno in the late 1950s. By the late 1960s, the salaries of Supreme Court Justices had fallen to the level of second rank civil servants. Yet during the New Order, the breakdown of the judiciary extended beyond under funding and low salaries to the core professional practices of the judicial system. The system of merit-based personnel management and continuous internal assessment, *eksaminasi*, was abandoned outright in the late 1960s, and decisions on promotion and transfer became discretionary. As the economy started to take off in the 1970s with the onset of the oil boom, this discretionary system of advancement and irregular rotations began to take their toll on the integrity of the legal system. Judges were exposed to political pressures and manipulation and the independence of the judicial system was undermined (Pompe, 2003: 17). Indeed, the judiciary did not find the State guilty in a single major case brought before the courts until *Reformasi*. Soeharto himself often played judge and jury in important cases. Meanwhile, continued underfunding bred corruption. Estimates suggest that state funds covered only 30 to 40 percent of the judicial system's routine budget (Pompe, 2002: 21), and thus court personnel were forced to rely on gifts, bribes and levies.

If the absence of an independent, competent judiciary both reflected and deepened the absence of formal institutions for regulating transactions in society, the chronic underfunding of the civil service likewise meant that the practice of government was not based on rules. This is not to say that the civil service did not grow: indeed it expanded rapidly during the 1970s as the government made heavy investments in education, health and physical infrastructure. Yet after almost ten years of rapid expansion both in the economy and the civil service, the World Bank's 1979 report on patterns of growth and social progress commented that 'the bureaucracy has not overcome the deficiencies of the previous regime, and is dealing with an expanded and more complex economy, vastly increased levels of government spending and increased responsibilities' and that 'it requires little exaggeration to say that the need to raise the general level of efficiency and reliability of the government bureaucracy remains one of the highest national development priorities. Discussion of Indonesia's development needs without drawing attention to this important constraint would be futile' (World Bank, 1979: 18–20). Low salaries had a clear knock-on effect in national institutions. They contributed to 'projectism,' the neglect or reformulation of routine activities in favour of *proyeks* that provided a bonus or allowance. Low salaries also contributed to moonlighting and petty corruption.

The New Order government, then, delivered a society without political institutions to allow for protest, questioning or scrutiny of government practice; with no effective institutions through which government or private enterprise could be held to account to society; and with a government bureaucracy that became ever more prone to both petty and grand corruption. The institutional basis to sustain the fruits of 'good' economic policy, to correct pathologies within the economy and to contest the rise of political corruption simply did not exist. The particularly sad irony in this case is that, with the windfall oil and other incomes in the 1970s and 1980s, Indonesia had had the resources to invest in such institutions. The centrality of the Presidency and his cronies, as well as the willingness of external actors to continue supporting the 'good policy, weak institutions' model, meant that such investment did not occur. Thus the 'good policies that went bad' (in Grindle's sense) did so because of the deliberate neglect of the institutional bases of a democratic society and of Weberian government.

The crisis

Few predicted the Indonesian crisis, and none its severity. While some observers expressed concerns about the economy's growing vulnerability, rising debt and appreciating currency, this concern was far from predictive of a crisis. Moreover, it was hard to argue with Indonesia's growth, which amounted to more than 7.5 percent in 1996. Indeed,

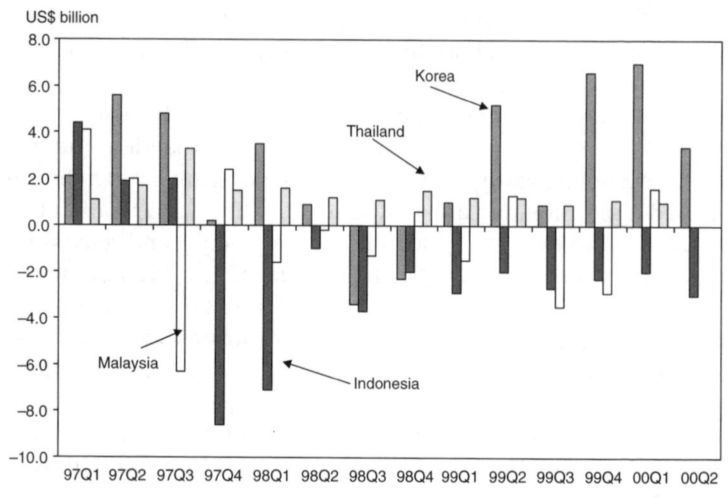

Figure 3.4 Private capital flow to Asian crisis countries, 1997–2000 (US$ billion, selected countries)
Source: BI, CEIC.

until just before the crisis, the authorities' were concerned about the strength rather than the weakness of the Rupiah, which had kept close to the lower end of the intervention band. But what started as contagion from the speculative attack on the Thai Baht soon became the deepest crisis of Indonesia's history. Indonesia was singled out for special punishment by the capital markets, and nowhere was the reversal in capital flows so sharp and so prolonged as in Indonesia (Figure 3.4).

The crisis deepened despite the early corrective actions that the authorities took to stem the growing outflow of capital. Initially, these measures were seen as another example of the skillful macroeconomic management for which Indonesia was known, yet they did not stop the outflow of capital. The driving force at that stage was the need for heavily indebted enterprises to cover their unhedged foreign exchange exposure. A decade of relatively stable exchange rates, combined with high domestic interest rates had greatly increased foreign debt, and an increasing share was short term. After Korea, Indonesia had the highest share of short term debt to reserves of the Asian crisis countries, and with the floating of the Rupiah and the halt of renewed capital inflows, firms were scrambling for exchange risk cover, which put continued pressure on the Rupiah. In addition, the contraction of liquidity in the banking system failed, as many banks were unable to meet their interbank clearing obligations. With hindsight, the exchange rate policies followed by Indonesia for over three decades may have been no longer suited for the early 1990s, which saw a sharp increase in international capital flows. Indonesia, as many other countries, did not try to restore a fixed or pegged system after the crisis, and the conventional wisdom has become that a country should either have an irrevocably fixed exchange rate – such as Hong Kong – or a freely floating one.

The trigger for the failure of the first IMF salvage programme, signed in November 1997, was the effective reopening (under a different name) of one of the closed banks – one owned by Soeharto's son. This shed doubts on the authorities' resolve to forcefully address the weaknesses in the financial system, doubts that were further fed by an announcement by the Finance Minister by end-November that no more bank closures were to take place. The public felt that more banks in the system were bad, but did not know *which ones*. This uncertainty combined with the limited deposit guarantee, caused a massive withdrawal of deposits from private domestic banks, and their transfer to state-owned banks seen to be implicitly guaranteed by the State,[14] or their use for further speculation against the Rupiah. The liquidity support that Bank Indonesia provided to banks short of liquidity was widely abused by the bank owners, often close associates of Soeharto.

Rupiah selling accelerated in mid-December, when the President cancelled an overseas trip, and rumours about his health started to circulate. As the World Bank (1998b: 18) wrote 'The combination of a financial crisis, an upcoming election and an ageing sick President ratcheted uncertainty to an unprecedented level.' The issue of Soeharto's succession may have played a broader role in the crisis. While no data are available on this, it may well be that a significant part of the Rupiah selling came from people closely connected to the Soeharto regime, beginning to prepare for a life without him. Indeed, even before the crisis, this had already induced moderate scale capital outflows of connected businessmen, at that time under the banner of 'international diversification.'[15] Soeharto himself had been aware of the problem of succession before. In 1996 he had declared that 'There is a need ... to prepare a new leader' (Elson, 2001: 289), but he had not acted on his awareness. Soeharto's decision to run for a sixth term on January 20, 1998 cost the Rupiah some 10 percent in value, although part of this loss may have been explained by the announcement on the same day of the Vice Presidential candidate, B. J. Habibie, a 'technologist' known for his expensive high-tech ventures, notably the national plane project.

The second IMF-supported programme was designed to restore the credibility of the Government. This credibility had received another blow in the draft budget published on January 6, 1998, which was considered by many to be based on unrealistic assumptions (World Bank, 1998b: 1.6). The programme included wide-ranging measures to address the distortions in the economy created to the benefit of Soeharto's family and business partners. The tax benefits for the National Car project of one of the President's sons, the subsidies to the national airplane industry, the clove monopoly, Bulog's import monopoly on wheat and sugar and the plywood monopoly were all to be abolished. The President himself signed the IMF letter of intent on January 15, the reasoning being that Soeharto should be seen to be willing to cut into the interest of his close associates and family members in order to save the economy. But the programme failed to turn around expectations, either because the markets felt that Soeharto would not live up to his promises, or because 'the absence of corporate and banking reform in the new policy package did not help' (World Bank, 1998b: 1.7).

Soeharto's reelection on March 11, 1997, Habibie's Vice-Presidency and the appointment of several of Soeharto's closest associates (including his eldest daughter and Bob Hasan, a close business associate) did not bode well. However, the 'crony cabinet' showed a surprising performance in implementing the measures agreed with the IMF, and a third letter-of-intent was signed on April 6. Part of the agreement was the *gradual* abolition of fuel subsidies (O'Rourke, 2002: 87). Instead the President announced on May 4 a fuel price increase of 70 percent and bus fare increase of 67 percent, to be implemented the next day. This triggered widespread protests across the country. During one protest organized by Trisakti University students, four students were shot and killed, apparently by the military. This triggered three days of rioting in Jakarta, in which hundreds of people died; property, especially that of Sino-Indonesians was damaged, and very many women were raped. In an unprecedented move, the rubber-stamp parliament called for Soeharto's resignation, and on May 21 he stepped down, making Habibie president. What had started as a financial crisis had turned into an economic, social and political crisis.

At that point, the economy was in freefall, with GDP declining at a rate of 20 percent year-on-year. Even exports, which should have benefited from the steep fall of the Rupiah, had collapsed because of the virtual absence of trade credit. Inflation had shot up to nearly 100 percent, with even higher price increases for rice and other staples for the poor, and as a result the poverty headcount doubled to over 27 percent. It can be debated whether the second IMF supported programmes should have addressed the broad range of interests of parties connected to the President, and there are those who have argued that Indonesia's crisis was deepened rather than relieved by the IMF's interventions (see for example Jomo KS, 1998). But even the narrower October 1997 programme was caught in delays and policy reversals because of the interests of Soeharto and his associates. The lack of a political system outside the President aggravated the crisis when he fell ill in December, because the markets (and cronies) could not manage the uncertainty entailed in a possible succession or change of political system – political uncertainty became a catalyst for capital flight. It also undermined the credibility of the stabilization programme itself, and thus the reversal of capital flows (upon which stabilization critically relies) never occurred while Soeharto was in power. Finally, the decay in social cohesion under the New Order can at least in part explain the widespread rioting and emergence of conflicts that had been suppressed for decades.

Indonesia's weak institutions also undermined the recovery. Nowhere was this clearer than in the banking system, a large part of which had failed during the crisis. In the absence of a functioning, reliable judiciary, sorting out the avalanche of bad debts in the system became an impossible task. The special agency created for the task, IBRA, never gained the clout and the political backing to pursue bad debtors in an efficient way outside judicial channels. Moreover, because the large debtors had the option to go to court, IBRA had to settle debts of former bank owners on highly unsatisfactory terms, and recovery even on those debts became a protracted affair. Consequently, costs to tax payers were larger in Indonesia than anywhere else, and few former bank owners were brought to justice.

Arguably, the country's weak civil service became a hindrance to poverty alleviation during the crisis. A social safety net with a multitude of measures to reduce the impact on the poor became mired in corruption. The World Bank cancelled a loan to finance part of the safety net on those grounds, and in the end only the rather weakly targeted subsidized rice distribution made some impact on the rising numbers of poor during the crisis.

At the end of 2003, political stability had returned, macroeconomic stability was settling in and growth was a hesitant 3–4 percent of GDP. However, income per capita still hovered 10 percent below pre-crisis levels and the recovery lagged behind that of other crisis-affected

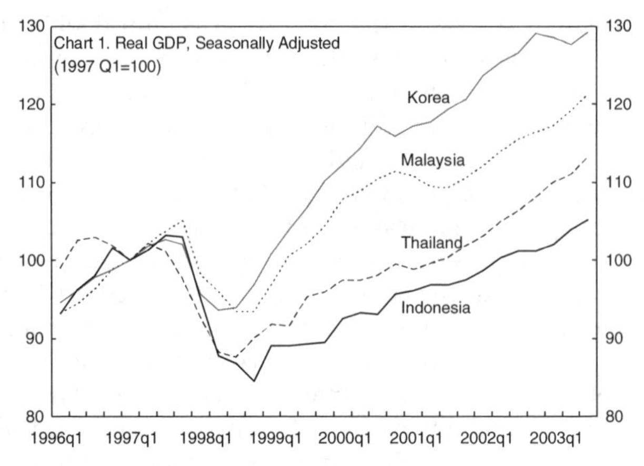

Figure 3.5 Lagging recovery
Source: IMF.

countries (Figure 3.5). Indonesia's crisis had been among the most costly in history. If one adds up the fiscal costs of bank restructuring with the output losses compared to trend (see Claessens *et al.*, 2003), Indonesia's crisis cost some 94 percent of GDP, more than Argentina's crisis of 1980–1982 (72 percent of GDP), Chile's crisis of 1981–1983 (88 percent of GDP), or Japan's protracted crisis of 1991–2003 (72 percent of GDP). The weak legal system had protracted the clean-up after the crisis, had aggravated the losses to the state because there was no legal threat to bad debtors, and delayed the economic recovery substantially. It had also greatly damaged the sense of justice among Indonesians, who saw that most of the corrupters of the New Order era and most of those who had ravaged the financial system remained outside the reach of justice.

Some lessons

Indonesia's growth success in the 30 years since 1966 was built on policies and institutions that promoted a (generally) conducive investment climate. The growth generated, together with windfalls from the oil price booms of the 1970s, allowed Indonesia to undertake numerous policies to include broader layers of the population in its success. A prime example is the expansion of education and health services during the 1970s, as well as the agricultural development policies in the 1960s and 1970s. The village grant programme (*Inpres Desa*) started in the 1970s further exemplifies this. Little recognized, but perhaps as important for rural development and poverty alleviation as targeted programmes, was the maintenance of a competitive exchange rate. The regular devaluations used to realign absorption gave a boost to tradable sector incomes; farmers and Indonesia's outer islands that relied to a much larger extent than Java on resources rather than manufacturing, also benefited from the move (Woo *et al.*, 1994).

Second, the presence of economically well-versed technocrats who could be relied upon in bad times, and who were by and large isolated from political interests, provided investors the confidence that sound policies would prevail, despite regular set-backs in trade and investment policies under the influence of competing factions. Several key policy rules also reflected the country's commitment to macroeconomic stability namely the balanced budget and open capital account that lasted throughout the New Order.

Third, the *way* in which Indonesia reformed its economy is of as much interest as the policies themselves. First, Indonesia's economic policies in the three decades of the Soeharto government can perhaps best be summarized in Hall Hills' line as 'Good Policies in Bad Times.' Although risky, using bad economic times as a window of opportunity to get good policies in place is likely to increase a country's chance at success in the long run. Second, 'packaging' measures that by themselves seem insignificant, but when taken together imply a major policy move, as was the case with the liberalization packages of the 1980s can be attractive as they have clear political benefits and strong signaling effects. Third, using pragmatic approaches to pressing issues – such as food security in the 1960s and 1970s, or fuel and rice subsidies during the crisis – may be preferable ideological policy stances.

Fourth, a strong partnership with the donor community played a role. The stabilization programme of the 1960s owed much to the support received from the IGGI donor group and the Paris Club. Again during the Asian crisis, rescheduling of Indonesia's debt and large pledges by donors were critical in stimulating Indonesia's recovery. In more normal times, the partnership with the donor community and policy discussions during the annual donor meeting, contributed to Indonesia's policies and programmes. It is no coincidence that the 1980s reform packages were often announced shortly before the annual donor meeting. In addition to official donors, others in the international community played a role as well. This includes the Ford Foundation that provided the scholarships by which many of the technocrats afforded their economics study in the United States back in the

1950s and 1960s. And it includes a group of advisors from the Harvard Institute of International Development, who, hired by the Indonesian government and based in the Ministry of Finance, advised on many of the economic reforms implemented in the 1980s and 1990s.

Fifth, institutions and policies have an expiration date. At some time, they may work well, but change in external or internal circumstances may render them less useful or appropriate. Indonesia's fixed exchange rate system exemplifies this. Since the crisis, and in this era of strong capital flows, a fixed exchange rate is no longer an appropriate tool of macroeconomic management for developing countries. In addition, the extremely open capital account that lent credibility to Indonesia's macroeconomic policies in the 1960s and 1970s posed problems in the 1990s when rapidly growing enterprises and a newly liberalized financial system exposed Indonesia to external vulnerabilities. Some economists now recommend limited restrictions on short term capital inflows in normal times and on outflows during a crisis. In that sense, Indonesia was a case of good policies gone bad (cf. Grindle, Chapter 2).

Sixth, strong institutions matter in development in general, and during a crisis in particular. Without the rule of law, an increasingly complex economy is hard to manage. Without independent oversight, the financial sector required for a modern economy is prone to crisis. Without popular participation in political decision-making, the increasingly difficult choices a government must make may lack the legitimacy needed to ensure their effectiveness. Without a clean, efficient civil service, implementation of those policies and their effects may diverge strongly from what policymakers intended. And without checks and balances on the political decision makers, a country runs the very real risk that leaders may endorse sound developmental policies at first and then pursue their own or their family interests later.[16]

Strong institutions are most needed when they matter most – in times of crises. A lack of strong institutions outside the President undermined Indonesia's ability to manage the crisis, and as a result Indonesia's crisis became deeper and costlier than in other affected countries. The absence of a functioning judiciary slowed the resolution of bankruptcies and bad debts in the aftermath of the crisis, thereby delaying economic recovery. It also made prosecuting those seen to have broken the law in pursuit of personal wealth almost impossible. The stopgap institutions to manage the economic crisis – IBRA and commercial courts – were only partially effective. The lack of strong political institutions prevented the deliberation of feasible policy packages which could have saved Indonesia from the worst of the crisis.

The conclusion of this chapter must therefore be that policies cannot be analysed independently from the institutions that generate and implement them. Indeed, neither proposals for nor critiques of policy make sense without a simultaneous treatment of the formal and non-formal institutional context. Understanding that institutional context in turn takes us back to contemporary and historical political economy if we are to understand why policy deepening and/or policy sabotaging institutions exist and operate in the way that they do.

Notes

1. This chapter does not necessarily represent the opinions of the World Bank, its Executive Directors, or its member countries. All correspondence should be sent to bhofman@worldbank.org. The chapter is partly based on a paper prepared for the Shanghai Conference on Scaling Up Poverty Alleviation, Shanghai, May 2004. The authors would like to thank the late Saleh Afiff, Jehan Arulpragasam, Anthony Bebbington, Mark Baird, Yoichiro Ishihara, Homi Kharas, Tamar Manuelyan, Peter Timmer, Adam Schwarz and Roberto Zhaga, and participants at the Shanghai conference, for comments on an earlier version of this paper, and a senior Indonesian economic policymaker who wishes to remain anonymous for extremely useful discussions on the topic of the paper.
2. Personal communication of a World Bank economist working in Indonesia.
3. The growth literature attributes economic development to three factors, broadly speaking: geography (natural resources and endowments), integration (trade and openness) and institutions (rules, norms and social capital).
4. We are grateful to Sir Tim Lankester for this thought expressed in a speech in Jakarta comparing Indonesia's and India's development paths.
5. There was an indigenous civil service largely recruited form the local nobility, the *priayi,* but these were restricted to the lower ranks of the colonial administration.
6. There are numerous studies on the contribution of productivity to growth in Indonesia, with different approaches yielding widely different results. See Stiglitz and Yusuf (2001) for an overview.
7. This increase in the national Gini Index reflects the rise in inequity in urban areas. Rural areas remained almost constant with the index moving only from .26 to .27. In the wake of the 1997 crisis, the Gini index moved relatively little, so some work has been undertaken recently to assess the possibility of measurement errors.
8. See Wie (2003) for a collection of interviews with some of the key technocrats.
9. Soeharto was acquainted with them because of the courses in economics they had delivered at the army training school in the late Soekarno period (Mohammad Sadli in Thee, 2003: 126).
10. Some observers highlighted the 1993 cabinet change. Under public pressure to alter the economic administration's image, in creating his new cabinet in March 1993 Soeharto dismissed three leading (Christian) technocrats and replaced them with Muslim economists (Schwarz 1994: 80–1). Two

economic advisors see this move as less significant, but acknowledge the generally declining influence of the technocrats in the 1990s.

11 Schwarz referencing McVey (1992).

12 Soeharto's administration channeled civilian political activity into a limited number of sanctioned social and cultural organizations that came under the government's direct control and would be used to implement policies and political agendas. Non-governmental organizations were given some leeway to operate but always were subject to dissolution. Other efforts at controlling popular political participation included the de-politicizing of university campuses and the closing of 'offending' publications which were considered 'harmful to development.'

13 Until 1967, the political parties dominated the People's Consultative Assembly (MPR), the body that is charged with selecting – and also impeaching – the president. In order to increase its control of the MPR, the government then granted itself the right to appoint a third of the members of the MPR, as well as over a fifth of the seats in the DPR (parliament). (Schwarz 1994: 31). In addition to ABRI representatives, these government-appointed legislators included regional representatives from around the country and delegates from various interest groups such as the professions. The intention was to secure representation from the widest possible cross-section of society, and avoid the 'tyranny of the majority' that was feared would result from a wholly elected MPR and DPR.

14 To a lesser extent foreign banks also benefited from the 'flight to safety'.

15 Interview with an Indonesian economic policymaker.

16 One Indonesian policymaker summarized Suharto's problem as 'Presidents should not have children.'

4

When Good Policies Go Bad, Then What? Dislodging Exhausted Industrial and Education Policies in Latin America

Merilee S. Grindle

Successful policies, those that 'have endured, met their aims and secured the acquiescence of those who initially opposed them,' sometimes succeed by adapting to new circumstances and realities, as Willy McCourt and Tony Bebbington point out in Chapter 1. Creative adjustment may therefore be one way that such policies endure over time and continue to provide benefits to significant sectors of a population. Sometimes, however, for development and poverty alleviation to continue in the wake of a successful policy, it may be necessary for the original policy to be superseded by a significantly different one. Indeed, policies that produce good results may, over time, cease to do so. Moreover, successful policies can create unintended negative consequences that need to be addressed through new policy initiatives. Thus, over the course of time, even policies that have strong records of generating growth and poverty reduction may need to be revised in significant ways or replaced by new policies that are more appropriate.

Nevertheless, while policy change may be an important factor in promoting successful development, political economists generally predict discouraging outcomes from efforts to alter existing policies. They argue that most policies – whether good or bad for development – create beneficiaries who use their political and economic influence to lock in place or deepen the policies that benefit them, and that these interests resist efforts to supersede or revise policies, even when changes or revisions would lead to more socially beneficial outcomes.[1] At the same time, interests that might benefit from new policies tend to be less powerful, less organized and less aware of the benefits they will receive in the future. Potential beneficiaries of policy change thus face significant collective action problems. As a consequence, good policies that no longer deliver development effectively can be trapped in place by a political equilibrium of powerful entrenched interests and weak coalitions for change.

In this chapter, I present two examples of political equilibria that constrained policy change in a number of Latin American countries in recent decades: one that emerged around import-substitution development strategies and another that supported access to education. In both cases, policies introduced to promote economic and social development produced solid benefits for broad sectors of the population, and they did so over several decades. They also generated political interests and institutional structures that maintained these policies in place long after it became evident to many citizens, development professionals and policymakers that they were no longer generating good results for the societies in which they were being carried out.

What is interesting in the case of import-substitution and education policies in a number of countries, however, is that political equilibria were altered and changed policies were introduced. How can this be explained? As it happens, the model of policy entrenchment adopted by many political economists does a good job of explaining how the mobilization of interests and institutions emerge to defend an existing policy *status quo*; but the same tools of analysis only partially explain the political dynamics of policy *change*.

In efforts to change policies, analysts not only need to consider the interests of past and future beneficiaries and the biases of institutions, but also to take account of the role of agency in political life. While much has been made of the 'policy champions' and 'policy entrepreneurs' who lead change initiatives, what is most important about these actors is their strategic use of resources in particular contexts, not the simple fact of their existence.[2] Those who lead change initiatives often try to undermine the power of existing interests and to alter the biases of institutions that constrain choice. Whether they are successful or not depends in part on their strategies and skills, and also on the context within which they seek to promote change.

The history of import-substitution policies and access to education policies provides insight into the interaction of interests, institutions and agency in policy change. In both cases, despite very significant opposition, a political equilibrium of interests and institutions around an existing policy was dislodged and new policy orientations became possible. The dynamics of the two cases are somewhat different, however, in terms of how much depended on the strategic actions of reform leadership. The introduction of new strategies for economic development – to replace the increasingly dysfunctional import-substitution policies – was encouraged by widespread perceptions of crisis that increased tolerance for change, by international pressures and by the availability of a powerful new development paradigm that supported policy reformers at high levels in government. In the case of educational policy change, contextual factors did not provide much support for change, and the burden of introducing new policies fell more directly on strategic reform leadership.

When new policies are introduced, despite the deep beliefs of their champions, they do not necessarily bring success in terms of generating broad and sustained benefits for large groups of citizens. Indeed, in the case of the market-oriented economic reforms that replaced import substitution as a development strategy in Latin America, and the quality-enhancing education reforms that were promoted to amend the deficiencies of access policies, results were not always what their proponents anticipated. What then? As with other cases, these policies have created their own political equilibria that may hold them in place, whether they deliver on their promises or not.

The purpose of this chapter is to reflect broadly on the politics of policy stasis and change when policies that have made significant contributions to development are no longer doing so. While building on my own prior research and that of many others on the policy reform process, it does not delve into the particular experiences of specific countries, nor does it seek to provide explanations for differences among countries in terms of their political experiences. Rather, it seeks to generalize about why policy change is politically problematic and why it sometimes happens. It explores the interaction of interests, institutions and agency in policy change initiatives. I suggest that analysis of whether particular policies are good or not needs to be joined by analysis of the dynamics of policy change.

Policies and political equilibria: two examples

Policies that have produced good results for development do not always continue to do so decade after decade. In Latin America (and in countries in other parts of the world) import-substitution policies generated significant growth in their early years, but became 'exhausted' as a development strategy when, over time, they encouraged inefficiencies in domestic production, limited competition, increased the hand of government in economic decision-making and added to debt and technological dependence. Many experts became convinced that this broad set of policies needed to be replaced by others, ones based on liberalized internal markets, more open trade and less government intervention in the economy.

In the same region, development policies that promoted access to basic education reduced illiteracy rates dramatically and made schooling possible for most children. But over the longer term, this policy failed to deliver on the quality of education. Children were able to go to school, but whether they were learning important and useful skills that could contribute to their future development was increasingly uncertain. After several decades of emphasis on the promotion of access to education, then, many of those concerned about the role of education in economic and social development and poverty reduction began to argue that policies to encourage access needed to be fortified by policies stressing the quality of the education being delivered.

In neither instance was policy change easy. In the case of import substitution, policies that had generated considerable growth and poverty alleviation also generated rent-seeking economic elites, politicians and bureaucrats who were loathe to see those policies rejected in favour of new ones. In the case of education, the development of strong teachers' unions and centralized bureaucracies was a consequence of access reforms; the principal barriers to improving the quality of education were these same teachers' unions and bureaucracies. Thus, in many countries, when it was important to alter economic and social policies such as these, it was challenging to do so because of the power accumulated by particular interests and the institutions that favoured the *status quo*.

The case of import substitution

In the 1930s, a number of Latin American countries introduced specific policy instruments to deal with drastically declining exports and foreign exchange crises. These policies stimulated industrialization of economies that had been primarily based on agricultural and mineral exports. In the late 1940s, through the work of Raúl Prebisch and others in the newly established United Nations Economic Commission for Latin America, the theoretical underpinning of the region's drive for industrialization was put in place.[3] It called for a broad development strategy based on import substitution. In this approach, industrialization would allow Latin American countries to escape from long-term decline in terms of trade and short-term boom and bust cycles characteristic of economies dependent on world prices for a small number of primary products.

According to theory, changes in the international capitalist economy meant that the development of the region's economies was inherently distinct from the process of development that characterized already industrialized countries. As a result of this different trajectory, the state would have to assume much of the role that private sector entrepreneurs had performed for earlier developers. For the efficient allocation of resources leading to industrial growth, the state would need to have control over important industrial infrastructure like public utilities and basic industries and to regulate imports to encourage domestic production. National development based on the idea of import substitution also encouraged the introduction of wage and price controls and economic planning. These and a variety of other instruments could be used to cajole, entice or regulate weak domestic private sectors into assuming a more active part in industrial growth.

In practice, in the decades after 1950, many Latin American states became the principal source of capital for industrialization through powerful national development banks and corporations, and the state invested heavily in infrastructure and basic industry to provide inputs for domestic manufactures. At the same time, states limited imports of basic products in order to provide protection for infant industries, setting up extensive bureaucracies in the process. They also encouraged the agricultural sector to produce cheap foodstuffs for urban consumers and to generate resources from export that could be invested in industry. In addition, planning and management as means toward economic development emerged as important emphases within Latin American bureaucracies.

By the late 1950s in many countries and by the 1960s in most others, the 'easy phase' of import substitution, emphasizing light consumer industry, had been accomplished. And in most of the countries where it was introduced, it produced a sustained period of broad-based economic growth and poverty alleviation. In particular, this was a period of expansive employment generation, as workers were hired to build industrial and urban infrastructure, as government bureaucracies grew to handle new tasks and as workers, managers and professionals were needed in new industries.

In much of Latin America, the decades of the 1950s, 1960s and 1970s were good ones, when growth brought improved incomes for many. Between 1965 and 1980, GDP in many countries grew at sustained high rates – Bolivia at 4.4 percent annually, Brazil at 9.0 percent, Colombia at 5.7 percent, Ecuador at 8.8 percent and Mexico at 6.5 percent. In Mexico and in Brazil, much of this period was known as the period of the 'economic miracle.'

Government revenues also grew during this period, while industrialization – and rural poverty – encouraged urbanization. As cities expanded, it was easier for governments to provide basic services to larger portions of the population. As a consequence, important indices of human welfare advanced rapidly. Life expectancy grew, on average, by 15 years between 1950 and 1980, and infant mortality rates declined from over 100 per 1000 live births in 1950 to about 40 by 1980 (IDB, 2000). Illiteracy rates declined, and public health infrastructure, such as water and sanitation, made major inroads in reducing mortality and the toll taken by diseases traditionally associated with poverty. Poverty, while still an insistent reality for large portions of the population, consistently declined as incomes and social infrastructure expanded and as incipient urban working and middle classes grew. Improvement affected major portions of Latin America's rapidly growing population, and per capita income growth was significant.

By the mid-1970s, however, there were increasing signs that the impact of import-substitution policies was not all good. Protectionism and a wide variety of subsidies to both capital and labour encouraged inefficient industries. In some cases, markets became saturated with domestically produced goods that could not be exported because of high production costs and poor quality. Moreover, import substitution actually increased demand for imports of capital goods and technology to encourage the industrialization process. The hefty fortunes made in the formerly weak domestic private sector increased pressure for the importation of luxury goods.

At the same time, incentives to the agricultural sector were repressed through policies to hold domestic food prices low for urban consumption and overvalued exchange rates that discouraged production for export.[4] With agricultural exports declining and domestic manufactures uncompetitive internationally, foreign exchange crises were inevitable. Combined with demand for consumption goods from urban sectors, this encouraged inflation. Urbanization, which offered improved standards of living for many, also outpaced the ability of government to provide social and physical infrastructure and the capacity of the economy to produce jobs: squatter settlements and unemployment created visible tensions and increased pressure on governments to provide a range of economic and social benefits. Rural poverty became more apparent as marketing boards and price controls provided cheap foodstuffs to urban areas, but few incentives to peasant farmers. Pressures grew for governments to pay more attention to rural conditions and to the problem of agricultural productivity. The public sector expanded to provide jobs for political supporters.

The rapid rise in fuel prices in 1973–1974 and again in 1979–1980 had a significant impact on economies whose industrial and institutional underpinnings were already weak. Most countries responded to rising energy prices, decreased industrial and agricultural productivity and increased demands for public sector investment by borrowing heavily abroad, an approach made very attractive by an excess of international liquidity and low interest rates in the 1970s. In fact, for a large number of countries in Latin America, public deficits were increasingly financed by external borrowing.[5]

Thus domestic policies for economic development, after fueling growth for a significant period and providing broad social benefits in employment and social services, created the basis for stagnation and decline. In the early 1980s, an altered international environment created a full-blown economic crisis for countries throughout the region. Tightened credit supplies and rapidly rising interest rates brought a sudden drop in international liquidity and triggered pressures for debt repayment. When Mexico announced that it was not able to service its 62 billion-dollar debt in August 1982, few countries were in a position to avoid the negative consequences of a new and harsher international economic environment.[6] Total and per capita debt burdens doubled and even tripled in many countries between 1980 and 1991 (World Bank, 1993b: 238). The decade was littered with intense negotiations with international financial institutions to reschedule this debt.

The 1980s is now widely remembered as the 'lost decade.' During this period, per capita growth rates became negative for most countries in the region and growth rates declined to 1.7 percent annually for the region as a whole. Wages declined by 20 to 30 percent in many countries, job loss was widespread and the number of people living in poverty increased significantly during this period. By the end of the decade it was estimated that some 30 million people were employed in the informal sector (Tokman, 1989: 1067).

By mid-decade, many policymakers, drawing on models promoted by U.S.-educated economists and under pressure from international financial institutions, agreed that substantial policy change was necessary. In large part, they revisited the wisdom of import-substituting industrialization and came to believe that this development strategy had significantly contributed to the current condition of economic crisis. In order to remedy the situation, they were convinced that major changes in existing policies were required; tinkering at the margins would not address the problem. Increasingly, the remedy they agreed upon was economic liberalization, more open trade and the withdrawal of the state from many of its accustomed roles in the economy.[7]

This meant deregulating the economy, eliminating many government functions and jobs; lowering barriers to trade, increasing competition for domestic private sectors; and reducing or eliminating subsidies to capital, labour and urban consumers. The privatization of state-owned enterprises would do much, it was argued, to increase their efficiency. Government budgets had to be trimmed – sometimes drastically – to control inflation and repay debts, and spending ministries were a principal focus of concern for those who advocated change. Neoliberal economic reformers called for market-oriented systems in which competition would lead to more dynamic growth and increased welfare. They wanted a smaller, more efficient and less intrusive state.

The problem they faced, of course, was that import-substituting industrialization had created a range of interests that benefited from the policies. Over the period of several decades, what had been weak domestic industrial sectors grew wealthy, they organized and they became more powerful. As influential individuals and interests, they were strong supporters of import substitution. Over the years, they had benefited from government-provided infrastructure, low interest loans, tax holidays, subsidies to labour and non-competitive markets. Public sector workers, whose numbers grew throughout the period, organized themselves to become important supporters of the continuation of government management of the economy, and of the jobs, budgets, functions, perquisites and power their responsibilities implied. Similarly, powerful managers in the large parastatal sector were loathe to accept the changes that privatization would bring. Those who received subsidized electricity, telephones, transportation and other services were reluctant to lose them. Strongly organized unions worried about the loss of jobs, security and services they enjoyed if privatization and economic liberalization were to proceed. Urban consumers stood to lose access to low food prices. Each of these interests was closely connected to political parties, political machines or political resources that increased their capacity to resist change.

Table 4.1 The politics of import substitution and neoliberal policies: a comparison

	Import substitution policies	**Neoliberal economic policies**
Typical actions taken	• Increase the role of the state • Restrict imports • Build basic and industrial infrastructure • Expand bureaucracies • Increase budgets • Hire administrators • Provide subsidies to capital, labour, and consumers	• Decrease and alter the role of the state • Deregulate economy • Downsize bureaucracy • Impose budget austerity • Privatize SOEs • Eliminate subsidies • Increase foreign investment
Typical political implications	Creation of benefits: • Jobs • Construction and provisioning contracts • Increased budgets • Increased power for ministries and managers • Cheap interest, transportation, housing, and food	Imposition of costs: • Loss of jobs • Loss of state-provided economic and social benefits • Declining public sector budgets • More competition • Higher prices • Greater insecurity
Typical political response	• Incipient domestic private sector welcomes reforms and collaborate with them • Bureaucrats welcome increased role and power • Unions welcome more members • Urban consumers welcome low prices for food • Politicians welcome patronage • Voters support changes	• Domestic economic elites seek to protect benefits • Public sector workers protest loss of jobs • Unions resist loss of jobs • Urban constituents protest against loss of subsidies and services • Politicians seek to protect patronage • Voters see change as detrimental (at least in the short term)

Thus changing import-substitution policies meant challenging a wide range of powerful interests and institutions inside and outside government. In contrast, in most countries there were few interests that were organized to support change. Table 4.1 demonstrates the characteristic political economy surrounding the introduction of import substitution – primarily the provision of benefits – and that surrounding the introduction of neoliberal economic policies – generally the imposition of costs.

The case of access to education

Achieving the dual objectives of access and quality are at the heart of good policies for health, education, sanitation, water, housing and social protection. Nevertheless, even while policymakers usually seek to ensure that both access and quality are delivered at the same time, it is difficult to ensure that this will happen. In terms of the time, effort and complexities involved, it is simply easier to build schools than to prepare good teachers; easier to expand health infrastructure to rural areas than to ensure that health care professionals there are well trained, show up for work and deal effectively with patients; easier to provide new tubing than to maintain a sanitation system. Thus in the history of many social services, access can expand quite rapidly even while quality lags behind. When this is the case, access-type policies need to be complemented by quality-enhancing changes.

Many Latin American countries promoted policies to increase access to education, and during the 1950s, 1960s and 1970s schooling was expanded to many rural areas and to poor children in mushrooming urban squatter settlements. By the early 1990s, all of the region's constitutions guaranteed education as a right of citizenship and most parents registered their children in school when they reached the appropriate age. And by many of the principal outcomes that specialists look for in assessing the accomplishments of an educational system – the adult literacy rate, enrollments and gender disparities – the region had made significant progress. In 1950, 42 percent of Latin Americans were illiterate; by 1990 this figure had declined to 15 percent; and by 2000 to 12 percent. By 1990, approximately 85 percent of the total primary school age group was enrolled in school. Literacy rates and enrollment figures for females trailed those of males, but not by much. In 1990, 83.3 percent of Latin America's female population was literate, compared to 86.4 percent of its male population, and girls composed 49 percent of primary school enrollments (UNESCO, 2000; World Bank, 2000).

There were, of course, major differences in achievements within the region. Some countries approached full literacy, for example, while in others, illiteracy and low enrollments continued to be significant problems. Despite these failures, by the 1990s, Latin America's national education systems had done a creditable job of improving access to basic education for the vast majority of children. By the definition of success adopted in this volume, then, education policies of the 1950s, 1960s and 1970s were successful.

The region's record in providing quality education, however, was much less impressive. Repetition rates were high, and dropout rates suggested real problems relating to system efficiency and effectiveness.[8] In the early 1990s, on average, children in Latin America remained in school for seven years, but the average level of education achieved was only up to fourth grade level (Schiefelbein and Tedesco, 1995, cited in Reimers, 1999: 16). Tests of language and mathematics skills in the third and fourth grades indicated that average scores were low on a test described as 'much more simple and less sophisticated than the tests administered in industrialized countries' (Wolf *et al.*, 2000: 319). Most countries in the region fit the terms used in a Colombian government study to characterize primary education in that country: 'the quality is low, the rate of school failure and dropout is high, there is insufficient class time, and the curriculum is of little relevance for students.' (Departamento Nacional de Planeación, quoted in Hanson, 1995: 108).

Education was also inequitably provided. Data for individual countries indicate that the poor were less likely than the rich to finish primary school and much less likely to finish secondary education.[9] The same kinds of differences characterized children living in rural and urban areas. Because indigenous peoples tend to be among the poorest in the population and among the most rural, they were disproportionately represented among school-leavers.[10]

Educational administration was also highly inefficient at the start of the 1990s. Although there were certainly extensive unmet needs for resources in all countries, the problem was not primarily resources, but the inefficient use of resources (Birdsall *et al.*, 1995). Management of public education was almost everywhere at fault. Central ministries of education in most countries determined curricula, contracted teachers and supervisors, established standards for teacher training and classroom learning, administered salaries, managed budgets for school construction and repair, commissioned and selected textbooks, and promoted and disciplined teachers and their supervisors. Indeed, *dirigiste* national ministries of education were accused of being 'better at repressing change...than operating a system for steady improvement.' (Navarro *et al.*, n.d.: 18).

Typically, teaching and administrative appointments were made on the basis of patronage. In many countries, national teachers' unions virtually controlled the education ministries. A recurrent problem was that of 'ghost' workers, to whom salaries were regularly paid but who never appeared for work; absenteeism among teachers and their supervisors was extensive. Patronage in some countries virtually ensured security of tenure regardless of performance; in others, it meant frequent changes and great insecurity. To add to the difficulties, teachers were almost universally poorly trained (Navarro *et al.*, n.d.: 11–15). Particularly among older teachers, university education was not widespread and, in rural areas and in poorer countries, teachers at times had only eighth or ninth grade educations. Most teachers and administrators had few incentives for professional development, and most had no expectation of improving their conditions through promotion or demonstration of their capacities as educators.[11]

It should not be surprising, then, that by the 1990s there were advocates throughout Latin America arguing persuasively that better education was critical if countries were to wage effective battles against endemic poverty and inequality, if they were to gain advantages from globalization and if they were to build and sustain democratic citizenship and institutions. Research centres, universities and think tanks produced numerous studies of the problems of current systems and the imperatives for change. Similarly, international discussions during the 1990s emphasized the importance of education to political, social and economic development.

Making changes to alter the focus from access to quality, however, was politically difficult. At the centre of access policies were efforts to increase education budgets, train and hire more teachers, build more schools, distribute more textbooks and administer more programmes. In general, these reforms were politically popular. Although they cost money and required some administrative capacity, access reforms provided citizens with increased benefits and politicians with tangible resources to distribute to their constituencies. They created more jobs for teachers, administrators, service personnel, construction workers, and textbook and school equipment manufacturers. They increased the size and power of teachers' unions and central bureaucracies. In fact, unions were often among the principal advocates for broader access to public education. Given these characteristics, it is not too much to argue that these reforms were easy from a political economy perspective.

This could not be said of most of the 1990s proposals in education. Efforts to improve quality in the basic education systems emphasized increasing their efficiency, decentralizing control over important personnel, curricular and monitoring functions, involving parents and local communities in holding schools and teachers accountable for better performance, and altering the pedagogical orientation of teachers, textbooks and classroom materials. Quality enhancement in education involved the potential for lost jobs, and lost control over budgets, people and decisions. Such changes meant that central government ministries of education would have to give up power, take on new roles and pursue new responsibilities more effectively and efficiently. Often, regional and local governments were expected to assume responsibilities they had never carried out before. As indicated in Table 4.2, the politics of quality-enhancing policies differed significantly from those of access policies.

Moreover, to be successful, quality-enhancing changes required long chains of implementation activities and decisions. Ultimately, education changes had to be adopted at the classroom level if they were to improve the extent to which children learned critical skills and abilities. This meant that consent was needed at several levels of implementation for new initiatives to succeed. At any point in a long chain of decision-making responsibilities, reform activities could fall victim to sloth, political contention, mistaken judgment, organizational jealousies or logistical tangles. And, to add to the complexity, the benefits of the reforms would become evident only over the long term when students began to demonstrate that their lives were more productive and that they had expanded choices about their economic and social destinies. Generating and sustaining interest in the reforms was therefore an additional challenge, not least among parents and politicians.

Opposition to introducing policies to enhance the quality of basic education systems was fierce (Grindle, 2004; see Chapters 5 and 6). Powerful teachers' unions charged that they destroyed long-existing rights and career tracks. Bureaucrats charged that they gave authority to those who 'know nothing about education.' Governors and mayors frequently did not want the new responsibilities they were to be given. Parents often did not understand the new policies or the responsibilities they were expected to assume. Because they did not see the results of change in the short term, and because of powerful links between unions, ministries and political parties, politicians were reluctant to espouse the new policies. Indeed, when reformers failed in efforts to

Table 4.2 The politics of access and quality policies in education: a comparison

	Access reforms	**Quality-enhancing reforms**
Typical actions taken	• Build infrastructure • Expand bureaucracies • Increase budgets • Hire administrators • Hire service providers • Buy equipment	• Improve management • Increase efficiency • Alter rules/behaviour of personnel • Improve accountability • Improve performance • Strengthen local control
Typical political implications	Creation of benefits: • Jobs • Construction and provisioning contracts • Increased budgets • Increased power for ministries and managers	Imposition of costs: • Loss of jobs • Loss of decision-making power for some • New demands, expectations, responsibilities for others
Typical political response	• Unions of providers welcome reforms and collaborate with them • Politicians welcome tangible benefits to distribute to constituencies • Communities are pleased to receive benefits • Voters support changes	• Unions of providers resist reforms • Administrators seek to ignore or sabotage change • Many politicians wish to avoid promoting reforms • Many voters are unaware of changes (at least in the short term)

Source: Grindle (2004: 6)

introduce significant quality-enhancing reforms, politicians were pleased to fill the gap by reverting to more popular activities like building schools and improving infrastructure.

Upsetting policy equilibria: interests, institutions, agents

In both cases of success that turned sour over time, powerful interests developed around the policies in place for economic development and educational access. In Latin America in the early 1980s, several decades of successful import-substitution policies had benefited a number of powerful groups: domestic industrial elites, public sector workers and administrators, labour unions and urban consumers. In the 1990s, several decades of successful access-to-education policies had contributed to the power and organization of central ministries of education, their employees and large teachers' unions. Similarly, institutions such as government bureaucracies, political parties and elections helped support existing policies. On the other hand, with the exception of some policymakers, academics and analysts, there were few groups advocating change.

The failures of the past were clear to important decision-makers and analysts, international as well as domestic, and new models of what needed to be done existed. Economic analysts, for example, argued strongly that import-substitution policies had failed, had led countries to the brink of economic ruin, and needed to be scrapped in favour of more market-oriented liberalization policies. For advocates of education reform, access to schooling was not enough; this approach had to be significantly bolstered by quality-enhancing education reforms.

Yet those who were opposed to change were highly organized, very vocal and politically important. In contrast, those who might benefit from change were generally unorganized, dispersed, politically quiescent and possibly unaware of how they might benefit from change. Moreover, political institutions tended to be biased against change. In fact, economic reforms proposed in the 1980s and 1990s and the education reforms of the 1990s were so politically contentious that it was reasonable to assume they would not be adopted, implemented or sustained.

Yet in both cases significant change happened. In the case of national development strategies, Latin American countries were among those that embraced the 'Washington Consensus' of neoliberal reforms earliest and most fully (Birdsall and de la Torre, 2001). In the case of education, about two-thirds of the countries in the region introduced significant quality-enhancing policies during the 1990s (Grindle, 2004: 9–10). While import substitution was largely scrapped, access policies were not eschewed but rather amended with quality-enhancing initiatives.

The stories of how these changes happened are, in many ways, unique to each country, so that summarizing the dynamics of change, as is done below, will do violence to important variations among countries.[12] There are, however, some characteristics that are similar across countries. In each case, policy change was the result of top-down initiatives: presidents, ministers and high-level public officials initiated the changes and tried to direct and manage the political dynamics of doing so. There were few organized interests that supported their initiatives. In general, these actors did not believe that change would lead to important electoral gains in the short term. They knew they were taking on causes that were very unpopular with some of the most powerful groups in their countries.

Although these important decision-makers acted with varying degrees of skill and success and the particular constraints they faced varied by country, they shared some common resources. Most Latin American countries have long had political systems, both democratic and authoritarian, in which presidents and the executive wield considerably more power than legislatures, courts or regional and local governments. Moreover, the lack of broad civil service systems provides country and organizational leaders with considerable patronage power.

The case of economic liberalization

In the case of import substitution, a changing context of international and domestic economic conditions affected the interests that supported policy stasis and provided advocates of a new development model a critical opportunity to introduce change. As we have seen, the interests supporting this development strategy or deepening it became highly organized and powerful over the course of several decades: industrial elites, urban workers, bureaucrats, urban consumers, and often the political parties they were linked to.

Yet the equilibrium that held this development strategy in place was unsettled by the economic crisis of the early 1980s. The crisis itself reduced domestic demand for goods and services, cut off the supply of imports and made access to capital extremely difficult. These factors significantly increased economic pressure on domestic industrial elites. Stabilization policies introduced to deal with the crisis followed and brought renewed hardship for powerful actors:

bankruptcies, job loss, downsizing in the bureaucracy, withdrawal of subsidies, high interest rates, and more. Overall, these conditions weakened the capacity of important interests to resist liberalization policies. In addition, in some countries, high and hyper-inflation created such widespread hardship for many citizens that governments were encouraged to take action – almost any action – that could halt the spiraling of prices. Tolerance for change, therefore, increased in the context of crisis.

But crisis and its effects on important economic interests are not sufficient to explain how new development strategies were introduced. Nor were new policies simply imposed on Latin American countries by international financial institutions. While these organizations – the IMF and the World Bank in particular – played central roles in the policy changes of the 1980s and 1990s, the policies adopted were generally a matter of deep conviction among policymakers, who had become convinced of the error of prior policies. Agents – presidents and ministers of finance in many countries – worked to alter the power of the interests and the institutions of decision-making so that those who favoured change gained power, while those who opposed it were weakened.[13] It was a combination of a changed context and strategic political action that made it possible to change long-existing economic policies.

Throughout the region, presidents used their resources to introduce new development strategies.[14] They centralized power in the executive, and often in the office of the president. They took power away from spending ministries and enhanced the power of ministries of finance and central banks. They created powerful economic cabinets, appointed economic 'czars,' and brought technical units into close collaboration with high-level decision-makers. They limited access to decision-making arenas, and often protected economic technocrats from political pressure. They sought to minimize the power of traditional political party leaders in economic decision-making. They also managed legislative relations in promoting packages of reforms, activating political pacts, majority parties or decree laws to introduce new policies. In some cases, they introduced social adjustment programmes to absorb some of the hardship caused by major economic restructuring. From a very general perspective, their strategic actions were geared toward further weakening the power of the interests that supported existing policies while enhancing their own room for manoeuvre, undercutting institutional constraints on their power and creating new institutions that supported their activities.

Some of the presidents and ministers who led the efforts to alter economic policies were highly skilled, such as Carlos Salinas and Pedro Aspe in Mexico, Carlos Menem and Domingo Cavallo in Argentina, Victor Paz Estenssoro and Gonzalo Sanchez de Lozada in Bolivia, for example. Others were less successful – a succession of presidents in Venezuela, Ecuador and Brazil, for example. Their actions were not necessarily democratic and they were often strongly criticized and protested against violently in some cases. In introducing change, their coalitions were often formed of technocratic elites and international financial agencies, neither of which could provide much electoral support. Indeed it is unlikely that they would have been so able to promote the policies they did had it not been for a context of sustained economic crisis that helped weaken the opposition to change.

The case of educational quality

One significant advantage that the economic policy change advocates had was that, for many of their preferred policies, however contentious, implementation followed relatively easily from decision.[15] In the case of education reform, this was not so. Education policies, as we saw, require long chains of implementation decision-making if they are to be effective. Moreover, those who sought to introduce quality-enhancing policies did not have the advantage of a widely perceived and strongly felt crisis that affected large portions of the population and weakened entrenched interests, nor did they have the convenient scapegoat of the international financial institutions in explaining why change was essential.

Yet in some ways their strategies replicated those of the economic policy reformers.[16] Presidents and ministers who championed educational change worked from the top down, sought to weaken the teachers' unions that they saw as the principal obstacle to change – they connived at changing their leadership, they created competing organizations, they marginalized the unions from discussions of reform, they confronted them in the press over quality and accountability issues. In addition, policy and political leaders used their powers of appointment to wrest high-level positions in education ministries away from the control of the unions, they selected cohesive teams to design the policies, they limited access to the discussions of change and they used connections to international financial institutions to acquire resources. Also, they relied on political pacts, party alliances or administrative decrees to introduce the changes without much objection from legislative bodies. They did not spend much time trying to mobilize support coalitions outside government.

Thus as with the economic change advocates, education reformers sought to undermine the interests that opposed them, alter the biases of institutions that resisted change and use their strategic advantages to further their ends. These strategies were adapted to the particular circumstances of each country, of course, and resulted in different degrees of success in terms of how much current policies were altered. In some cases they chose to negotiate with the still powerful teachers' unions; in other cases they chose not to; in still other cases, they found they had little choice when unions refused to discuss change. There were tradeoffs in these choices. Negotiated policies could be implemented fairly quickly and uniformly, but often targeted goals that had been modified during negotiation; policies introduced in more confrontational settings had more coherence, but of necessity had to be introduced slowly or piecemeal in the face of ongoing resistance and conflict (Grindle, 2004: see Chapter 7).

In the case of education reform, then, leadership strategy was extraordinarily important in explaining the ability to make changes. The most powerful interests were strongly committed to resisting change, and institutions tended to enhance their power. Unlike the economic policy changes, contextual conditions had not significantly undermined the capacity of the interests to resist. They went on strike, marched in the streets, camped out in front of the ministry of education, brought traffic to a standstill in capital cities. At times their protests turned violent, as cars were set on fire, shop windows broken, and police called in to restore order. In many cases, they proposed alternatives to the policies being promoted by presidents and ministers, and they used their ties to political parties to discourage policy change.

Skilful use of political resources helped a number of countries embark on quality-enhancing education policies during the 1990s and 2000s. Yet because education policies are more implementation-intensive than is characteristic of neoliberal economic reforms, their success in institutionalizing new systems of quality and accountability is not yet certain. Moreover, because education policies tend to be more 'chosen by' than 'pressed upon' policy decision-makers, in Albert Hirschman's terms, in some countries even skilful advocates of change were overcome by other issues that claimed their attention or that overwhelmed their leadership (Hirschman, 1981). As a result, it was more possible for the advocates of economic liberalization to congratulate themselves on their progress in changing policies than it was for those who promoted improved educational quality.

Conclusions: moving targets

Most development policymaking proceeds in the firm belief that new policies will pay off in terms of enhanced growth and social welfare. Whether they do or not is an empirical question that is generally answerable only in hindsight. Moreover, as we have seen, policies may deliver on initial promises but fail over the longer term, or may need to be enhanced with other initiatives. To the extent that this is true, policymaking for development is the pursuit of a moving target.

Neoliberal economic policy champions of the 1980s and 1990s were firmly convinced they had an answer to the development problems of Latin America. They could cite theories and studies to demonstrate the wisdom of their policy preferences. Education reformers in the 1990s were similarly deeply committed to their ideas about how schools could do a better job of educating children for productive and satisfying lives. They had the research to demonstrate the soundness of their policy visions.

Yet it is not at all clear that the new policies will become development successes. They replaced or revised failing policies, but did they in turn deal effectively with the problem of economic growth and poverty alleviation? Certainly, with the exception of Chile, neoliberal economic reforms have not led to sustained growth in Latin American countries nor has their positive impact been broad-based – poverty, unemployment and social distress advanced in many countries in the 1990s and 2000s.[17] Quality-enhancing education initiatives have suffered implementation setbacks and have not yet provided much evidence that they are making a difference to the destinies of poor children in the region.

In recent years, development professionals have become more committed to the view that development policies must be tailored to the individual circumstances of particular countries.[18] Thus, long lists of pre-conditions that must be 'got right' for development to occur are increasingly being eschewed in favour of thinking about a limited number of policy interventions that focus on a few critical constraints that are particularly important in a specific country. For many development economists, for example (see especially Rodrik, 2003), these kinds of targeted changes were critically important for sustained economic growth in China, Vietnam, India and several other countries.

To the extent that this kind of thinking gains ground, a successful development policy would be one that deals effectively with the bottlenecks, constraints, or adjustments deemed to be most important for unlocking the potential for growth and poverty alleviation in a specific country. Of course, understanding the nature of these constraints – which obstacles are most important and how best to address them – continues to be a source of significant debate, not least among economists. Yet many are now ready to acknowledge that the contents of a successful policy can and do change across countries and across time within countries. This is a hopeful development.

Even with a more catholic approach to the factors that contribute to development, however, the issue of the political equilibria that surround existing policies continues to constrain policy change initiatives. Whether new policies for economic development and educational quality in Latin America pay off or not, for example, they have created new political contexts that are important if efforts are made to alter or replace them.

In the case of economic development policies, a wide variety of financial sector interests, urban, professional and technocratic elites and foreign investors are among the new interests that have benefited from the policies and that will seek to maintain and deepen these policies. Institutions such as central banks, stock exchanges and regulatory agencies have grown in power. In the case of education policy, decentralization (a central component of most of the reforms) means that much of the conflict over subsequent education policies will not be centred in national capitals but will be distributed widely in the states, municipalities, or school districts where the important decisions about resource allocation and personnel are made. While teachers' unions have been weakened in some cases, they remain significant actors in education policy in almost all countries. In the future, state and local departments of education or local school councils may be the institutions that hold new distributions of power in place. Results of change initiatives are likely to be increasingly varied as the sites of conflict and change multiply.

Thus the politics of development success is also a moving target. Even when policies that have outlived their usefulness are changed, they put in place new policies that create both winners and losers and that can have unintended consequences. New interests, new institutional biases and, no doubt, new agents will contest change in new contexts. In such cases, development may be the result of the capacity to change and revise policies as well as the ability to generate good ideas.

In this chapter I have argued for the importance of agency in explaining how policy change happens. But, as the cases of import substitution and educational quality indicate, agency is always constrained by the particular context within which it is exercised, and by the mobilization of interests that support existing policies and the biases of institutions that sustain them. In fact, the politics of policy change reflect a dynamic interaction of interests, institutions and agency in a particular (and sometimes changing) context that unfolds over time.

Figure 4.1 presents a basic framework for understanding the factors that tend to be most influential in explaining the process of policy change. This process is a complex one that includes how issues come to be part of public agendas, how they are designed, what factors affect how they are negotiated, agreed to or rejected, and what influences whether they can be implemented and sustained over time. Of course, these phases are not independent of one another. How an issue gets on a policy agenda may easily affect who is involved in designing it or who needs to agree to its reformist content, for example. Equally, although the figure suggests a linear process of decision-making and implementation, in fact there are feedback loops and constraints that operate at each phase to promote, alter, or stymie opportunities for change: a reform can be redefined during negotiation or implementation, for example.

Of course, policy change initiatives occur in particular economic, political and social contexts. History matters: these contexts represent different configurations of interests, institutions and actors, and the legacies of prior political interactions. They represent distinct state-society relationships, political cleavages, prior policy initiatives and a range of distinct social and political conflicts. Efforts to introduce and implement new policies are not written on a political tabula rasa. Thus Figure 4.1 is only a general schematic of the factors that enhance or hinder policy change processes. Its purpose is to provide some guidance about the interactions of interests, institutions and agency.

To simplify, each of the phases of the reform process is an arena shaped by the variety of interests involved in a particular issue and the institutions that shape their relative power, resources and influence. Over time, those who seek to introduce policy change may have opportunities to work within these arenas to affect such interests and, in some cases, the institutions, in ways that can promote change; opponents of reform also have such opportunities. Thus, strategic actions and choices can, at times, affect the prospects for change. The figure emphasizes, however, that opportunities for change are always

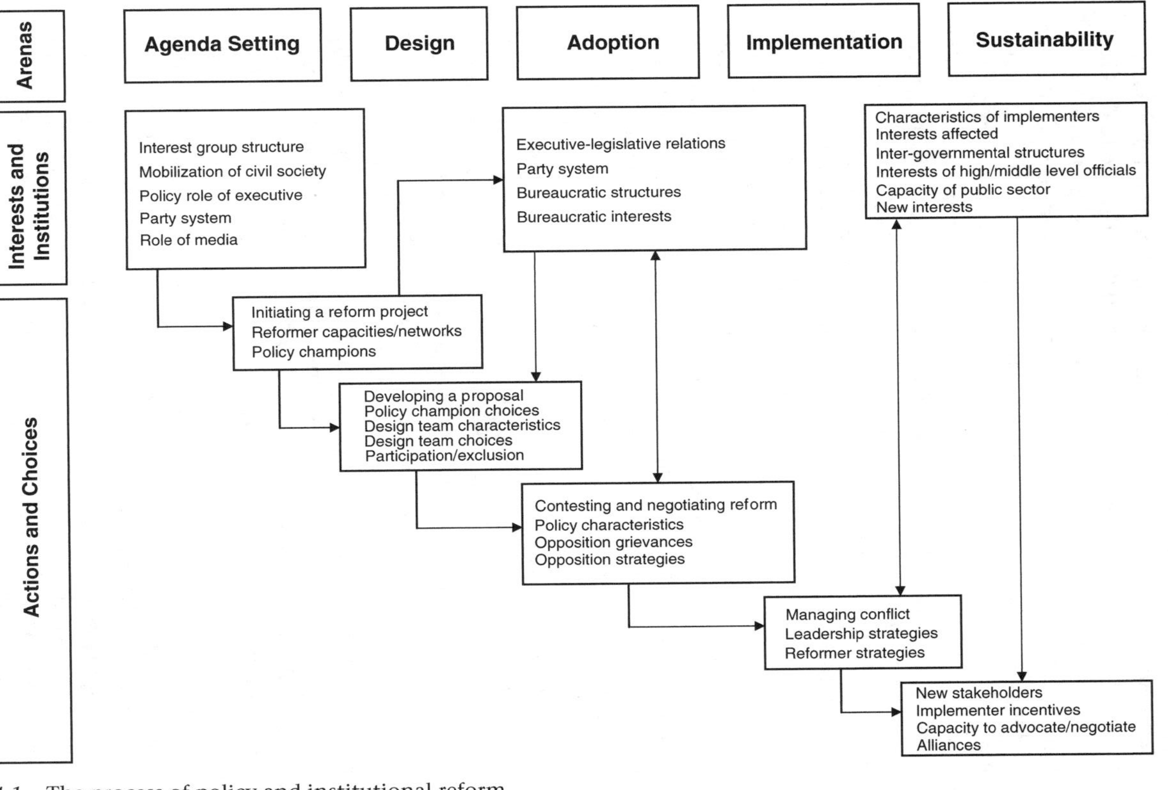

Figure 4.1 The process of policy and institutional reform
Source: adapted from Grindle, 2004.

constrained or even nullified by the histories of existing institutions, structures of political power and capacities.

Can countries increase the likelihood that policies will be changed when they are no longer delivering benefits that contribute to development? Interestingly, in the case of the readiness to make policy changes, developing countries may have some advantages over already developed countries. Policy change is inevitably difficult in all countries. Well-institutionalized political systems, such as those that characterize most industrialized countries, have some characteristics that should make policy change easier. They have, for example, extensive capacity to invest in information and analysis of the consequences of existing policies; they have well-educated populations and extensive media institutions that play a role in promoting public debate about important issues; and in some, programmatic political parties and parliamentary systems ease the difficulties of mobilizing legislative majorities for policy change. Yet these are also countries in which interests are powerfully organized, money has enormous impact on politics, political executives are constrained by custom, law and the media, and decision-making takes place in well-institutionalized settings that often provide little room for manoeuvre. Given these characteristics, policy changes face considerable obstacles.

In contrast, developing and transitional countries tend to have policymaking systems that are easier to change than those in already developed countries. Their institutions tend to be weaker and more flexible, the role of their political executives less constrained, their political parties more personalistic and clientelistic, the capacity of external actors to exert pressure greater and their vulnerability to external shocks much more significant. These are factors that actually facilitate change of policies, even while they also often undermine their durability. In such circumstances, are there remedies that would enhance opportunities for changing failing policies?

The response to this question is only speculative. Certainly, the establishment of states that are widely viewed as legitimate and that are not simply tools of particular elite groups or leaders is one way to open up debates about what is an appropriate policy. Certainly also, the broader spread of information about conditions and analyses of their causes can spark broader policy debates within countries. In this regard, the expansion of university research units, think tanks, independent media and other resources for generating information and analysis and sharing them broadly among populations is important to stimulate debate and encourage the production of new options. The development of programmatic parties that compete in regular and fair elections can give voice to alternative proposals for development. Political reforms that institutionalize the circulation of political elites can also lead to the critical analysis of existing policy and opportunities to introduce new ones. Creating institutions with some autonomy to adjust policies, such as central banks that monitor and correct for emerging macroeconomic problems, is also relevant.

There may be some possibilities for increasing the effectiveness of political institutions in monitoring, informing and debating policies, and undermining the power of elites who benefit from existing policies. Ultimately, however, the politics of policy change remain a moving target, as do the remedies for underdevelopment.

Notes

1 The political economy literature making this point is extensive. In the 1970s, Anne O. Krueger (1974) wrote an influential article on the politics of rent-seeking. Robert Bates (1981) explored the relationship between policy and its beneficiaries in a widely cited book. For an overview, see Geddes (1995). In my own research, I have been impressed by the extent to which development policy *creates* interests and institutions (see Grindle, 1986). This stands in some contrast to a pluralist perspective on political economy, in which government is a more or less passive recipient of pressures from interests that already exist and is closely constrained by already existing institutions.

2 See, for examples, Grindle (2004); Haggard and Kaufman (1992); Nelson (1990); and Williamson (1994).

3 Raúl Prebisch led a team of economists at the United Nations Economic Commission for Latin America and published an influential treatise about opportunities for economic growth in Latin America in 1950. See Prebisch (1950).

4 See Grindle (1986) for a discussion of the role of agriculture in industrial development.

5 For discussions of the problems of macroeconomic stability under import substitution, see Dornbusch and Edwards (1991).

6 For discussions of the crisis, see Grindle (1996: Chapters 1 and 2).

7 Useful discussions of the role of ideas and professional training in the neoliberal 'revolution' are found in Bierstecker (1995). See also Stallings (1992).

8 According to a UNESCO/UNICEF study, in 1989, only 38 percent of Dominican children graduated from the sixth grade, of Brazilians, only 35 percent, and of Nicaraguans, only 19 percent. Data presented in Larrañaga (1997: 331).

9 Unless otherwise indicated, data in this paragraph are taken from Reimers (1999: 8–9).

10 In the late 1990s, non-indigenous adult Guatemalans had received, on average, five years of education; their indigenous counterparts, two years; in

Peru, the gap was about three years and in Bolivia, it was five years (PREAL, 2001: 10).

11 For an extended discussion of the paucity of incentives for greater professionalism among Latin American teachers, see Navarro (2002).

12 A very large literature addresses these issues for individual countries. For a sampling, see Smith, Acuña, and Gamarra (1994).

13 At times, those who led the process of policy change were elected to office with the expectation that they would introduce policies to return their countries to the better days of the past. This was the case, for example, with Carlos Menem in Argentina and Carlos Andres Pérez in Venezuela.

14 For case studies, see Dominguez (1996); and Grindle (1996).

15 Good examples of this are devaluation and deregulation. In the former, little is needed other than the agreement of the ministry of economy, the presidency and the central bank. In deregulation, the state ceases to do things it had done in the past.

16 See the case studies in Grindle (2004).

17 Economists familiar with the experience of Latin America disagree about whether yet more market-oriented reforms are necessary, or whether the reforms introduced thus far have been an inappropriate response to the problems of the region.

18 Thus for example, for some countries, establishing peace and security is a major step toward introducing conditions more conducive to economic growth and poverty alleviation; for other countries, further development may be contingent upon dealing effectively with the AIDS epidemic; for yet others, improved possibilities for development may hinge on introducing complex institutional changes to allow for participation in an international or regional trade regime; for still others, a critical constraint on development may lie outside national borders, as when large debt burdens severely restrict government investments in infrastructure.

5

Why has Microfinance been a Policy Success in Bangladesh?

David Hulme and Karen Moore[1]

Introduction

If you ask a rich world citizen with an interest in development to name a development policy that works, there is a very strong chance they will say 'microfinance', and tell you that they have heard it works wonders in Bangladesh. In the public eye, and according to many analysts, microfinance has been successful. The microfinance industry now has global outreach, with more than 92 million clients reported in developing countries.[2] It is very difficult to find a Poverty Reduction Strategy that does not include microfinance as an element.

The most common account is that the microfinance industry has its roots in Bangladesh with the Grameen Bank, and it is on Bangladesh that this chapter will mainly focus. According to this account the initial success of microfinance in Bangladesh has diffused across the world.[3] If we step back to the late 1970s this seems a most unlikely scenario. The precursors of microfinance – rural credit and small farmer credit – had a history of dramatic policy failure, charted by the Ohio State School. At that time, it was widely acknowledged that attempts to provide poor people (at that time synonymous with small farmers) with small loans had been disastrous (see Adams *et al.*, 1984 and others). They failed to get credit to poor people, did little to improve agricultural yields and had high rates of default, so that viable rural finance institutions could not be established. Poor people were viewed as not being 'bankable'. The high unit costs of transactions, the inability of poor people to repay loans and the political manipulation of credit initiatives meant that development policy would be well advised to withdraw from this domain and leave all banking to the private, for-profit sector.

This chapter charts the overturning of this orthodoxy. After a brief discussion of the meanings of key terms, we provide a rapid history of the development of the microfinance industry in Bangladesh. Building on this, we examine the evidence of the success of the microfinance industry in Bangladesh – in terms of outreach, economic and social effects on its predominantly female clients and their households, broader national-level effects, processes of institutional development, and the export and replication of the Bangladesh experience outside its borders – and touch on critiques of the microfinance paradigm.

In the second part of this chapter, we use the framework developed by McCourt and Bebbington (Chapter 1, this volume) to explore the reasons why microfinance has performed well. On one hand, there is the innovative design and specification of microfinance policy, the ways in which it has been implemented on the ground, and the processes of learning and adaptation underlying the broader development of the microfinance industry. On the other, there are the ways in which microfinance institutions have managed a favourable demographic, infrastructural and political-economic environment, and the crucial role of the exceptional ability and performance of both the leaders of the microfinance movement, and of the millions of poor people who make up its clientele. We conclude by briefly describing the diffusion of microfinance around the world, and drawing out a number of general lessons about the processes that lead to successful development policy.

In this account, development policy is not seen as something that only governments do. Rather, as McCourt and Bebbington articulate, it is seen as any action that has, or is intended to have, large-scale developmental effects, so that it can be something involving both governmental and non-governmental organizations, as well as individuals, and their networks. As we detail below, while the microfinance industry in Bangladesh has been closely associated with the experiences of NGOs and largely remains within their domain, government has always 'participated' – to a limited extent as providers and regulators, but more crucially in terms of creating an enabling environment for microfinance institutions, or at least not hindering them. Recent institutional and regulatory developments suggest that microfinance in Bangladesh has truly come of age as public policy, with microfinance institutional approaches moving from 'parallel', to 'competitive substitute', to 'transforming the mainstream'.[4]

What is microfinance?

As noted above, in the post-war period farmers' lack of access to credit was identified as a major obstacle to the development of impoverished rural areas, leading to the establishment of subsidized government lending schemes and rural cooperatives throughout the developing world. However, it became apparent that these endeavours were not able to overcome the screening, monitoring and enforcement problems that restrict poor people's access to the formal financial sector. In most cases, the poor were not reached, nor were the institutions financially sustainable (see Adams *et al.*, 1984; Hoff *et al.*, 1993). Experimentation in 1970s Bangladesh with community development models in the form of the renowned 'Comilla Model' – is a case in point. Only isolated success was achieved, due to the model's disregard of the diversity of village social structure and the co-option of inputs and institutions by richer farmers (Chowdhury, 1989; Wood, 1992).

In order to confront the problems inherent in lending to the poor, there have been large-scale innovations in the provision of financial services over the past three decades. Generally, these new systems have been called 'microcredit' – provision of small-scale loans to the poor – and more recently 'microfinance' – provision of a range of the poor's financial service requirements, including credit, savings, insurance and remittance management. The majority of microfinancial interventions have been targeted at off-farm small and microenterprises (SMEs). Generally, those businesses which produce goods and services utilizing few employees and limited capital are described as SMEs, although this basic definition masks a world of diversity. For instance, whereas microenterprises usually exhibit a home-based ownership and labour structure, small enterprises often hire outside labour.

In the developing world, innovation in microfinancial services has been most notably demonstrated through the credit-focused peer-monitoring model targeted at poor women developed by the Grameen Bank of Bangladesh. However, throughout low-income and marginalized communities in Asia, Africa and the Americas, models have emerged that represent important adaptations of the Grameen model, as well as some very different approaches to financial service provision.[5] Microfinance service providers (often known as microfinance institutions or MFIs), are most often non-governmental organizations (NGOs). However, there are also a number of government-sponsored MFIs as well as statutory banks involved in microlending, and institutions that act as intermediaries between banks and borrowers. As noted, these 'of non-poor, for poor' programmes (Copestake, 1995) take a variety of approaches to the provision of credit and, to varying extents, other financial services. Furthermore, different types and amounts of non-financial inputs – from skills training and marketing, to organizational support, health and education, for example – are also provided by many MFIs in accordance with their particular goals.

Poverty alleviation or reduction is an ultimate goal of most MFIs, with either direct or indirect links to immediate objectives. Objectives are in turn determined by the organization's ideological outlook, in particular how the organization perceives the relationship between poverty alleviation and access to credit. The ease with which a poverty-focused intervention can be carried out and the efficiency with which it can be monitored and evaluated, are also very important factors. For instance, Hashemi (1997: 250) states that Professor Muhammad Yunus, founder of the Grameen Bank,

> discovered that while the credit market was the scene of the most brutal exploitation of the poor (with high interest rates leading to persistent indebtedness leading to forced sale of assets and destitution), it was also the arena where interventions were easiest for allowing the poor to break out of their cycle of poverty.

If financial liquidity problems are seen as a central reason for poverty, as perceived by Yunus, the organization will more or less confine its role to the provision of credit – this has been called the 'credit minimalist' approach. These organizations tend to evaluate their success in terms of financial indicators of outreach and repayment, although consideration of impact is certainly not unknown. If, on the other hand, poverty is viewed as a result of a more complex process, involving liquidity problems as well as other factors, the organization's objectives will tend to incorporate the provision of a larger range of financial, economic, social and organizational interventions – this has been called the 'credit plus' approach. The immediate goal in this case is generally not service provision in itself, but rather the provision of services that will have a positive and observable impact on poverty (Copestake, 1995).

A brief history of microfinance in Bangladesh – experiment, expansion, innovation[6]

A thumbnail sketch of the major MFIs in Bangladesh is provided in Appendix 1.

In 1971 Bangladesh emerged as an independent nation, ravaged by war and natural disaster, with many destitute people but also a significant cadre of young activists full of hope, energy and commitment to reconstruction and nation-building. As the new government failed to meet its substantial challenges, even with overseas assistance, small non-governmental organizations emerged over the 1970s to organize relief and rehabilitation through community development. As noted above, however, elite capture of resources plagued community development experiments, so targeted approaches began to be tried.

The Grameen Bank started as an action research project in 1976, when a Chittagong University team led by economics professor Muhammad Yunus began to lend small amounts of money to poor households in a few nearby villages. Borrowers were organized into small 'peer monitoring' groups of four or five people (soon becoming single sex groups, with a focus on women's groups) that met weekly with other groups to make loan repayments. Demand for credit grew rapidly and repayment rates were good, so the project was able to secure loans for on-lending from the state-controlled Bangladesh Bank and other commercial banks. In 1984, the Grameen Bank became a government-regulated bank through a special government ordinance, and remains the only body regulated in this way.

Early on in its evolution the Grameen Bank focused on women, and currently more than 95 percent of its active members are female. There were two main reasons for this. The first was targeting. In Bangladesh, women are often the poorest and most marginalized citizens, and this was particularly the case after the 1971 war. The second reason was organizational performance: women's groups functioned better than male groups, and there were significantly fewer problems with repayment. Many other MFI's in Bangladesh and elsewhere have replicated this focus on women.

Over the next two decades NGOs grew in number and scale, and by the early 1990s the experiences of BRAC, Proshika and ASA, as well as the Grameen Bank, dominated development discourse in Bangladesh. The early 1990s in particular was a period of rapid expansion of access to microcredit. Procedures were by then established and standardized, and computerization became more common, allowing the MFIs to intensify disbursement and repayment monitoring. The Grameen Bank and NGO MFIs used donor funds and, increasingly, member savings and interest payments, to open new branches across the country. During this period, a wholesale financing institution (PKSF) also emerged (see below).

But by the mid-1990s it seemed that the very success of 'first generation' MFIs led by the Grameen Bank was hindering the development of new and different approaches (Hulme in Rogaly, 1996). The movement of the integrated, socially-focused programming of ASA in particular, but also of BRAC and other NGOs, towards that of the finance-minimalist Grameen Bank was clear and noted by many.[7] Zaman (2004: 51) notes that 'the benefits of a narrow focus on microcredit during the expansion phase was that it kept costs low, operations transparent, and management oversight relatively straightforward.'

From the mid-1990s, however, a range of 'second generation' innovations began to emerge, as it became increasingly clear that the poor required a wider range of financial services; that the existing services, particularly savings, needed to be made more flexible; that the needs of vulnerable non-poor micro- and small entrepreneurs were not being met; and that the poorest were often excluded from microfinance. This change in focus was based on feedback from the field in Bangladesh and internationally, and a large amount of research, conducted both in-house (by BRAC and Proshika researchers in particular) as well as by national and international academics and consultants. The emergence of SafeSave in 1997 as an experiment dedicated to investigating the possibilities of savings-led, individual-oriented microfinance was a forerunner of the period.

As noted in Appendix 1, not even the Grameen Bank was exempt from this trend. In 2001–2002, all Grameen Bank branches began to operate the new, simpler and much more flexible 'Grameen Generalised System' (also called 'Grameen II'), which offers four types of loan products: basic loan, housing loan, higher education loan and struggling members' (beggars') loan. There is also a facility for larger small enterprise loans, and there is a range of companies (both commercial and not-for-profit) in the Grameen family.

What has been achieved by microfinance in Bangladesh?

McCourt and Bebbington define development success as the tangible enhancement of the human capabilities of a significant population of otherwise disadvantaged people, whether through direct investments and improvements in their assets or through the improvement of the environments in which poor people pursue their well-being. It is clear that microfinance in Bangladesh at least reaches 'a significant population of otherwise disadvantaged people': people with low and unstable incomes, little or no land or assets, low social status and few if any alternative sources of financial services that are both accessible and affordable. The extent to which there has been a 'tangible enhancement of their capabilities' is of course a normative and debated question, but on balance the evidence suggests that this is the case, particularly through asset enhancement but also via positive effects on the socio-economic environments in which the poor work and live.

The numbers

The selection of which statistics to highlight is, of course, also a normative decision, and unsurprisingly different institutions and networks, in Bangladesh and globally, choose different statistics to collect and publish.[8] Here we touch only on the immense scale of the Bangladeshi microfinance sector, in terms of numbers of MFIs and numbers of clients, both in absolute terms and in relation to the microfinance sector globally. We also note the dominance of a few large MFIs.

Most NGOs are involved in microfinance to a greater or lesser extent. According to the Credit and Development Forum (CDF), in 2002 there were as many as 1200 MFIs; a more recent CDF estimate suggests that about 1500 MFIs currently operate in Bangladesh, with another 500 entities soon to join the industry. Most MFIs (except those run by government bodies) consistently report repayment rates of 98 percent or more.

In 2002, about 13 million poor households had access to credit and other financial services through the 1200 MFIs. This figure excludes over three million Grameen Bank borrowers, but also is likely to overestimate the total number of poor households with access to microcredit due to the practice of individuals and households borrowing from more than one source. On its website, PKSF notes that 'There is debate ... on the extent of overlap ...(but the) general consensus is that a national average would be that 15 percent of all borrowers are borrowing from more than one MFI'.[9] In this case,

> the effective coverage is about 11 million households. Out of 11 million households covered by (microcredit programmes), about 80% are below the poverty line and so about 8.8 million poor

households are covered by microcredit programmes. With an estimated number of households of 26 million, out of which about 46% are poor households, the total number of poor households is approximately 11.96 million. Therefore, there is still scope for extending the coverage of microcredit programs to an approximate 3.16 million households.

From this estimate, it seems that at least 80 percent of poor households are covered by microfinance services. While the figure is certainly substantial, the assumptions about the proportion of MFI clients who are among the poorest are questionable and open to redefinition and debate.

According to data gathered by the Microcredit Summit Campaign, by the end of 2004 330 'verified' Bangladeshi MFIs (which include the Grameen Bank, NGOs, MFI networks, government bodies and commercial banks offering some form of microfinance) had 24.4 million active clients, three-quarters of whom were poor and two-thirds of whom were poor women (see Tables 5.1 and 5.2 below). The majority of borrowers are clients of the handful of very large organizations discussed above: the Grameen Bank, BRAC, ASA and Proshika. Of the

Table 5.1 Bangladeshi MFI data verified by Microcredit Summit, in a global context

	Number of MFIs	Number of poorest clients (millions)	Number of active clients (millions)	Proportion of active clients who are 'poorest'	Number of poorest who are women (millions)	Proportion of poorest who are women
Verified Bangladeshi MFIs	103 (31%)	18.4 (31%)	24.4 (29%)	75%	16.1 (33%)	88%
Total verified MFIs	330	58.5	77.9	75%	49.2	84%
Total reporting MFIs	*3,164*	*66.6*	*92.3*	*72%*	*55.6*	*84%*

Source: Daley-Harris (2005) (Appendix 1 and personal communication with Microcredit Summit team).
Notes: Figures pertain to the end of 2004; figures in parentheses represent the proportion of total verified MFIs made up by Bangladeshi verified MFIs; 'poorest clients' are those estimated to have been living on less than US$1/day, or in the bottom half of those below the national poverty line when they took their first loan; 'active clients' are those with an outstanding loan; figures do not take into account 'membership overlap' – those who borrow from more than one MFI.

Table 5.2 Top 10 Microcredit Summit-verified Bangladeshi MFIs, based on number of poorest clients

	Number of 'poorest' clients (31/12/04)	Number of active clients (31/12/04)	Proportion of active clients who are 'poorest'	Number of 'poorest' who are women	Proportion of 'poorest' who are women
Grameen Bank	4,060,000	4,060,000	100%	3,897,600	96%
BRAC	3,630,000	3,990,000	91%	3,630,000	100%
Bangladesh Rural Development Board (BRDB)*	3,528,041	3,713,728	95%	2,399,068	68%
ASA	2,490,000	2,770,000	90%	2,390,400	96%
Proshika	1,236,104	1,545,130	80%	803,468	65%
Sonali Bank**	500,000	3,800,000	13%	365,000	73%
Caritas	251,273	284,947	88%	173,378	69%
Thenamara Mohila Sabuj Sangha (TMSS)	250,664	278,516	90%	238,131	95%
BURO, Tangail	221,366	221,366	100%	219,152	99%
Rangpur Dinajpur Rural Service (RDRS)	175,713	228,199	77%	140,570	80%
TOTAL	**16,343,161**	**20,891,886**	**78%**	**14,256,767**	**87%**

Source: Daley-Harris (2005)
Notes: *Government body acting as a network of MFIs not included elsewhere; **nationalised commercial bank.

remaining organizations, only 12 have over 100,000 borrowers, but many of the smaller MFIs join ASA, BURO Tangail and TMSS as the most profitable MFIs in South Asia (Tazi, 2005).

Evidence of economic impact

There are three pathways through which improved access to financial services is held to improve household food security and well-being (Zeller *et al.*, 1997):

- Yunus' now famous virtuous circle of 'low income, credit, investment, more income, more credit, more investment, more income...'

asserts the primary process by which microfinance is envisaged as improving the economic well-being of borrowers: loans for investment in income-generating activities (Hulme and Mosley, 1996). This can be divided further into two streams:

- First, additional capital can be used to enhance the level of the household's productive human and physical capital (i.e. learn new skills, hire workers, rent land, purchase tools and inputs etc.) – 'this is the traditional argument for credit' (Zeller *et al.*, 1997: 25).
- Second, with improved access to credit, the risk-bearing capacity of the household can be increased so that riskier but potentially more profitable activities or technologies may be adapted.

- The second pathway has been identified as a positive effect on the composition of assets and liabilities. In terms of credit, this is chiefly manifested in a reduced need to obtain credit at high cost from informal sources (e.g. the notorious usurious moneylender), or to sell off productive assets at a low price in emergencies (see also Hashemi *et al.*, 1996; Todd, 1996). Instead, storage of crops and other products for sale at a later time and a higher price may increase with improved access to credit.
- The third pathway is through 'consumption smoothing'. This pathway remains generally discouraged by MFIs, as it is seen to detract from the potentially larger and more sustainable impacts of credit through income-generating activities. However, there is an increased awareness of the long-term importance of maintaining, for example, nutrition and education inputs to children, and Bangladeshi MFIs have adapted their procedures to take this into account.

Does all this work? Have poor Bangladeshis economically benefited from their enhanced access to microfinance, and if so, to what extent? Over the past 15 years, much research has been undertaken on this issue, from professionally-run large-scale impact assessments and village-level ethnographies to journalistic and anecdotal field reports. Different definitions and different methodologies, more or less rigorous, have been employed (see Sinha, 2005). Understandably, evidence on the economic impact of microfinance is often contested.

On balance, however, there is evidence that microfinance, on average and in general, does have a positive economic impact on clients in terms of income growth and reduced vulnerability, although the effects are often small (see Mayoux, 1995), and all clients do not benefit equally. This is the finding of Khandker's recent study on the effects of microfinance on poverty, and his review of previous studies therein. Referring to a joint World Bank-Bangladesh Institute of Development Studies research project in the late 1990s, one of the most comprehensive and rigorous impact studies to date, Khandker (2005: 266) finds 'strong evidence that the programs help the poor through consumption smoothing and asset building' and that 'microfinance helps women acquire assets of their own'.

Further, based on the analysis of panel data spanning the 1990s, Khandker reports that microfinance 'raises per capita household consumption for both participants and nonparticipants' (*ibid*: 285), increasing the probability that program participants will escape poverty. In 1991/2, the average return to women's cumulative borrowing was 18 percent, and by 1998/9 this had risen to 21 percent. This resulted in an annual decline of the poverty rate among programme participants of five percentage points in 1991/2, and two percentage points in 1998/9. The lower rate in 1998/9, argues Khandker, is due both to diminishing returns to borrowing as well as to overall better economic conditions, as microfinance also has village-level 'spillover' effect, reducing both extreme and moderate poverty even among non-participants. Microfinance accounts for more than half of the overall observed annual poverty reduction of three percentage points among programme participants, and up to 40 percent of the overall village-level annual poverty reduction of one percentage point. Khandker finds that for both participants and non-participants the effect of microfinance is stronger for the extreme poor compared to the moderately poor, and that the effects of female borrowing are much stronger than for male borrowing.

If so many MFIs are involved in lending to so many poor, primarily rural Bangladeshis, and on average it helps them and their neighbours improve their economic condition, why does the rural poverty rate remain so high? First, economic improvements that are significant but insufficient to lift a household above the poverty line do not contribute to declines in headcount poverty rates. Second, microfinance participation is high but nowhere near universal, and active participation is rarely continuous. And it is important to note that, modest as an annual two percentage point decline in poverty rates among rural microfinance participants seems, it still represents up to half a million people escaping poverty each year. Most importantly, however, the quantity and quality of growth remain crucial factors in determining levels of rural poverty (Sen and Hulme, 2006), both directly and through constraining the gains achieved by MFI clients. Microfinance helps, but it is not a panacea. Other economic and non-economic interventions are also required.

Evidence of social impact and women's empowerment

Although microfinance's initial objective was not primarily in the 'social' realm, if at all, most MFIs do now identify one or more social goals: women's empowerment, children's school attendance, awareness of and demand for health services, for example. Evidence of the social impact of microfinance in Bangladesh has also been mixed, but again, on balance, it suggests that microfinance and the associated activities of MFIs have had positive social effects. Indeed, it often seems as if this fundamentally economic approach has performed best in the social domain. Khandker (2005: 266) notes that the earlier WB/BIDS study 'supports the claim that microfinance programs promote investment in human capital (such as schooling) and raise awareness of reproductive health issues (such as the use of contraceptives) among poor families', and that microfinance helps women 'exercise power in household decision-making'.

It is widely recognized that access to credit can foster social, psychological and even political empowerment. Credit services for the poor, and particularly poor women, reverse their systemic exclusion from access to public or private funds, thus altering systems of hierarchy and power (see, for example, Todd, 1996). Access to alternative means of finance can reduce dependence on moneylenders; at the same time, access to institutional credit can also be used as a bargaining chip in order to secure informal loans. In general, a levelling of the playing field occurs, allowing the poor to participate more effectively in the social, economic and political workings of their community. Thus, Hedrick-Wong *et al.*'s (1997) assertion – that credit provision in itself does not challenge any of the structural reasons for poverty – is not valid.

Structures of power at the household level are also affected. Credit becomes a bargaining chip for many women, in terms of both improving their fall-back position, and allowing them to 'negotiate transfers' with those who hold some form of social control. In Bangladesh, women's economic contributions to the household are traditionally in labour and kind, and as such are often invisible. Access to an institutional loan in cash 'may induce a revaluing of women's contribution to household survival', so that women's status within the household, their access to resources for themselves and their children, and familial stability may all rise' (Goetz and Gupta, 1996: 53–4). Similarly, widows with loans have been noted by Todd (1996: 84) to have a stronger claim of support on sons who want access to credit.

Further, for a woman who has seldom if ever come into contact with a significant amount of money, an MFI loan can result in greater self-confidence and self-worth. Women can use credit as a bargaining chip with their male relatives to gain access to a group of community women – the credit group – and to any other services that an MFI might be offering in the way of skills training, education and health services. Thus a woman's access to credit enables her broader participation in community social networks and social programmes, in turn enhancing her wider opportunities and empowerment. Hulme and Mosley (1996: 125–8) also suggest that 'the creation of a regular forum at which large numbers of poor women can meet and talk represents a breakthrough in the social norms of rural Bangladesh', and reduction in the isolation experienced by many women is bound to follow.

In Hashemi *et al.*'s (1996) examination of the relationship between microcredit programmes and women's empowerment, 1225 married women under the age of 50 – members of Grameen Bank, BRAC, non-members in Grameen-served villages, and a comparison group – were observed and interviewed over a period of three years. Eight indicators are used as proxies for empowerment: (1) mobility, (2) economic security, (3) ability to make small purchases, (4) ability to make larger purchases, (5) involvement in major household decisions, (6) relative freedom from domination from within the family, (7) political and legal awareness, and (8) participation in public protests and political campaigning. Each of the programmes was shown to have a significant effect on four empowerment indicators (2, 3, 4 and 7) as well as on the woman's contribution to family support and to the composite empowerment score. Grameen Bank alone significantly affects women's involvement in major decisions (5), and BRAC alone significantly affects mobility (1). Even those members with little or no control over their loans and income-generating activities were shown to be more empowered than non-members.

National-level impacts

> We have received a lot of things from the international community, but we have given the model of microcredit to the world.
>
> – Prime Minister Begum Khaleda Zia

Unfortunately Bangladesh is known internationally not for its cultural heritage or beautiful natural environment, but for problems like poverty, floods, famine, disease, war, overpopulation, oppression of women, corruption, ferryboat disasters and water contaminated by arsenic. But Bangladesh is now also famous for the 'invention' of microfinance; for the commitment and insight of Muhammad Yunus and other NGO leaders; for the vast cadre of competent and honest NGO field staff who put the microfinance model of poverty alleviation into practice every day; and even for narrowing formerly huge gender gaps in economic participation, education and health[10] (arguably largely through microfinance and the other activities of NGO MFIs).

Employment creation by the MFIs themselves – above and beyond the effects on clients – has been enormous. We estimate that there are at least 50,000 credit officer-type positions across the country, and considering their own households, many times this number of people indirectly derive their livelihood from the provision of microfinance services. Moreover, while we will discuss the crucial role played by the early 'social entrepreneurs' as creators and developers of MFIs and the microfinance industry in Bangladesh, an important and overlooked effect of the current industry is its role in creating the *next* generation of social entrepreneurs.

Palli Karma-Sahayak Foundation (PKSF)

> If you think a state-run organization is always doomed to fail you are wrong. Better look at Palli Karma-Sahayak Foundation ... (Shahiduzzaman, 1999)

The Palli Karma-Sahayak Foundation (Rural Employment Support Foundation) is an 'apex organization', a parastatal involved in loaning government and donor funds (World Bank, USAID, ADB and IFAD) to its partner organizations (POs) for on-lending as microcredit. When PKSF was established by the Government of Bangladesh in 1990, it was a signal that microfinance was coming of age. While the organization took a few years to establish itself, it is now a major channel through which Bangladeshi MFIs access funds, and may be both the largest and most successful of such organizations globally. By the end of financial year 2003–2004, the cumulative loan disbursement of PKSF POs at field level stood at over US$2.2 billion (PKSF, 2004). These funds have been on-lent to 5.1 million borrowers, of whom 90 percent are women.

In financial year 2003–2004, PKSF provided over US$58 million in loanable funds to 206 POs: three big organizations (ASA, BRAC and Proshika), 195 small and medium ones and for the first time, eight 'pre-PKSF' organizations. PKSF POs operate in every district in Bangladesh.[11] This is an exceptionally large number of MFIs relative to apex bodies in other countries, but there are still well over 1000 small MFIs in Bangladesh not funded through PKSF.[12] In 2002 PKSF funds made up only about 15 percent of the total microfinance industry in Bangladesh, compared to Grameen Bank's 37 percent (Levy, 2002; calculated from PKSF, 2002). At the same time, PKSF funds made up 24 percent of the on-loanable funds available to NGO-MFIs, with 25 percent from (largely compulsory) member savings and 17 percent from 'service charge' (interest), and only 16 percent directly from foreign donors. In 2003–2004, PKSF POs were able to maintain a loan recovery rate above 98 percent at the field level. In turn, POs were able to repay PKSF, including interest ('service charges'), as per schedule, so that PKSF itself was also able to maintain a loan recovery rate above 98 percent.

A large majority of PKSF credit was issued under the rural microcredit programme: 74 percent and 71 percent of all mainstream funds, and 69 percent and 62 percent of total funds in 2002–2003 and 2003–2004 respectively. Both urban microcredit and microenterprise credit are, however, growing in importance in PKSF's portfolio. PKSF also assists POs in strengthening their institutional capacity, in an attempt to enhance their sustainability and ability to repay loans. While PKSF claims that it favours no particular model of microfinance, instead encouraging innovations and different approaches based on experience, Matin *et al.* (2000) note that it does in fact 'prefer its partners to use the dominant product' – in this case, the Grameen-style group lending approach.

Many commentators note that the success of PKSF is predicated on the fact that its development was preceded by that of a large and stable microfinance industry, as well as on the strong and independent decision-making that its management has been able to pursue, attributed to the prominence and commitment of individuals on its Governing Body and General Body (Levy, 2002). In May 2005 the Managing Director of PKSF, Dr Salehuddin Ahmed, was designated the ninth Governor of Bangladesh Bank. He has committed himself to turning the central bank from a purely regulatory body into a 'bank of the people devoted to alleviating poverty', with a focus on microcredit for small and medium enterprises (*Independent*, 2005). If PKSF's emergence in 1990 was a signal that microfinance was coming of age as a public policy, Dr Ahmed's appointment may be read as an indication that it has also become integral to mainstream public policy.

Export, replication and transfer[13]

Bangladeshi microfinance models have been exported both formally and informally around the world. The Grameen Bank Replication Program of Grameen Foundation USA was established in 1999 to support institutions and social entrepreneurs throughout the world who seek to replicate the Grameen Bank approach, or scale up existing programs to provide financial services to the poor. Through 52 partners in 22 countries (including the US), the Grameen Foundation USA currently affects close to 1.2 million of the world's poorest families (Annual Report, 2004).

BRAC is unique as a southern NGO that has now spawned offshoots in two other countries. In June 2002, BRAC Afghanistan was launched, and in May 2005 BRAC was registered as an NGO in Sri Lanka, having arrived in the country with a relief and rehabilitation programme following the tsunami in 2004. Of course, BRAC is not only a microfinance success. Its non-formal primary education programme is internationally well-regarded, and BRAC Afghanistan and Sri Lanka, like their parent, are active in health, education and social development as well as microfinance. Nonetheless, by September 2003 BRAC Afghanistan had lent almost US$1 million to over 10,000 borrowers, with a 100 percent repayment rate.

The status of microfinance, particularly in its Bangladeshi version, as a 'magic bullet' in the development industry has also been exemplified by several international bodies.

- In 1996, the World Bank set up the Consultative Group to Assist the Poorest (CGAP), and committed US$200 million to MFI programmes globally. Dr Fasle Abed, founder of BRAC, was a member of its first Board. When CGAP decided to focus on poverty reduction, it recruited two Bangladeshi staff to spearhead this function.
- The Microcredit Summit in February 1997 successfully raised donor and commercial funds in an effort to reach 100 million of the poorest families by the year 2005 (now extended to 2015). It is headed by Professor Yunus of the Grameen Bank.
- Also in February 1997, UNDP and UNCDF launched MicroStart in order to foster transparency and good institutional and financial performance among MFIs. Since its inception, MicroStart has

> begun operations or is being developed in 20 countries, and grants have been approved for 68 MFIs. ASA is a MicroStart International Technical Service Provider, and has been instrumental in MFI development in Nigeria and the Philippines as well as India.

Jain and Moore (2003: 2) note several reasons why the 'Grameen model' has become the one most often imitated. Some of these are to do with the Grameen Bank itself – its relatively early development, and, as discussed below, its leadership, which 'has been especially active and effective in publicizing the virtues of the Grameen model – and in doing so in terms that appeal to ... donors'. The other reasons are to do with characteristics of Grameen's two biggest global microfinance rivals. The BancoSol approach in Bolivia, it is argued, doesn't seem to offer an alternative *rural* model, and its development is grounded in recent Bolivian history. BRI's success in Indonesia is dependent on 'the unusual capacity of Indonesian village-level authorities to monitor and influence individual households'. For many reasons of design and implementation discussed below, the Bangladesh experience, at least as portrayed by its advocates, seems to have grabbed the attention of practitioners and policymakers internationally as being both simple and flexible enough to apply to different contexts.

While gender relations vary significantly between cultural contexts, Grameen replicators throughout the world have found that women experience greater exclusion from formal financial institutions than men, and that women are generally more creditworthy. As a result they tend to focus on women borrowers. The donor emphasis on trying to improve the position of women has supported that focus. As a result microfinance and women's empowerment are often seen, rightly or wrongly, as being closely linked.

Critiques

Not everyone in Bangladesh or elsewhere is happy with the 'microfinance paradigm'. In some cases, the entire microfinance approach to poverty alleviation has been criticized, often from a neo-Marxist perspective, for its focus on the market and poor people's financial liquidity rather than on the socio-economic structures that underlie poverty (see Mayoux, 1995). Others contend that the very success of microfinance as an industry is based on its failure to challenge the foundations of class structure and patriarchy, and that the home-based self-employment often emphasized by MFIs limits the potential for people to escape poverty and marginality.[14] A handful of Bangladeshi NGOs, such as

Nijera Kori, have maintained their commitment to fostering radical social movements through awareness-building and mobilization against injustice and barriers of access to public entitlements – *without* recourse to providing microcredit (Kabeer, 2002).

Most critiques today, however, focus on refining the models, not discrediting the approach in general. For instance, the degree of achievement of the oft-stated goals of poverty alleviation and empowerment of the poor, and the extent to which different groups benefit, have become important topics of research and debate. Hulme and Mosley (1996) have highlighted the overall lack of knowledge about those for whom microcredit is just 'micro-debt': loan defaulters and programme dropouts. An increased understanding of these groups has facilitated innovations in financial services for the poorest that emphasize flexibility, savings, and the central role of assets (Matin and Hulme, 2003). Further, the perceived trade-offs between the achievement of goals of poverty alleviation and empowerment, the evolution of financially sustainable MFIs and the provision of a broader range of financial and non-financial services to a more diverse clientele have come under increased scrutiny by practitioners and scholars, as have the best ways of reducing costs to both MFIs and their donors, and to poor people themselves, and the role of technology in this struggle.

It is also important to note that there have been failures among Bangladeshi MFIs. These include the collapse of Gano Shahajyo Sangstha (GSS), a large NGO-MFI, due to allegations of misuse of donor funds and gender discrimination in 1999. It is also clear from fieldwork that an unknown number of poor people have suffered because of bogus NGOs. In such cases, tricksters establish savings groups with premises of loans once people have built up a savings fund. However, before the loans start, the organizers disappear with the group's savings.[15]

Explaining the success of microfinance in Bangladesh

How can the success of microfinance in Bangladesh be explained? Here we apply McCourt and Bebbington's framework to try to identify and explore the key factors.

The policy: Innovation, design and specification

As we saw in the previous section microfinance in Bangladesh started as an experiment. Muhammad Yunus operated a small-scale action research project out of which emerged a number of lessons which he, and later others, applied to microfinance. Both the process adopted (experimenting on a small scale, improving the efficiency of the service once it became effective and phasing expansion over several years) and the design features selected (see below) have contributed to success. The process appears to be similar to what David Korten (1980) described in a seminal work as a 'learning process' approach.[16]

There are many overlapping explanations of why the Grameen model worked. They suggest that it produced a product that met client needs, developed relatively low-cost delivery mechanisms and generated resources that permitted it to survive and expand. Here we extract findings from Hulme and Mosley (1996). (Jain and Moore (2003) provide a critical perspective on many of these explanations.)

Targeting: In order to reach those most in need, or those best able to use credit effectively, Bangladeshi MFIs have adapted combinations of direct targeting, using an effective indicator-based means test (e.g. a combination of effective landlessness and involvement in manual labour combined with being female), and indirect targeting through self- and peer-selection. Bangladeshi MFIs allow for self-selection through a combination of initially small loans with market-level interest rates and strict repayment conditions, as well as time-consuming and potentially stigmatizing membership obligations such as compulsory attendance at meetings.

Screening out 'bad' (non-poor and too poor or non-viable) clients: Charging market-related interest rates and client involvement in group selection.

Ensuring repayment: Intensive borrower supervision by field staff, peer group monitoring,[17] performance incentives to staff, progressively larger loan sizes and compulsory savings.

Reducing costs: Accessing no-interest or low-interest loans from donors, building up low-cost client savings to on-lend and cost recovery by charging market-related interest rates.

Administrative efficiency: Working with groups, transferring transaction costs to clients and standardized products and procedures.

Thus, the perceived financial soundness of microfinancial services targeted at various subgroups of the poor – women, the landless, small business owners etc. – is not only based upon the replacement of subsidized credit by market-rate loans (indeed, most Bangladeshi MFIs continue to depend on subsidized donor credit, and few are sustainable). Innovative targeting, screening and monitoring mechanisms are equally important. As Besley and Kanbur (1991: 70) state, '...policy-makers can have their cake and eat it too – improved targeting means that more poverty alleviation can be achieved with less expenditure!'[18]

For an extended period between 1985 and 1995, other MFIs in Bangladesh (especially BRAC and Proshika) copied this specification, with modifications and improvements. After 1995, there was a growth in MFIs that signed up to the Grameen Bank story – that the poor are bankable and sustainable institutions can be created to meet their microfinancial needs – but adopted very different models. Prominent amongst these are ASA, BURO Tangail and SafeSave.

An important feature to note, in relation to the main innovations in Bangladesh and elsewhere, is the central role of public and non-governmental organizations (Hulme and Mosley, 1996). While much of the performance of MFIs has to be understood in terms of the adoption of private sector practices – charging market-related interest rates, treating individual branches as cost centres, stripping out administrative costs – the for-profit sector has played only a small role in experimentation and innovation.

Implementation

Pilot projects around the world have shown that high levels of motivation and resourcing can achieve success on a small scale in virtually any field. Once the innovation has been identified, the task that emerges is how to shift to service delivery on a large scale (see Rondinelli, 1993 for a discussion of scaling-up pilot projects). In Bangladesh there were three main components in this process.

First was the scaling up of the Grameen Bank itself. This required the standardization of its 'model' (cells of 5, groups of 30, 12 month loans, standard repayments etc.), the creation of an administrative structure that could steadily expand with only limited losses of effectiveness, and efficiency and access to financial resources. Fuglesang and Chandler (1987) describe the processes that permitted the Grameen Bank to expand without over-reaching itself.[19]

In particular, Grameen Bank managed to create a human resources system that could turn out high numbers of effective fieldworkers and field-level managers. Key elements of this included selection (taking only new graduates who have not learned bad practices in the state or commercial sectors), practical training, a rewards package based on market rates, merit-based promotion and the active promotion of an organizational myth. Professor Yunus fully understood the invisible management benefits that arise from staff feeling they are part of a high-performing organization. Jain and Moore (2003) also note the importance of the relatively unhierarchical campus-style living that Grameen Bank and many other MFIs promote, through which field staff are insulated from many of the pressures of both the people with whom they work and their own families, so that they are able to focus on operating as an effective team.

As Grameen Bank expanded and developed, its management information systems, based until the late 1990s on paper rather than computers, were sufficient to maintain its functioning. Access to financial resources for continuation and expansion was made possible by charging clients interest rates around twice those charged in government rural credit schemes and through access to donor funds. There were so many donors in the 1980s and 1990s wishing to finance poverty reduction in Bangladesh, and so few good projects to fund, that Professor Yunus was able to select the donors from whom he would take grants.[20]

The second path by which the microfinance industry was expanded was by competitor organizations copying the Grameen model (usually with some modifications). This is most obvious in the case of BRAC which operates a microfinance programme that is now of a similar size to the Grameen Bank in terms of numbers of active borrowers. Although BRAC staff like to argue that they invented their own model, it is clear that over the 1980s BRAC found it hard to compete with the Grameen Bank, and so it adopted the Grameen model into its 'integrated' rural development approach to produce a 'credit plus' model providing clients with group-based microcredit and technical advice.[21] Even more remarkably, Proshika, a consciousness-raising, peasant mobilization NGO with origins in radical socialism, began to adopt the Grameen model in its programmes in the early 1990s. This created the basis for it to expand (its clients seemed to prefer microcredit to consciousness-raising), and by the late 1990s microcredit was its major activity.[22] Countless smaller NGOs have followed BRAC and Proshika to such a degree that many observers are concerned that microfinance has crowded out other roles that NGOs should play.

The third path to expansion has been through microfinancial innovation outside the Grameen model. Organizations such as ASA, BURO Tangail, and SafeSave have been persuaded that the poor are bankable, but have sought to provide them with products that are better than the Grameen model. This has meant a greater emphasis on savings, individual rather than group-based approaches and greater flexibility in terms of loan size, repayment schedules and access to savings.

To a significant degree the success of the Grameen Bank encouraged these organizations to seek to do better by undertaking their own experiments.

Learning and adaptation

In the mid-1990s the Grameen Bank was sometimes accused of not learning, of having locked itself into a rigid model and discouraging other organizations from moving away from it. We can say this with confidence, as we were among the accusers! At the time there were some grounds for that case, but one must admit that the Grameen Bank and Professor Yunus have learned and innovated over the 1990s and early 2000s. In 2001–2002 the Grameen Bank relaunched itself as 'Grameen II' with a promise to transform its services to clients. The new products include flexible loans, voluntary savings and 'micropensions' (the latter are proving especially popular). Grameen has also been innovating in other areas including mobile telecommunications, reported to be very successful (Sachs, 2005).

Men's leadership – or women's agency?

Organizational and policy success is often explained in terms of the exceptional ability and performance of leaders (Leonard, 1991). This has been especially true for the Grameen Bank, where there is a vast literature idolizing Muhammad Yunus. Similarly, both BRAC with Fazle Hasan Abed and Proshika with Dr Qazi Faruque Ahmed have been seen internationally as achieving great results on a massive scale. There can be no doubt that Bangladesh's microfinance industry has been inspired by Yunus and developed through other effective leaders.

However, the contribution of the Grameen Bank's and other MFIs' clients must also be recognized. Millions of 'little' women (in terms of social status as well as height and body-mass index) have shown extraordinary agency and capacity to use MFI services, improve the well-being of their households, and repay their loans.

What then can be said about the practice of targeting women, towards which the Bangladeshi MFI community shifted in the 1980s? In many ways, the success of microfinance in Bangladesh is based on poor women's agency (and lack of agency).

On the surface, the rationale for the MFI focus on women is obvious. Women are often the poorest and most vulnerable people within low-income communities, with households nonetheless depending on their income-generating and expenditure-saving activities. It is surmised that providing women access to affordable credit can empower them economically in the same manner as men: through enhancing their ability to invest in productive human and physical capital as well as risky technologies, to avoid emergency sales of assets and usurious rates of interest, and to smooth consumption (Zeller *et al.*, 1997). Further, it is important to note that fostering women's role as the 'brokers' of the health, nutritional, and educational status of their families, in particular that of their children, is also an important goal (Goetz and Gupta, 1996). Thus women's participation in microfinance programmes has been considered critical, not only to their own socio-economic well-being, but also to that of their families.

However, two studies in particular (Ackerley, 1995; Goetz and Gupta, 1996) have challenged these ideas. According to these studies, women borrowers in Bangladesh manifest a range of levels of control over loan-funded enterprises, returns from those enterprises, and responsibility for loan repayments. A significant proportion of women have limited or no control over loan-funded business and returns, yet shoulder the burden of repayment. In this case, 'the developmental objectives of targeting credit to women can be eroded if a direct relation between personal loan use and repayment responsibility is ruptured' (Goetz and Gupta, 1996: 54).

Why then are women still being targeted? Analysts increasingly note another reason for targeting women: as Rogaly (1996: 106) succinctly puts it, it is not 'access for women'; rather, 'women are accessible'. Women have been found to be much better credit risks than their male relatives. In many countries, women are relatively easy to locate, as they work in the home compound. Further, they are perceived as more susceptible to repayment pressure, both in terms of the social network and training opportunities they stand to lose, as well as the social norms they conform to that make them easier to intimidate. This alternative rationale suggests that simply targeting women with microfinance does not necessarily imply that gender issues and gender relations have been adequately addressed (Johnson, 1999). In this view, woman-targeted microfinance programmes exploit gender norms so that women assume the costly job of ensuring repayment of male or household credit, actually increasing women's dependence on male decision-making and their vulnerability to male violence and economic shocks.

Mayoux (1995, 1998) distinguishes between three main paradigms of women-targeted microfinance provision:

- The *financial sustainability* paradigm is based on an instrumentalist, market approach which focuses attention on women's high repayment rates as a means of achieving the wider goal of assisting individual entrepreneurs to increase their incomes.
- The *poverty alleviation* paradigm targets women because they are among the poorest, and more likely than men to spend extra income on their families.
- The *feminist empowerment* paradigm aims to enhance the bargaining power as well as the incomes of poor women, and sees gender equity itself as an inseparable part of any wider development goal. In this framework, without parallel interventions fostering women's access to markets, technology, decision-making structures, legal rights and social capital, the positive discrimination inherent in targeted credit is of little value.

Household power structures, however, can be affected by a targeted infusion of credit in several different ways, so that the line between strategic–empowerment–feminist and practical–instrumentalist–market becomes blurred. Credit can become a bargaining chip for many women, allowing them to 'negotiate transfers' with those who hold some form of social control. In Bangladesh, women's economic contributions to the household are traditionally in labour and kind, and as such are often invisible. As discussed above, access to an institutional loan in cash may lead to a revaluing of women's contribution (actual or perceived) to the household, so that women's status within the household, their access to resources for themselves and their children, and familial stability may all rise (Goetz and Gupta, 1996).

Based on an analysis of the opposing perspectives on gender and microfinance in Bangladesh, as well as field data on a Bangladeshi MFI targeted at a relatively well off group of women and men, Kabeer (1998) constructs a much more nuanced argument. Her analysis not only reminds us of the importance of defining 'empowerment' in women's own terms, but also highlights the importance of the characters of individual women and men, the nature of their poverty and how a financial service is delivered in determining the impact of credit upon investment choices, asset accumulation and household decision-making structures. While many Bangladeshi women certainly suffer a strategic disadvantage at home, one must also recognize that in many cases the household is conceived as a joint venture in which women and men have different rights and responsibilities in terms of asset control and decision-making. The idea of separate control over separate earnings may not be very useful (Todd, 1996).

It is important to recognize that women's ability to use financial services in the way they wish can be both constrained and facilitated by the gendered socio-economic relations that operate at the household level as well as in business and the local and national communities. 'There is an extremely fine line between recognizing constraints on women's freedom of manoeuvre and reinforcing the terms of those constraints by taking them as givens' (*Ibid.*, 59).

A favourable environment

Bangladesh is often perceived as having difficult environmental conditions. With poor governance, catastrophic flooding every few years and high levels of corruption there are many systemic and unpredictable challenges to deal with. But, there are also a number of environmental factors that supported the microfinance industry. In particular:

- The country's high population densities lower the cost of service delivery.
- The basic infrastructure for service delivery, notably bank branches with security facilities and roads, is available in all but the most remote areas.
- There is a regular supply of new university graduates with few other employment opportunities.
- Relatively secure law and order means that fieldworkers and bank branches are fairly safe.[23]
- Foreign aid donors have had large budgets available to support viable projects.

The political economy of success

Establishing a successful policy requires much more than simply getting the right design. In particular, it requires a careful analysis of the domestic and international political economic environment to ensure that the policy can function, and that groups who might oppose the policy can be co-opted or out-manoeuvred.

As a starting point one must note that the human agency behind the early Bangladeshi MFIs grew out of the political economy of

Bangladesh in the early 1970s. Professor Yunus was one of many young Bangladeshis who observed the terrible poverty and deprivation of the country at that time, after the War of Liberation and the floods of 1974, and decided that they had to do something. Similar sentiments informed the founders of BRAC, Proshika, ASA, RDRS and many other agencies. While we know the names of the leaders of those initiatives, this socio-political environment of the early 1970s also shaped the actions of thousands of other Bangladeshis who became the senior and mid-level staff for poverty reduction initiatives. The wave of human agency, energy and creativity that swept across Bangladesh at that desperate time created capacity, in terms of both knowledge and institutions, upon which the country continues to draw today.

Where the Grameen Bank is concerned, it has to be observed that it has been skilfully managed since inception so that it is both embedded in Bangladeshi society and able to exploit changes in that society. Professor Yunus has been able to use his personal status, as a member of Bangladesh's elite with a PhD from the USA, to steer Grameen Bank around potential obstacles in the country's political economy. While the country was under authoritarian rule, Yunus negotiated Grameen Bank's path to becoming a statutory organization. This gave Grameen Bank the freedom to escape having to lend as part of a patronage system, to set its own interest rates and to be officially regulated in ways that did not constrain the institution. Subsequently, Grameen Bank has been able to avoid challenges from the country's various democratic governments – BNP, Awami and Coalition – by careful management. This involves closely following politics, managing elite relationships and a public image in which Grameen Bank is prominent but not identified with any political group.[24]

Internationally the Grameen Bank's image has also been effectively managed so that it has garnered support from many different quarters. Indeed, Grameen has been foundational in creating a global image of microfinance as a policy that can appeal to both right-of-centre and left-of-centre ideologies. Its discourse of micro-entrepreneurs, micro-enterprise, investment, loans not grants and cost recovery garnered support from those who see private sector development as the pathway out of poverty, and as superior to social grants and welfare. At the other end of the political spectrum, its discourse of the agency of the poor, group formation, participation, empowerment and women's rights met with the approval of those who believed social change was the way forward. By telling two stories at the same time, but in differing proportions to different audiences, both the idea of microfinance and the image of the Grameen Bank were able to appeal to a wide audience and avoid criticism from all except the more extreme elements of the right and the left. A broad consensus was achieved that permitted national governments, bilateral and multilateral donors and NGOs to support the Grameen Bank and microfinance.

This consensus did not mean that everyone was happy about the Grameen Bank. It has faced opposition. Domestically, the greatest threat has been from Islamic fundamentalists who see it as challenging the position that women should play in Islamic society and as flouting the prohibition of usury. At times this has been a physical threat, with offices attacked and field staff threatened and harassed. However, the Grameen Bank (and other MFIs and NGOs) have countered this by making the case that they are not anti-Islamic and honour all the laws of the country, and by encouraging government to take stronger action against fundamentalists. In the mid- to late 1990s many MFI leaders and staff felt that fundamentalism could become a major threat. This position seemed to have moderated, but in the last couple of years, it has revived.

A further challenge has come from the media and especially journalists with socialist or far-left leanings. Bangladeshi newspapers have regularly issued a challenge to the MFIs to explain in detail what has happened to the foreign aid they have received, and to respond to the claim that their activities have weakened the role that the government plays in poverty reduction. Such arguments may have fuelled elite and middle class debates, but they do not appear to have created a practical threat to the Grameen Bank or the country's microfinance industry. Clients have not withdrawn from MFI services, government has not tightened up regulations or controls,[25] and foreign donors continue their support (although Grameen Bank has not requested any donor funds since 1995, nor received any new donor funds since 1998).

Finally, within the Grameen Bank itself, management have had to handle their relationships with staff carefully. In the early 1990s there was pressure from Grameen Bank employees to form a trade union. Professor Yunus and senior managers were concerned about this. It would clearly give them less control over staff terms and conditions and, as they pointed out, most trade unions in Bangladesh are dysfunctional: they do not serve their members' or their customers' interests.

As with so many of the process factors that explain success, the exact means by which this issue was resolved are undocumented, but the outcome was clear. After negotiations, the staff agreed to a 'Staff Federation' which created a channel for two-way communication between staff and management, but which did not have the full status of a trade union. According to Grameen Bank this meant that poor clients continued to have the upper hand in determining policy. According to trade unionists and left-wing academics it meant that the legitimate rights of workers were not honoured.

Beyond Bangladesh

As mentioned earlier, the ideas and methods of the Grameen Bank have not simply diffused across Bangladesh; they have spread across the world. The global image of microfinance is shaped by Grameen Bank and there are at least 52 direct Grameen offshoots operating worldwide, including in the US. Professor Yunus' office has numerous photos of meetings with world leaders, with Bill and Hillary Clinton taking pride of place. Yunus has received numerous international awards, and when the media look for a poverty reduction success story, they usually turn to Grameen Bank or an MFI influenced by the Grameen Bank.

Formally, there are two direct mechanisms through which this policy transfer operates. First, the Grameen Bank runs scores of international seminars each year that train people from other countries to learn how to replicate Grameen Bank. It provides field visits and manuals, it puts participants into a replicators' network and can even provide start-up grants through a link with the Grameen Bank Replication Programme. The Grameen Trust's newsletter (*Grameen Dialogue*) lists 131 partner organizations in 35 countries (April 2005) with a client base of over 1.8 million in October 2004. The second mechanism is the Microcredit Summit, which we have touched on already.

Conclusion

We conclude that microfinance has been a policy success in Bangladesh. This has probably been the case in other places, but nowhere else is the evidence so clear. This is a firmer conclusion than we reached in earlier studies eight to ten years ago. Why is that? Partly because we have mellowed and perhaps are not so idealistic! Partly because microfinance's institutions and impacts have stood the test of time, and because microfinance has expanded what it is doing and achieving. There is clear evidence that microfinancial services have helped millions of poor people in Bangladesh to achieve their personal and household goals, and it has also helped place poor women on the development agenda as active agents of their own development rather than mere passive recipients. Partly also, it is because the microfinance sector in Bangladesh no longer exaggerates the claims about its impact in the way that it did ten years ago, when MFI leaders and staff insisted that all their members were 'the poorest of the poor', that every loan was a success for the borrower, and that the gender and class empowerment being generated was rapidly producing a more egalitarian society.

But, has microfinance been a public policy success? As we pointed out earlier, this depends on what you mean by 'public'. It has certainly been a success in terms of the broader concept of 'public action' that Amartya Sen floated in the early 1990s (and then seemed to abandon). It started as a public action project: Professor Yunus and his colleagues were members of a civil organization (a university), but also public servants. They were financed by public monies and by NGOs. The Grameen Bank became a statutory body but the 'replicators/adaptors' that scaled up microfinance were mainly NGOs, and thus part of civil society. Subsequently, a major vehicle for scaling up has been the PKSF, a public-private partnership. Behind much of this activity, both innovation and replication, has been donor resources from the public sector in wealthier countries. All of this is set in a regulatory and macro-economic framework that has been supportive (or at least has not been too disruptive) and is part of the public sector. We can label this as networks, co-production or anything we choose as long as two things are noted.

First, the main players are the state and civil society: this is public action by any other name. Second, the private-for-profit sector has played only a minor role in this success. Private sector concepts like profit/loss, unit costs, performance related pay, market-based interest rates, competition have been an important part of the story, but for-profit organizations have played only a minor role. The case Hulme and Mosley (1996) made ten years ago – that commercial businesses do not invest in creating pro-poor innovations, that they are followers but not leaders in service provision for the poor – still seems to hold.

Finally, why has microfinance been a policy success in Bangladesh? We agree with Zaman (2004) that visionary leadership, a supportive (or more accurately, not unsupportive) policy/regulation environment, effective action by donors, a suitable physical and social environment and, recently, PKSF to provide scaling-up finance and improve industry standards have been key factors. We would also add that microfinance's visionary leadership needs not only to be technically able but also to have the skills and social resources necessary to manage the domestic and international political economy. In addition, the institutional processes have to permit learning and allow effective implementation systems. It must also be noted that millions of 'little' women (see earlier), the clients, have contributed to making microfinance a success.

But is there any over-arching explanatory framework or does 'success' boil down to a mere list of attributes? The best we can find is Uphoff's (1992) concept of 'social energy'. This postulates a process by which dynamic leaders and the ideas they promote, diffuse through society, gaining momentum and persuading individuals and organizations to adopt different values and do things differently. This raises the productivity and creativity of leaders and lower-level workers, and promotes the ideal of helping others and providing services to the poor. It also generates useful knowledge, encourages skills development and helps to shift attitudes in a progressive direction. The spark of social entrepreneurship that Yunus set off has energized scores of leading Bangladeshi social activists and thousands of others to try to get microfinancial and other services to poor people. The diffusion process has moved into the public sector through PKSF and, with the appointment of the Director of PKSF as governor of the central bank, this social energy seems set to sweep into the financial sector more widely. Maybe it will stop here. But maybe not. Providing services to poor people was not previously an exciting or 'sexy' activity; microfinance in Bangladesh has changed that. That is a great achievement! And a policy success in the 'failed field' of poverty reduction, in a 'basket-case' country like Bangladesh, shows the agency of the poor, and remains inspirational.

Appendix 1 Major MFIs in Bangladesh

In order to represent programme diversity, examples of Bangladeshi MFIs can be placed on a matrix (Figure 5.1). On the horizontal axis is the continuum between pure credit provision and broader financial service provision; on the vertical access we have the continuum between credit or finance only, credit or finance plus business-related services, and credit or finance plus social programmes.[26]

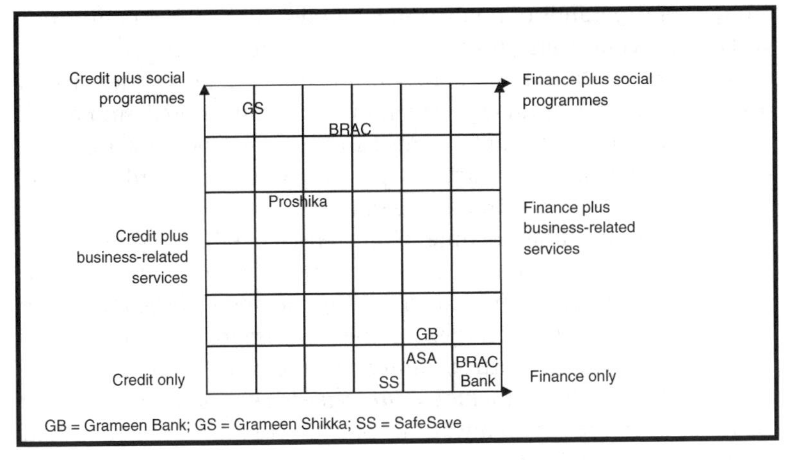

Figure 5.1 Matrix of microfinance (and related) institutions in Bangladesh, 2006

BRAC, originally known as the Bangladesh Rural Advancement Committee, is a 'finance-plus' NGO established in 1972. It houses a very large range of non-financial 'social' programmes. Zaman (n.d.: 51) notes that 'the know-how and confidence to implement large programs arose, in some cases, from the experience of scaling up programs not related to microcredit. For instance, in the case of BRAC, its first major experience with a nationwide programme came when it implemented an oral rehydration program to combat diarrhoeal disease. Thirteen million women were trained ...'

Over the past decade in particular, it has developed its range of financial services to include a greater variety of savings products and credit for small business. More recently, in 2001 and 1997 respectively BRAC Bank and the Delta BRAC Housing Finance Corporation were established as commercial interests to meet the financial requirements of non-poor Bangladeshis. In 2001, BRAC established a university, and in 2002 and 2005 respectively, it started work in Afghanistan and Sri Lanka.

As of September 2005, BRAC was working in over 68,000 villages and over 4000 urban slums in every district of Bangladesh. It claimed over 5 million members, almost entirely women, and a cumulative disbursement of over US$2.95 billion. Nearly 1 million children were enrolled in a BRAC school, and over 3 million have graduated. The NGO employed over 34,000 staff, over 62,000 community school teachers and tens of thousands of poultry and community health and nutrition workers and volunteers (BRAC At a Glance, September 2005).

The **Grameen Bank** is a 'finance-minimalist' bank that offers a wide range of financial products with limited organizational support. It started as an action research project in 1976, and became a government-regulated bank through a special government ordinance in 1984. In 2001–2002, all Grameen Bank branches began to operate the new, simpler and more flexible 'Grameen Generalised System' (also called 'Grameen II'), which offers four types of loan products: basic, housing, higher education and struggling members' (beggars') loans. There is also a facility for larger small-enterprise loans, and there is a range of companies, both commercial and not-for-profit, in the 'Grameen family'. They include ***Grameen Shikka*** (GS), established in 1997 to promote the education of non-literate Grameen Bank members, provide financial support in the form of loans and grants for education, and promote innovative ideas and technologies for educational development.

In March 2005, the Grameen Bank was working in almost 51,000 villages. It claimed over 4.3 million members, over 95 percent women, and a cumulative disbursement of over US$4.7 *billion* (Grameen Bank At a Glance, March 2005).

Proshika, also established in 1976, started microfinance programmes in the 1990s. It matches member savings with credit, and provides technical and marketing assistance where needed. Initially it fulfilled its social intermediation objectives through group formation and conscientization rather than service provision, but it has moved into the provision of a wider range of social programmes. Its status is unclear, as it clashed with the government in 2002 and its registration as an NGO has been cancelled.

At the end of 2004, Proshika reported over 1.5 million active borrowers, 80 percent of whom were among the poorest, of whom in turn 65 percent, or 0.8 million people, were women (Daley-Harris, 2005).

The Association for Social Advancement, known as **ASA**, was established as an NGO in 1978, with a focus on consciousness raising, group development and training among the rural poor. It started its microfinance operations in 1991, recreating itself as a finance-only MFI. It is now the third largest MFI in Bangladesh, and offers a range of savings, credit and insurance facilities. Its non-financial activities are now limited to providing capacity development to small Bangladeshi NGOs and MFIs worldwide.

At the end of 2004, ASA had over 2.7 million active borrowers, about 90 percent of whom were among the poorest, of whom in turn 96 percent, or almost 2.4 million people, were women. (Daley-Harris, 2005)

BURO, Tangail began as a five-branch pilot project in 1989 in Tangail District, and established itself as an NGO in 1990. Today it operates in eight districts in north-central Bangladesh. BURO's savings system in particular and financial products in general were at the forefront of the movement in the 1990s to make microfinance products more flexible.

At the end of 2004, BURO, Tangail had almost 220,000 active borrowers, of whom almost all were poor women. (Daley-Harris, 2005)

SafeSave was initiated as a research experiment in 1997 to explore sustainable methods for providing individual financial services (i.e. not based on peer groups) to poor and very poor slum dwellers in Dhaka. Female slum-dwellers were employed to make daily doorstep visits to clients. In 2002, SafeSave became a permanent, self-sustaining microfinance institution, and by 2004 was on a firm organizational footing.

SafeSave remains small (at the end of 2005 it was serving about 11,000 clients from eight branch offices) and geographically limited to urban Dhaka. In mid-2002 it established a rural experimental project called Shohoz Shonchoy (EasySave) in an area northeast of Dhaka. By the end of November 2005 Shohoz Shonchoy had over 1100 clients. It was established as a cooperative in 2005 (SafeSave website).

Notes

1. Corresponding author: David.Hulme@manchester.ac.uk. The authors gratefully acknowledge insightful comments from Anne-Marie Goetz, who acted as discussant at the ESRC-funded *Seminar on Policy Success in Developing Countries* (Institute for Development Policy and Management, Manchester, 20 May 2005) at which this paper was originally presented, as well as from other participants in this seminar. Comments received from Stuart Rutherford, Malcolm Harper and others at a presentation made to the Microfinance Club (London, 5 October 2005) are also acknowledged. David Hulme's work for this paper was supported by the ESRC's Global Poverty Research Group (GPRG).
2. According to *The State of the Microcredit Summit Campaign Report 2005*, at the end of 2004 3164 microcredit institutions reported reaching 92,270,289 clients, 66,614,871 of whom were among the poorest (<US$1/day, or among the bottom half of those below the national poverty line) when they took their first loan. Data from 330 institutions, representing 87.7 percent of the poorest clients, was verified by the Campaign.

3 This is not to deny the importance of much earlier, often centuries-old innovations in informal and formal financial services by and for low-income people in, for example, West Africa, Europe and South Asia; or that today's microfinance practitioners, policymakers and academics should not learn from those experiences (see Siebel, 2003). It does assert, however, that the current global dominance of microfinance as a development intervention is largely based on the Bangladesh experience over the past three and a half decades. (Indeed, as this chapter went to print, Professor Muhammad Yunus and the Grameen Bank were jointly awarded the 2006 Nobel Peace Prize 'for their efforts to create economic and social development from below'.)

4 Thanks to Anne-Marie Goetz for suggesting this terminology.

5 Important centres of innovation include ACCION International in Latin America (and now Africa and the United States), BancoSol in Bolivia (see Rhyne, 2001), and Bank Rakyat Indonesia (Robinson, 2002).

6 This section draws heavily on an excellent article by Hasan Zaman (2004).

7 See for example Buckley (1996: 280–1); Todd (1996: 160); and Wood and Sharif (1997: 35).

8 For example: borrowers, savers, or total clients (members, customers); active, total or cumulative clients; the poor or the poorest (with all the problems of definition implicit in these terms), or all clients (with an assumption that anyone using MFI services has little or no access to other forms of finance); women, men or both; total credit disbursed or total deposits collected; repayment rates; a range of financial performance indicators including productivity, efficiency, leverage and profitability; and, not least, economic or social effects at the household level.

9 A higher estimate is given by Rahman (2005, cited in Tazi, 2005), who suggests that 'it is widely believed that overlap constitutes up to a third of reported outreach'.

10 For example, the World Economic Forum's 2005 global gender gap ranking places Bangladesh 39 out of 58 countries, above India (53) and Pakistan (56), but also Italy (45), Greece (50) and Mexico (52). It is ranked 18th on economic participation, surpassing the UK (21) and US (19), and 37th on both educational attainment and health and well-being, surpassing Austria (38) on education and the Baltic countries (44, 46, 48) on health and well-being.

11 Reflecting the industry as a whole, however, MFI activity is still highly concentrated. There are nine districts where only one PKSF PO operates, and 24 districts with 8 or more POs operating. In Dhaka district, 16 POs operate.

12 Levy (2002: 14) noted that 'little more than 10 percent of MFI applications for a first disbursement are accepted.'

13 People involved in promoting microfinance typically talk of 'replicating' the Grameen Bank. However, there a variety of different transfer approaches ranging from straightforward replication, to adopted models of the Grameen Bank, to experimenting with quite different models following the inspiration of the Grameen Bank.

14 Thanks to Anne-Marie Goetz for her elaboration on this point.

15 After four years in government administration, GSS was cleared of the charges, and has recently resumed its educational activities on a limited scale (PREM 2005).

16 Indeed, 'learning by doing' has come to be considered the mark of the successful (yet modest) Bangladeshi development organization. BRAC was perhaps the first official 'learning organization', and even PKSF has adopted the label.

17 Jain and Moore (2003: 9) rightly note that neither the 'strong' form of group liability (where group members assume the debt of defaulters), nor its weaker form (where the group is denied further loans when a member defaults), is commonly enforced in practice, and that the group acts more as a means of building on social norms to instil a culture of discipline and financial responsibility.

18 They go on to point out that 'Alas, the real world is not quite so straightforward.'

19 Do note that these authors were great fans of the Grameen Bank and tend to describe Grameen Bank practice as if it were the perfect implementation of its policies.

20 Professor Yunus fell out with one of his early sponsors, IFAD, for reasons that are not clear. This was not a problem as he simply identified new donors.

21 Most notably in chicken rearing (for eggs and meat) and moriculture (silkworms). The chicken rearing has proved highly successful. Moriculture was technically sound, but collapsed in the face of cheap silk from China.

22 There is a fascinating but undocumented tale behind Proshika's microfinance success. Proshika moved into microfinance with a senior management that had little relevant experience, being more acquainted with revolutionary theory than with double entry book-keeping! However, skilful technical assistance inputs from its donor consortium (and especially DFID) led to the installation of a highly effective financial reporting system that guided field staff and senior management behaviour.

23 Some recent targeting of branch offices of large NGOs by terrorists insisting that Bangladesh should move to strict forms of Islamic law suggest that this may change, but as yet this has done little to undermine NGO activities.

24 This contrasts with Proshika, which took a political position that led to bad relations with the present government. Its foreign funding has been blocked and the organization has been attacked and raided at local and national levels. It is now only partly functioning.

25 This is beginning to change. In 2000, GoB formed a Microfinance Research and Reference Unit (MRRU) based in the Bangladesh Bank. Its high-level membership, drawn from government, PKSF, Grameen Bank and BRAC, has worked to develop a regulatory framework for all MFIs. The framework is likely to include an interest rate ceiling, and PKSF has already been taking steps in this direction. In early 2006, reports in the media suggested that the framework would soon be passed to legislators for approval. The appointment of the PKSF director to the post of governor of Bangladesh Bank may well facilitate this process.

26 An important third axis is the continuum between programmes oriented to the individual, and those with a more collective focus. This distinction is far from straightforward, however, and beyond the scope of this paper.

6

Behind 'Win-Win': Politics, Interests and Ideologies in Housing Subsidy Programmes

Diana Mitlin

This paper discusses four large-scale, well-regarded housing subsidy programmes (in Chile, Mexico, the Philippines and South Africa) in order to explore the political and social dynamics of pro-poor development success. In particular, it argues that – at least for the programmes considered here – success has been achieved through alliance-based policymaking, and has always been accompanied by both compromise and contestation. Such processes may be inevitable if state programmes that aim to secure a degree of redistribution are to achieve any significant success.

The programmes discussed here and summarized in Table 6.1 have all worked, primarily in urban areas, to address poor people's need for secure tenure, housing improvement and access to basic services. All are state programmes of notable scale – even the smallest of them has assisted 140,000 households – and each has been in place for an extended period. The Chilean housing subsidy programme (in various components) dates from the 1980s, although similar schemes emerged in the late 1970s. In Mexico the discussion concentrates on the initial years (1982–1988) of the Mexican National Popular Housing Fund (FONHAPO), although the programme extended beyond this period. In the Philippines, the Community Mortgage Programme was set up in 1986. In South Africa the housing subsidy programme discussed here was launched shortly after the democratic government took office in 1994.

All the programmes involve a range of civil society, state and (in three cases) private sector agencies. As noted in Chapter 1 (see also Houtzager with Pattenden, 2003), non-state pro-poor agencies face a dilemma: state intervention is essential for policy change, and state resources are required for large-scale programming, yet the involvement of the state may dilute the policy goals pursued by non-state agencies. It is with this dilemma in mind that these programmes illustrate the evolution of alliances among state and non-state agencies aimed at addressing the needs of the poor. Each has also involved NGOs within the policy process, while also incorporating a role for grassroots organizations in implementation. More specifically, they illustrate how groups in an alliance use their need for resource acquisition as well as their ideological position to establish and then to influence pro-poor policies and programmes.

Each programme aims to reach lower-income households although the emphasis on poverty reduction differs considerably across the programmes. To varying degrees, each programme acknowledges the need for complex and integrated approaches to poverty reduction, with the strengthening of social capital accompanying the accumulation of material assets and an improved living environment, and with anticipated benefits to health. The specific approaches followed have changed as the programmes have evolved.

The chapter argues that pro-poor policies and programmes, even when successful (and in some cases because they are successful), are vulnerable to amendment by powerful economic and political interests which are not pro-poor. In two cases, the programmes have privileged private enterprise interests. In the third case, the programme has been overtaken by bureaucratic delays, exacerbated by pressure from private construction firms to divert funds away from the programme. In the fourth programme, political elite interests have come to dominate. In all four cases, other groups, primarily NGOs, have sought to move the programme towards approaches that offer integrated poverty reduction support with material assets and stronger organizational capacity. In respect of organizational capacity, NGOs have sought to move the programmes in a pro-poor direction. Ideological contestation has run alongside the tussle over programme mechanisms, affecting the ways in which resources are distributed. These programmes are ostensibly narrow ones that target housing need (secure tenure and services) for low-income families through an enablement[1] approach, but they also have a political meaning. At one extreme, they have been an opportunity for companies or politicians to gain money or votes. At the other extreme, they have been an opportunity for poor people to come together in social associations that recognize and address their oppression.

The paper proceeds as follows. It begins with a summary of debates on housing improvement strategies in order to locate the programmes within these broader debates. It then describes each of the four programmes, and goes on to consider the themes outlined above. The paper closes by considering the value of the development success framework introduced in Chapter 1 as a way of understanding the housing programmes considered in this chapter.

Housing improvement: debating strategy and policy

The UN estimates that 900 million people live in accommodation which is inadequate in terms of tenure, infrastructure, services, safety or security (UN-Habitat, 2003). Adequate shelter (safe and secure housing together with secure tenure and access to basic services) is widely considered to be important to poverty reduction, and the Millennium Development Goals include a target for reducing by 100 million the number living in urban slums by 2015.[2] Lack of infrastructure and services together with inadequate housing (Hardoy *et al.*, 2001) are major causes of ill health, itself a major factor responsible for pushing people from transitory to chronic poverty (Pryer *et al.*, 2005). Save and secure shelter also delivers less tangible but important benefits, such as reduction in the stress caused by tenure security, a sense of citizenship, and the establishment of local networks to assist with access to other needs, including employment.

There have been many state initiatives to address such shelter needs. Programmes to provide complete houses have generally been criticized for their high unit cost and small scale (Hardoy and Satterthwaite, 1989: 106–112). For example, high unit costs in Nigeria meant that between 1971 and 1995, the government built only 13 percent of the units they intended to build (Ogu and Ogbuozobe, 2001: 477). As a result, housing allocations and subsidies are often inadequate, and end up going to the wrong people as governments try to recoup cost overruns and respond to political pressure. There were significant transfers of public funds to the few who benefited, while many people remained without adequate housing. In Mexico for example, in the period prior to FONHAPO, housing policy provided a small number of very visible, mostly high-rise apartments of good quality, and housing estates to be rented or sold at subsidized rates to middle-income people (Connolly, 2004a). In Chile prior to 1970, the government consistently failed to reduce the housing deficit, with those few units that were built being priced beyond the means of the poor (Gilbert, 2002a: 309). Likewise, to participate in one Indian programme intended to improve housing for the poor, beneficiaries had to own land. To enable the inclusion of the poorest, land was allocated free to some people squatting on public land with plots of less than 85 square metres. A basic permanent structure was provided using funds provided by the state housing finance company at a subsidized interest rate of 9 percent. However, party-political leaders allocated and sold titles together with half-completed houses for political reasons. Repayment rates were less than 15 percent (Smets, 2002: 150).

The work of John Turner (1976) widened awareness of the process by which low-income households secure their housing through informal markets and self-help activities, with reference to the development of low-income settlements in Peru. He described the considerable investment that households make over time, even though tenure is not formal and insecure, and services might not be provided.

As a result of his and other work, architects and planners have increasingly come to believe that housing providers should build on residents' energy and creativity, and take account of the investment they have already made. Development agencies have undertaken 'site and services' programmes which seek to provide legal land tenure and basic services at low cost (Hardoy and Satterthwaite, 1989: 127). Some of these programmes were effective, but others were not, for several reasons. First, supply of plots did not match demand, and so plots ended up being sold at a premium price. Second, even when low-income families did obtain a plot, they often did not stay on it. There were two reasons for this. The first was as a result of 'gentrification', where a poor household sold its plot, especially where the site had been upgraded, and then moved to a worse location. The second, opposite reason was where site locations were poor, so that people made it their business to move somewhere better.

Despite such problems, NGOs continued to innovate (Turner, 1986). Particular attention was paid to the provision of small loans to enable improved and rapid consolidation of settlements (Arrossi *et al.*, 1994). In some countries, provision of housing loans converged with the growth of microfinance (Daphnis and Ferguson, 2004; Mitlin, 2003; see also Chapter 5 in this volume). However, providing small loans did not help the poorest families, who needed to acquire land prior to household consolidation and securing services. In response, collective loans for land purchase and infrastructure investment have developed, sometimes with state subsidies and/or international development assistance grants (ACHR, CODI and IIED, 2004; Mitlin 2003; UN-Habitat, 2005).

Table 6.1 The four programmes

Country	Chile	Mexico	Philippines	South Africa
Programme	**Housing subsidy programme**	**FONHAPO**	**Community Mortgage Programme**	**Housing subsidy programme**
Dates	Policy started in 1977, expanded in scale in mid- to late 1980s	1982–1988: continued after that date but changed in nature	Formulated following 1986 and institutionalized in 1989	Formulated in 1995 and developed from that date
Scale	1.3 million subsidies allocated by the end of 2003	More than 250,000 households supported between 1982–1988	141,000 households reached by the end of 2003	1.4 million approved subsidies by end of 2003
Main strategies	A mix of three components: beneficiaries' savings, government subsidy and (except for the poorest) loans to finance complete units. Regional government contracts a commercial company to construct housing, or household buys through the housing market	Subsidized loans to encourage a range of housing solutions including upgrading and incremental development as well as new build. Emphasis on strengthening the collective capacity of the community through shelter improvement	Subsidized group loans to enable those at risk of eviction to purchase land. Some loans for upgrading land	Individual subsidy entitlement realized through contractor built housing developments. Options for self-build through People's Housing Process. Recently added requirement for savings or sweat equity
Key participants	Central government, local government and private building contractors. Social organizations help with sub-programmes for groups wanting to build	Central government agency finance supported a range of public and social housing institutions including NGOs and local government. Some participation by the private sector	Central government, 'originators' (community support agencies includes local government and NGOs)	Central, local and provincial government, commercial contractors, social housing organizations

Table 6.1 The four programmes – *continued*

Country	**Chile**	**Mexico**	**Philippines**	**South Africa**
Programme	**Housing subsidy programme**	**FONHAPO**	**Community Mortgage Programme**	**Housing subsidy programme**
Significant problems	Delays in securing subsidies, peripheral location of contractor housing, poor quality	Popularity of scheme led to it being subsumed within partisan politics; poorest struggled to participate equally	Delays in securing subsidized loans, limited finance, lack of central state commitment. Poorest struggle to participate	Location of housing units and poor quality of (small) units
Scale of subsidy	Various sub-programmes for different groups with unit subsidies of up to $7500. Savings contribution of over 3 percent of the value of the subsidy	An initial subsidy of between 15 and 25 percent was offered on the value of all loans (higher subsidies for the smaller loan values) and a further 15 percent subsidy was offered for prompt repayment	Interest rate of 6 percent on available loans. Small subsidy for technical assistance. Average loan amount of $700	Maximum value of capital grant increased from about $2000 (1995) to just over $3000 (plus $350 own contribution)

Housing improvement in practice: four national programmes

It is in the light of these general debates on housing programme design that we consider the four programmes discussed in this paper. We now describe those programmes (see Table 6.1 for a summary).

Chile: housing subsidy programme[3]

Chilean housing policy is notable for its continuity as well as its scale. Since the mid-1980s, housing policy in Chile has focused on subsidizing the demand for housing, with between 70,000 and 100,000 units provided every year.[4] There are a number of sub-programmes, all of which mix three financing components: beneficiaries' savings, government subsidy and (except for the poorest) loans. The cheaper the housing, the higher the proportion of its costs covered by the subsidy. All programmes require the beneficiaries, even the poorest, to make a savings contribution, in order to reduce dependency and promote a sense of ownership. Most programmes have included a credit system or support for a loan system of private mortgages. However, an increasing number of subsidies – about one-third in 2003 – have been given to the poorest without loans.[5]

In most cases, people apply for assistance through the regional office of the Ministry of Housing or through the local authority. There are clear rules for applicant assessment and transparent selection procedures, with results published in newspapers. Subsidies are given to individual households or groups consisting of at least ten families. The organization of the group is managed by a registered and approved external institution such as the municipality, an NGO, the regional housing office, a housing cooperative and a housing foundation.

While the approach has been successful in addressing Chile's housing deficit, there have been problems. Applicants have sometimes had to wait several years for a subsidy.[6] New housing developments have mainly been built in the urban periphery where land costs are lowest, and a host of factors combine to reduce quality of life, including cramped and poor quality units, lengthy and expensive travel, social segregation, poor security, unequal access to urban services and environmental contamination. Illegal land invasions, the traditional way for the poor to get better land, are no longer a way out.

Mexico: FONHAPO[7]

The Mexican National Popular Housing Fund (FONHAPO) was created in April 1981 to reach low-income families too poor to benefit from existing housing loan schemes. Over the following six years, with only 4 percent of the total public sector investment in housing, FONHAPO supported 23 percent of all new housing financed by public funds and reached about 250,000 households. The process was quite transparent and the recovery rate was high, compared to other Mexican public housing schemes. The programme was considered a success especially by NGOs and left-leaning academics. However, after 1988, FONHAPO's operating principles changed, leading to a sharp reduction in its activities. At present, it no longer offers a housing assistance to the urban and rural poor.

The design of FONHAPO drew heavily on the experience of an NGO called COPEVI[8] (Ortiz, 1996: 17). COPEVI was founded in 1965 by a group of young architects and social workers to improve housing for the poor and to promote democratic housing and urban development policies. Some key FONHAPO concepts, such as the organization of and support to groups like cooperatives, are present in COPEVI's original statutes.

FONHAPO was established as a state body which aimed to provide housing to people who were not benefiting from existing housing programmes because they were poor or unemployed. The majority of its beneficiaries were previously tenants. FONHAPO could not do much to help extremely poor people, for example those outside a regular family. FONHAPO financed intermediate organizations which could be public (belonging to the federal, state, municipal or quasi-state sector), private (such as financial institutions and development trusts) or social (cooperatives and other legally constituted social organizations). In contrast to many other housing institutions at that time, FONHAPO did not exclusively finance finished dwellings, but also supported the provision of sites with services, incremental housing development, home improvements and building material production.

Partly as a result of FONHAPO's work, by the mid-1980's the main actions of the urban housing movement had shifted substantially from defensive measures – such as resisting evictions, opposing land tax charges, or getting rid of corrupt community leaders – towards more active demands. *'Protesta con propuesta'* (protest with proposal) became the dominant theme, leading to the development of housing and urban projects designed and controlled by the community organizations themselves. The aims and achievements of many projects went beyond housing issues. Communities also addressed employment, health and education, women's organizations, communal facilities, alternative technologies, ecology and integral neighbourhood development. Some were also interested in community democracy, emphasizing decision-making in assemblies and obligatory participation in the commissions established to address project needs. By the end of the 1980s, the major task of Mexico City's urban movement was the development of community housing projects.

However, during the 1980s the loose agglomeration of community-based organizations that made up the Popular Urban Movements was also influenced by the general pattern of political reform. Initially, these mostly Maoist-inspired mass organizations steered away from party politics, but as the opposition parties expanded and mobilized around electoral campaigns,[9] the Popular Urban Movement was drawn into electoral politics. Party politics began to seep into community housing, and housing loans were used to buy votes. Increasing political competition generated the very clientelism that the housing projects had tried so hard to keep out.

FONHAPO changed in other ways too. The housing professionals were supplanted by career politicians from the ruling party. Decision-making became more vertical, and access to credit became increasingly dependent on poor people's capacity to mobilize as pressure groups, rather than on negotiations between FONHAPO officials and community representatives as had previously been the case (Ortiz, 1996: 59). The market orientation became stronger with the withdrawal of explicit subsidies on the value of loans, increased effort in loan recovery, the suppression of FONHAPO's previous land banking policy and the elimination of loans for land purchase. There was a steady increase in the proportion of 'home improvement' loans which were just large enough to secure an electoral return. Meanwhile, the unit value of loans for core housing went up, making them less accessible to the very poor. FONHAPO made ever fewer and ever more expensive sites and services loans after 1990. In short, more bureaucracy, more clientelism, less community.

Philippines: Community Mortgage Programme (CMP) (1990–present)[10]

The CMP in the Philippines allows low-income households, particularly squatters with no secure tenure, to get housing they can afford. It offers subsidized loans to communities facing eviction from land on which they are squatting; to enable them to buy the land and build dwellings. Between 1989 and 2003, the Programme has assisted 140,650 poor families in 1126 communities.

Established in 1986, the CMP derived its inspiration from the community organizing and housing experiences of NGO leaders who were invited to contribute to the policies and programmes of the Aquino government, experiences that owe a great deal to the 18-year resistance to the Marcos dictatorship. The programme requires target beneficiaries to form community associations to obtain funds to buy property and develop land without collateral. All developments are supported by an NGO, a local authority or a national housing agency in a process known as 'origination'. Individual members of the association may obtain further loans for house construction and improvement after securing land titles. The CMP is considered to be the most responsive and cost-effective among state housing finance programmes in the Philippines. Its loans are six times smaller than other housing programmes', and its collection rate, at 75 percent, is the highest of all the government housing loan programmes.

Despite this, CMP has faced a number of difficulties in helping its clients. The government has been reluctant to commit long-term funds, partly because officials object to the legitimization of squatting; relevant state agencies are inefficient; CMP has great difficulty in getting money from the National Home Finance Mortgage Corporation (NHFMC); and land prices, especially in Metro Manila, have risen above CMP's loan ceiling in some cases. Thus over 90 percent of CMP loans are used only for lot acquisition; borrowers have to find the money themselves for any subsequent improvements. Underlying all this is the unresolved question of whether CMP's incremental housing approach, centring on on-site land purchase, is valid or not.

The programme has had to cast around for support. The government pays lip-service, but housing is still used to buy votes, just as in Mexico. Decentralization to local authorities has complicated funding arrangements. In response to all these problems, there has been the suggestion to create a new institution with social housing at its core, but it was too early at the time of writing to assess its impact.

South Africa: housing subsidy programme (1995–present)[11]

At the advent of democracy in 1994, South Africa faced a massive housing challenge. Nearly 70 percent of the population had been regarded as temporary residents of 'white' South Africa, and the apartheid government had neglected housing development for the poor to discourage black urbanization. There was only one formal brick house for every 43 Africans compared to one for every 3.5 whites. The housing backlog was estimated at 1.5–2 million households.

When the ANC government took office, it promised to build one million houses within five years. It introduced a capital subsidy programme for land purchase, infrastructure and housing, funded by the state but operated by the private sector.[12] Households had to consist of at least two members who should be legal South African residents on low incomes (generally under US$542 a month) who had not received state housing assistance before.

The government launched a People's Housing Process policy in 1998 to support self-build activities. The policy enables communities to provide voluntary labour and avoid paying money to contractors:

> This policy and programme encourages and supports individuals and communities in their efforts to fulfil their own housing needs and who wish to enhance the subsidies they receive from government by assisting them in accessing land, services and technical assistance in a way that leads to the empowerment of communities and the transfer of skills.[13]

There is some funding for NGOs to play a role. However, less than 1 percent of housing subsidies have been allocated to the People's Housing Process. The other 99 percent of subsidies have been allocated to private developers.

By 1999, despite the evident success in large-scale coverage, some of the limitations of the strategy were becoming apparent. The subsidy system is designed around the house itself rather than settlement need, and therefore poorly integrated with other aspects of settlement development. Providers are encouraged to find the most efficient way to build an adequately sized house on a serviced plot of land using a fixed subsidy amount. The subsidy system does not cover any non-housing costs, such as social and economic amenities, and coordination between government departments is weak. As a result, the units have been of poor quality, and poorly located on low-cost land, often far from services. Tomlinson (2002: 380) suggests that the subsidy system has reinforced apartheid urban spatial forms. Some residents have sold their dwellings at knock-down prices, creating a 'new homeless' class which has no remaining subsidy entitlement.[14]

Understanding success

Safe and secure housing is important for poverty reduction, both directly as a basic need and indirectly through reducing household expenditure and enhancing earning capacity. The four programmes we have considered all seek to improve housing access for the poor. With the partial exception of FONHAPO, they have been successful in reaching large populations, they have endured, and in Chile and the Philippines they have also survived regime change. We now discuss what we can learn from these programmes about the dynamics of development success.

All four programmes are notable for involving multiple agencies, with commercial companies and NGOs working alongside state authorities in three of the four.[15] The participation of NGOs has been particularly notable. In Mexico and the Philippines, NGOs have prepared groups to take up subsidies and loans. In Chile and South Africa, NGO involvement is restricted to supporting communities which go down the minority group route. In three of the countries, NGOs played a significant founding role in developing the programmes. In Mexico and the Philippines, the government recruited NGO staff to develop the programmes, while in South Africa the subsidy programme emerged through the National Housing Forum which had NGOs among its members. In South Africa and Chile there has also been strong participation from commercial companies.

As noted by others (Houtzager with Pattenden, 2003), such interagency alliances entail costs: compromises which dilute programme objectives. After discussing the nature of success in these programmes, we assess those costs. Complete houses provided by contractors, we will argue, satisfy the interests of commercial providers and, sometimes, politicians. Conversely, a prominent role for community groups, together with the use of an 'incremental development model' which targets improvements to existing dwellings rather than new constructions, is conducive to the provision of large-scale affordable housing, and has the added advantage of strengthening local grassroots organizations.

Scale and poverty orientation

As indicated by Table 6.1, all the programmes have operated at scale. While not denying that housing needs remain acute, there is no doubt that these programmes have made a significant contribution to broadening access to improved shelter. All are 'pro-poor' in that they involve the allocation of resources to low-income people who need housing. All involve similar components, albeit with different emphases. The subsidy component is smallest in the Philippines, where it only extends to the interest rate subsidy (although the CMP's squatter clients often negotiate a further indirect benefit in the form of a discount on the cost of the land). It is largest in South Africa, where the full capital subsidy can be secured by the poorest households with only a sweat equity component. In Chile, for the sub-programmes directed to the lowest-income households, the savings requirement is less than 10 percent of the value of the capital subsidy, and the state contribution is substantial. In short, as a group these programmes have reached citizens, including the poor, at scale, have delivered substantial benefits, and have redistributed resources and improved housing conditions.

However, there is a downside. For one thing, there are limitations in the groups that have been reached. Neither FONHAPO nor CMP reaches very low earners, even though CMP is more successful than other government housing programmes in reaching low-income people (Connolly, 2004a; Porio *et al.*, 2004). We might expect Chile and South Africa's more heavily subsidized programmes to impose fewer financial constraints on the poorest households, but constraints there still are. For example, it takes time for the poorest Chilean households to accumulate the required savings.

A more intractable problem is that it will always be difficult to address poverty through the transfer of housing assets alone. The poorest households are likely to need an integrated programme with support for income generation and employment as well as savings, community capacity-building and housing-related improvements. Investing in housing and land development is only a suitable first step in a poverty intervention when a community is in immediate danger of eviction (Boonyabancha, 2004). The high cost of that development and the potential need for relocation may make vulnerable livelihoods more vulnerable still.

All the programmes have had to manoeuvre to obtain funds, sometimes in difficult circumstances. In South Africa the government has been criticized for having prioritized economic growth at the expense of the needs of the poor in its economic strategies (Human Sciences Research Council, 2004; Peet, 2002: 74–6; Van der Berg *et al.*, 2005: 6–10). Whilst the housing subsidy has sometimes seemed at risk, funding has continued and actually increased. In Chile, the government introduced the housing subsidy at a time when the government was trying to reduce the role of the state and hold down government expenditure. Gilbert (2002a: 310) argues that the government put its neoliberal agenda on one side in order to continue the tradition of providing housing subsidies to the poor, recognizing the scale of housing need and the necessity for even a dictatorship to maintain popular support. In the Philippines, NGOs have been active in lobbying the state to maintain funding for the CMP, and CMP has struggled on, albeit with low levels of funding. For five years, FONHAPO's supporters were equally successful until, as we saw, the changing political context resulted in the politicization of housing. In each case, there has been a formal or informal coalition of interests that has kept the programmes going.

These programmes have sought intangible political benefits as well as the tangible financial and physical ones. For example, all of them have tried to offer financial support transparently and predictably. In Chile there is an elaborate process for publicizing subsidy allocations. In South Africa, applications are validated against a national database identifying entitlements. In the Philippines, allocations have more to do with land status and the risk of eviction, rather than the entitlements of individuals.

All programmes support the formation of social or political capital through collective lending and urban development, but the degree to which they emphasize loans as opposed social solidarity is one of the most significant differences between them. Loans offer an individualized solution to poverty through enabling the accumulation of physical assets, in this case through financial markets. By contrast, social solidarity offers a collective solution both through enhancing the value of self-help (it is cheaper to buy land in a group) and through creating social capital in the form of stronger relationships with other community groups, NGOs and local authorities. Both FONHAPO and the CMP put more emphasis on group development, offering subsidized loans to groups which provided incremental housing packages. Coming together as a group, strengthens the community which has, as it were, two for the price of one: both housing finance and increased 'voice'. In Chile and South Africa, however, group loans were only available to a small minority that was already well enough organized to take advantage of them.

Private and political interests as a brake on programme effectiveness

Despite the ostensible political commitment to them, it appears that neither of the Chilean nor the South African governments has put in serious money: the percentage of state expenditure allocated has been less than 1.25 percent (Gilbert, 2004: 20). In the Philippines, the CMP remains small and orientated to higher income groups (Llanto *et al.*, 1998). Between 1993 and 1998, only 19.5 percent of the total state expenditure on housing was allocated to poverty-oriented housing projects, and only 1.33 percent to the CMP (*CMP Bulletin*, January 1998). Even when funds have been allocated, it has been difficult to get them disbursed. For the year 2000, for example, CMP was allocated P2.7 billion for 2000, but in the first quarter it saw only P199 million.

Moreover, all this has happened while the situation of the urban poor has been worsening. Despite the subsidy programme, 16.4 percent of all South African households were living in inadequate dwellings at the time of the 2001 census, and the housing backlog had increased to an estimated 3 to 4 million houses as population growth, migration to urban areas and new household formation have outstripped housing provision. In Chile, 6 percent of the population is living in temporary housing, with half a million of them, or 100,000 households, living in squatter settlements. In the Philippines, the urban poor face rising land prices (with 25–50 percent increases per year) and declining urban real incomes (5–7 percent increase per year); and millions are still squatting (Porio *et al.*, 2004: 56).

Thus while some successes have been achieved, these programmes have only had a small impact on housing poverty. As we try to explain why that is, we have to take account of two tensions: first, the way in which private and political interests have steered the programmes away from incremental development and towards the construction of complete units that maximize benefits to the construction industry; and second, the tension between collective and individualized provision.

Private and political interests versus the needs of the poor

The interests of the poor are best served by developing housing incrementally (with adequate services) with plots in locations that make it easier for residents to earn a living. This strategy would enable available state finance to be shared as widely as possible with residents adding to state support through their own savings, sweat equity and small loans. In this model, large numbers of well-located serviced plots keep prices low and reduce the likelihood of families reselling for short-term profits. But this model rarely materializes. As we shall see, commercial interests dictate completed units provided on low-cost land to maximize the added value of construction investment, and political interests play a part too.

In Chile and South Africa, the focus on large capital subsidies was arguably a response to the needs of private commercial enterprises. In Chile, construction companies have used their influence to favour higher standards and to oppose self-help housing (Gilbert, 2004: 28).[16] In South Africa, the resort to a capital subsidy for addressing housing need emerged from the business representatives and consultants who dominated the National Housing Forum between 1992 and 1994, when nine of the 16 founding members were either from business or pro-business (Baumann, 2004: 6; Gilbert, 2002b: 1923; Huchzermeyer, 2003: 604).

The Forum saw low-income housing finance in terms of a new capital subsidy deployed by private developers in large-scale construction projects.

Similar interests have had a less direct influence on the success of the CMP in the Philippines. NGO staff there believe that commercial developers are partly responsible for the problems that they face in securing their share of funds from the administration. The CMP has had to compete for funds of the NHFMC within which it is located. Contractors' interests are served when the Corporation maintains a flow of mortgage finance for complete housing units aimed at middle-income households. In the Philippines, the NGOs involved in supporting the CMP have come to the conclusion that the best option is to have a distinct entity for supporting 'poor people's initiatives for self-help and incremental housing' (CMP Bulletin, 2003). In Mexico, FONHAPO sought to find a role for the commercial sector, enabling their participation within a broader mix of activities.

Recent housing programmes in Mexico have drawn on the Chilean experience of demand subsidies. However, support for incremental development remains insignificant, as new construction absorbs 92 percent of funds (Connolly, 2004b: 4). The average subsidy in 2004 was US$4540 for a finished basic house and US$184 for home improvements. The high cost of the complete housing meant that only 33,000 new houses were built in 2002 (World Bank, 2004a). The new houses are isolated, with only costly access to jobs and services.[17] The needs of the poor have carried less weight than the interests of commercial contractors.

Chile and South Africa's experience is similar to each other (Gilbert, 2002b: 1929). Once again, analysts suggest that this is a result of the dominance of the private sector, concerned to maximize profits, reduce the cost of land to a minimum and spend as much as possible on construction. In South Africa, 'This is entirely in keeping with the logic of private sector housing delivery under a fixed output price (the subsidy)' (Baumann, 2004: 1), while in Chile

> 'the policy offers few location options for the urban poor. The construction focuses on new housing developments that have mainly been built in the urban periphery where land costs are lowest' (Jiron and Fadda, 2003).

In both countries there are concerns about the quality of the construction, with small units, sub-standard building and resulting maintenance problems.[18] In Chile, this issue was highlighted in 1997, when heavy rains damaged as much as 10 percent of the social housing stock

(Perez-Inigo Gonzales, quoted in Gilbert, 2004: 28). In South Africa, criticism resulted in a minimum size requirement in the late 1990s, and increased funding in order to improve size and quality.

The building industry sometimes shares its interest in large-scale programmes with politicians. In both Chile and South Africa there is an emphasis on completed houses. We have already noted the weak support for the People's Housing Process (Huchzermeyer, 2003: 592). Incremental development is not lucrative for the building industry. It is also not very attractive for politicians because it does not produce 'facts on the ground' that they can attach their name to. (To be fair, politicians also sometimes worry that incremental housing will be low-quality housing, and will antagonize other residents.[19])

The pattern in all this is that the initial combination of commercial and civil society demands to press for a commitment to provide housing for the poor translates into pressure, once government commitment is forthcoming, to ensure that the provision satisfies the needs of the construction industry. The complexity of policymaking mean that setting up the programme is only the first step towards policy success: the way in which the policy is implemented is equally important. Moreover, programme evolution is not 'path dependent'. Rather than the policy being set on an irrevocable course at the outset, both policy and implementation may change as the balance of power oscillates among different actors. Changes in the political context, citizen complaints about housing provision, NGO research on the outcomes of the programme – all these and more can have an effect. FONHAPO, for example, developed a number of strategies to consolidate its work. Likewise, the People's Housing Process in South Africa had little support when it was first launched but has become more popular as the advantages of local ownership of the construction process have been more widely recognized. In the Philippines, the fortunes of the CMP have waxed and waned during the last 20 years as local pressure groups have contended with political and bureaucratic interests. And, as noted above, quality has improved in Chile after the 1997 rain damage fiasco.

Whilst commercial interests are generally easy to assess, political interests are more diverse and more opaque. They depend on the ideological persuasion of the state, the extent to which government wants to be seen as a housing provider for poor people, the political acceptability of incremental housing, public expenditure constraints faced by the government, the salience of the voice of the poor and the degree of political competition.

The individual versus the collective

Perhaps reflecting the reluctance of the government to strengthen community capacity especially their capacity for autonomous action, the second of the two tensions to which we referred earlier concerns providers' attitude to individual and collective neighbourhood processes. This bears directly on the ways in which the poor are able to exert their own influence.

We have argued already that multiple pro-poor benefits can be achieved through the provision of shelter. One of them is through the strengthening of community organizations. These organizations are an essential part of an incremental development strategy, as development decisions have to be made by all the residents. As these neighbourhood organizations become more effective, services such as water and security can be provided collectively, neighbours can help each other with housing construction, sharing labour and buying materials together at a discount. The organizations can lobby the state to improve the infrastructure, and to address poor people's needs in general. In addition to lobbying for infrastructure and services within their settlements, strong local organizations can work together to ensure that the city addresses the needs of the poor. As noted above, the process of strengthening local organization has been built into the Philippine and Mexican programmes, and the People's Housing Process in South Africa also recognizes the empowering nature of collective development (Baumann and Mitlin, 2003). Strengthening community organizations is an important way of tackling the lack of political voice which is an aspect of poverty.

The problem with the individualized approach is that it works well only for residents who have jobs and can access the commercial housing market, but not for others. Despite that, there is always pressure to individualize benefits, and often subsidies are released in ways that do not strengthen local organization, as in South Africa, where Huchzermeyer notes that community leaders find it hard to challenge this approach.[20] In the Philippines also, the CMP faces pressure to turn collective loans into individual loans because of concerns about the likelihood of default on collective loan repayments, especially when community organizations are weak and unable to enforce repayments. In part this is related to characteristics of the communities themselves. Small communities have a better repayment rate; at 88 percent in communities with fewer than 200 households against 69 percent where there are more than 350 households. Similarly, in on-site settlements (where people have not had to move), the average repayment is

87 percent against 79 percent in off-site settlements (Ballesteros and Vertido, 2004).

In Chile, there has been a clear preference for individualized allocation to households who meet qualification criteria. Interestingly, this emphasis now appears to be changing as greater priority has been placed on the solidarity housing fund for families below the poverty line who apply in groups of ten or more. The numbers of houses supported under this programme has increased from 2225 in 2001 (when the programme began) to 19,118 in 2003, equivalent to 19.8 percent of total subsidy approvals. Once again this illustrates again the way the balance shifts between the different stakeholder interests: housing programmes do not develop in a straight line.

The first tension between an incremental self-build process and finished units is a conflict between commercial and community interests over the share of physical assets and how much is spent on land (on which the contractor cannot make a profit), and how much on physical construction (on which the contractor can). The second tension is between the political system and the community, and the ways in which redistributed state finance may be used to strengthen the political capacities of the poor. The transformation of local organization and the strengthening of capacities and skills all enable local groups to negotiate more effectively with the state. As illustrated in the case of Mexico, when confronted with new options such strengthened groups could be more assertive and demanding (shifting from protest to proposal). Within a clientelist system they might negotiate for more, and within a more explicit formalized political culture they might also succeed better. But the state is often ambivalent about the extent to which it will support the development of such local (unaffiliated and unco-opted) political capacity. Governments may be reluctant to finance processes that support a more critical electorate and which break with more traditional clientelist ways in which communities and the state relate to each other over the allocation of resources and the management of votes. As is evidenced in the Mexican study above, empowered and energized communities may not offer support to the state that is financing the programme.

Political competition may help to shift the process back in favour of the strengthening of collective capacity. It is notable that the South African Homeless People's Federation who pioneered the realization of the People's Housing Process subsidy route in South Africa found it easiest to access these subsidies in the Western Cape which has a provincial government (the actor that allocated subsidies during this period) that did not have an ANC majority. In places where the ANC prevailed, it proved harder for this people's movement to access subsidies and the emphasis was instead on processes led by the local authority (for example in Port Elizabeth in the Eastern Cape) and/or private contractors (for example, Gauteng) (Baumann and Bolnick, 2001). This is not to argue that there was any deliberate attempt to undermine local community organization, but it is to suggest that in these cases faith was placed in different strategies – a redistributive government believed in its own capacity to deliver and in the capacity of the private sector to perform the functions outlined in its housing programme. But once more there is evidence of no simple process. The People's Housing Process option emerged in part because the local communities linked to the South African Homeless People's Federation demanded a more community driven collectivized process; their case benefited both from having access to external development assistance to allow for exemplar projects and receiving a special grant from Joe Slovo, the first minister of housing in the ANC's government.

Conclusion

The success of these programmes lies in the transfer of resources on a large scale and over an extended period. The assets transferred have been material, in the form of secure housing, but there has also been some social benefit in the form of stronger organizations. All four programmes have a significant non-state element, with communities and private sector being primary providers. In Chile and South Africa, and to a lesser extent in Mexico, there has been significant collaboration with the private sector. The programmes are ideological mixtures, involving state redistribution, private enterprise involvement, self-help by beneficiaries together with limited enabling approaches (in two programmes), and savings/loans components (in all four programmes).

Just as Chapter 1 suggested, the political economy of the policy process has been important, *via* the informal alliances that have shaped and sustained the programmes, partly through links with other political actors. Commercial and/or political interests have influenced all four programmes to the detriment of the poor. Private interests have done their best to maximize profits rather than build to the advantage of families, and in ways that will reduce future infrastructure costs. Political interests have also played a part, using housing to attract electoral support. While the popularity of housing subsidies explains why they continue despite the neo-liberal orientation of broader government policy, politicians remain lukewarm at best towards shack houses,[21] and seek to promote programmes that offer the finished product regardless of their capacity to provide them at scale. The question is not so much whether political will is present in the area of housing, but rather the form that political will takes.

The last decade has been notable in development for the emphasis on consensus politics and programming. Policies and programmes are lauded for being inclusive of civil society, the private sector and the state. The programmes discussed in this paper show the advantages of an inclusive approach, but also the costs that it entails. When powerful interests are part of a programme alliance, the poor lose out. The programme is skewed to the needs of the providers rather than the intended beneficiaries. In Chapter 4, Grindle argued that policies are maintained by those that benefit from them. Slightly differently from that, we argue that at any one time several groups can benefit from policies in quite distinct ways, and that the distribution of benefits depends on the detail of policy design and implementation. Programmes are continually renegotiated, and outcomes at any one time reflect a shifting balance of power between the different interests. Thus programmes that have an impressive record of continuity in outward appearance may in reality have changed fundamentally. FONHAPO in Mexico is an example of that.

In our discussion we have emphasized the ways in which the interests of the poor have not had priority in the development of housing programmes. However, this may overstate the case. Whilst commentators in South Africa were predicting the demise of the capital subsidy programme in the early years of the 21st century, subsidy amounts have in fact been increased. In the Philippines, the government has committed itself to setting up an institution for social housing, although progress in the last two years has been slow. In Chile, there has been a significant increase in group housing initiatives for the poorest. The programmes have represented a real transfer of assets from the state to those in housing need; the recipients have been poor, even if not the very poorest.

These experiences illustrate how NGOs' role need not be confined to filling service gaps, but can extend to shaping policy (see Chapter 1). Poor people themselves are also a significant group influencing policy. However, the experience of 'development success' in the area of housing suggests that the accumulation of tangible assets is an important but insufficient element. A successful development policy, in the end, will be one that enhances the ability of poor people to contest for political power and influence policy.

Notes

1. 'Enablement' refers to an approach which emphasizes the contribution of the state to facilitating the production of housing by the poor themselves or by the private sector.
2. They also recognize the need to improve water and sanitation services.
3. This section draws on Cummings and DiPasquale (1997), Fernandez (2004), Gilbert (2004), Jiron and Fadda (2003) and Rojas and Greene (1995).
4. See Gilbert (2004) for a discussion of its earlier history in the 1970s, and notably its emergence within the military dictatorship in 1977.
5. For example, the Solidarity Fund for Low-Income Housing.
6. Gilbert (2004: 26), quoting Astaburuaga (2000), notes that the average wait for a subsidy is 15.6 years. However, Fernandez (2004) in a more recent assessment suggests that waiting times are now below three years.
7. This section draws heavily on Connolly (2004a).
8. *Centro Operacional de Vivienda y Poblamiento AC* (Operational Centre for Housing and Human Settlement).
9. In 1988, for the first time in more than 50 years, the governing Revolutionary Institutional Party faced serious opposition in the presidential elections.
10. This section draws on Porio *et al.* (2004).
11. This draws on Baumann (2004) and Baumann *et al.* (2004) and www.housing.gov.za.
12. This was the recommendation of the National Housing Forum, a multi-sectoral group set up in 1992 to guide housing policy. See Gilbert (2002b) and Huchzermeyer (2003).
13. South African Government submission to Istanbul plus five, UN-Habitat (2001: 4).
14. Gilbert (2004: 31) documents this trend. But as he notes, there is no information on the scale of the problem. He suggests that a further problem is that people cannot afford the costs of services, although the high rate of non-payment suggests that this is not the only problem.
15. In the Philippines, there has been little involvement from the private sector.
16. Viviana Fernandez, an NGO activist who has worked in the housing ministry and who is now an academic, suggests that 'there has always been a great influence of the Chilean Chamber of Construction (all the building enterprises belong to this Chamber) in the design of housing policies'.
17. An analysis of housing subsidies in Europe also suggests that when subsidies are attached to the purchase of newly constructed housing, similar problems arise, with the housing being built in unpopular locations to take advantage of lower land costs (Bosvieux and Vorms, quoted in Scanlon and Whitehead, 2004).
18. While it is risky to assume bad practice, the issue of control does appear to be significant. There is a classic 'third party problem': the construction is being financed by the state for someone else.

19 The experiences of the author in subsidy-financed greenfield developments is that the emphasis on standards is considerable, and an incremental development approach is resisted.
20 The author's experience with the South African Homeless People's Federation confirms this tendency.
21 The most recent example of this has been the events in Zimbabwe in 2005. Hundreds of thousands of urban dwellers, including those who had legal title, were evicted from their shacks, even when they legally owned the land they were built on, in the government's *Operation Murambatsvina* (Restore Order). Operation Murambatsvina was followed by *Operation Garikai / Hlanlani Kuhle* (we promise things will be better), which aims to resettle the homeless and provide better trading sites for small businesses, but not on the same scale as the evictions.

7

Realizing Health Rights in Brazil: The Micropolitics of Sustaining Health System Reform

Alex Shankland and Andrea Cornwall[1]

Introduction

Brazil's 'Citizens' Constitution' of 1988 established health as 'the right of all and the duty of the state'. It also guaranteed the right of citizens to participate in the governance of the *Sistema Único de Saúde* (National Health System; SUS for short) through institutions created at municipal, state and national level. Nowhere else in the world have such ambitious and far-reaching efforts been made to institutionalize citizen participation in the governance of health systems. Yet the dominant tone in the literature on participation in Brazil's SUS is largely negative, with many observers questioning whether these institutional arrangements have had any significant impact on improving efficiency, shifting priorities towards the needs of the poorest or promoting genuinely accountable health system management.[2]

In this chapter, we argue that such negative perspectives risk ignoring the importance of the *political* role played by the institutionalization of participation in the architecture of the SUS – which, we argue, has been central to sustaining the 'SUS project' for almost two decades in a largely adverse macropolitical and macroeconomic climate. In the introduction to this volume (Chapter 1), McCourt and Bebbington highlight the significance of policy durability, both in analytical and political terms. They also emphasize the importance of paying close attention to the scope and depth of policies, drawing attention not only to the potential of policies with a broader scope to generate broad-based alliances but also to the potential of the policy negotiations that are part of alliance-building to strip policies of their more radical features. The 'SUS project' is particularly interesting for precisely these reasons, as it has given rise to durable policies, with broad scope, but with little attenuation of its more radical principles.

The SUS is a universal, publicly-funded, rights-based anomaly in the continent which pioneered 'neoliberal' health sector reforms.[3] It was conceived during the democratic transition which followed Brazil's 1964–1985 military dictatorship, gained institutional form in the 1988 Constitution and 1990 Basic Health Law (*Lei Orgânica da Saúde*), survived the 'neoliberal shock' of the Collor government and secured additional funding through hypothecated taxes during the fiscally conservative first Cardoso government, laying the groundwork for a steady expansion during the second Cardoso government and into the Lula government. Between 1988 and 1996, a period when federal government policy was dominated by attempts to impose orthodox macroeconomic austerity and to shrink the state through widespread privatization, annual federal health spending increased by over 50 percent in real terms, from around US$11 billion to some US$17 billion (Silva, 2003).

Defenders of the SUS model can point to significant improvements in Brazil's health indicators since the system's creation. By 1996 the proportion of pregnant women receiving at least one antenatal consultation had risen to 84 percent and the proportion of births attended by trained staff had risen to 88 percent (WHO, 2005), up from 60 percent and 73 percent respectively in 1990 (WHO, 1995). Between 1992 and 2004, under-five mortality fell from 65 to 34 per 100,000 and DPT3 immunization coverage rose from 69 percent to 96 percent (WHO, 1995, 2005, 2006). The proportion of the poorest households[4] accessing health services rose by almost half, with the PNAD household survey recording an increase in the number declaring that they had used these services in the preceding two weeks from 9.73 percent in 1986 to 14.18 percent in 2003 (Silva, 2003; IBGE, 2005). In the terms defined by McCourt and Bebbington, the SUS therefore qualifies as a development success which has expanded the human capabilities of the poor as well as demonstrating durability.

This picture of solid progress towards the fulfilment of health rights for all Brazilians is complicated, however, by a number of factors. First, there is the question of the counterfactual: health indicators were improving in Brazil before 1988, and there is no way of knowing the extent to which this improvement may or may not have been accelerated by the introduction of the SUS. There is also the question of persistent inequity: despite the expansion in coverage of poorer groups, the differential in health service use between the poorest and the richest segments of the population has remained, exacerbated by a massive rise in private health spending.[5] The inequitable distribution of health spending between Brazil's richest and poorest regions is a further aggravating factor, which combines with discrimination and social exclusion to perpetuate the inequalities in health status which are revealed when data are disaggregated by gender and race (Oliveira, 2002). Finally, there is the question of public perception: when popular and media images of the SUS are dominated by 'horror stories' of contamination, abuse or service collapse, it is hard to maintain a positive impression of the system's achievements.

For all the multiple failings of the system, and despite the fall from fashion of the state-centred, universalistic ideology which underpinned its creation, the 'SUS project' has endured and to this day remains largely unchallenged as the hegemonic model for health system development in Brazil. Writing in 2003, Marta Arretche described the establishment and consolidation of the SUS as a 'paradigm shift' through which the country 'replaced a centralized health care model based on contributory principles with one in which the *legal right* of free access to health actions and services at every level of complexity is universal and in which service provision is organized through a decentralized hierarchy' (2003: 332 – our translation, emphasis in the original). Arretche's conclusion was that while there would be an ongoing process of adjustments to the system's management arrangements, the rights-based SUS paradigm itself had become institutionalized to the point where it was unlikely to undergo any significant changes (*ibid.*).

In this chapter we begin by sketching the origins and development of the SUS and its framework for citizen participation. We outline the trajectory of the system and some of the most common explanations for its survival and growth, before going on to suggest an alternative explanation based on the micropolitics of inclusion as played out in the participatory institutions of the SUS. We then go on to examine the dynamics of citizen participation in three very different sites: the Health Council of a medium-sized municipality in north-eastern Brazil, the Special Health District established to serve the indigenous population of a remote area of the Amazon and the most recent National Health Conference. Our analysis seeks both to explore the links between micro-level inclusionary practices and the political success of the SUS, and to draw lessons from the Brazilian experience to address a broader set of questions about the possibilities – and limits – of citizen engagement in the shaping and management of health services.

The SUS: origins and trajectory

Citizen participation and the SUS

Emerging from a context marked by authoritarian and clientelistic forms of governance, Brazil's legendary participatory governance institutions appear all the more remarkable. The fruit of intense struggle by social movements over the course of decades of dictatorship, the provisions of the Constitution and *Lei Orgânica da Saúde* mapped out a radical plan for institutionalizing citizen action to hold the nascent democratic state to account for health spending. These institutions – the *Conselhos de Saúde*, or Health Councils – were to have parity of representation from organized civil society and the state, and were to be put in place in all of Brazil's 23 states and 5000 municipalities. They were to be complemented by a regular cycle of Health Conferences at the municipal, state and federal levels, whose role was to debate and agree the strategic priorities for health system development.

Until the mid-1980s, the Brazilian health system was characterized both by centralization and by exclusion. State curative services were concentrated in urban-based hospital care and open only to the relatively small proportion of the population who were in formal-sector employment (Costa, 2004: 2). For the most part, the rural and peri-urban poor only encountered state health services in the shape of vertical programmes such as the military-style vector extermination campaigns run by the malaria control agency SUCAM. Where sporadic outreach initiatives did extend some state curative services into rural areas, as in the case of the field hospital network run by FSESP, these services were generally under direct federal control and little effort was made to engage the local population in their management.

As the deepening economic crisis of the late 1970s and early 1980s weakened both the military dictatorship's grip on power and the state's ability to fund even the limited existing public health services, policymakers began to cast around for alternative models (Coelho *et al.*, 2002: 66). This provided an opening for reformers who had been involved in piloting more inclusive 'community health' approaches in local projects sponsored by universities or the Catholic Church to begin to occupy key positions in the federal and state-level health bureaucracy, while maintaining their links with the emerging grassroots health movement (Costa, 2004; Melo, 1993; Weyland, 1995).

This movement had gathered strength under the dictatorship as health emerged as one of the few arenas where popular mobilization was not met with immediate repression and where middle-class professionals were able to engage with communities without attracting the attention of the secret police. One of its key centres was in the East Zone of São Paulo, where community activists set up the first *Conselhos* as popular spaces for demanding health service accountability. Though they were initially created outside the health system's legal framework, these *Conselhos* were to prove highly influential in shaping the provision for participation and accountability in later Constitutional and sectoral reforms (Costa, 2004: 5). The struggle for democratization in the concluding years of the military dictatorship was marked both by deep mistrust of the 'bureaucratic-authoritarian' state among social movements and by the desire on the part of reformers aligned with these movements to maintain the centrality of the state in the implementation of policies to tackle the country's profound social and economic inequalities. This led to the framing of participation both as a right in itself and as a mechanism for *controle social* or 'citizen oversight' of state-implemented social policies.

During the 1980s, ad-hoc alliances between community activists and progressive professionals coalesced into the *movimento pela reforma sanitária* (movement for health reform). The movement became known more colloquially as the *movimento sanitarista* (public health movement), as a result of the prominence of public health specialists (notably those based at the FIOCRUZ National School of Public Health in Rio de Janeiro) among its leading figures. Marcus Melo has described the movement as the paradigmatic case of an 'issue network' led by technically-minded reformists, while recognizing that health reform had also become a 'key demand of the popular sectors' (1993: 149–50). As leading *sanitaristas* increased their penetration of the redemocratizing state and secured key posts in the Ministry of Health, they were able to open new spaces for the popular health movement and other non-elite actors (such as CONTAG, the rural workers' confederation) to voice their demands for reform. Through this process, the movement took on the characteristics of what Fox (1996) describes as 'state-society convergence'.

This convergence was evident in the symbolic high point of the *movimento sanitarista*, the 8th National Health Conference of 1986. Orchestrated by *sanitaristas* based at FIOCRUZ and in the Health Ministry and attended by thousands of community activists from across the country, the Conference proclaimed health to be 'the duty of the state and the right of the citizen' and enshrined key principles of universality, decentralization and participation as the normative basis of health system reform. Two years later these principles were written into the Constitution, and in 1990 the framework for operationalizing them was established by the *Lei Orgânica da Saúde*, creating the SUS as the mechanism for universalization of services.

This framework included a requirement for municipalities to establish *Conselhos* with 50 percent user representation and extensive powers of service and spending oversight, as a condition for federal transfers of funding for health services. While the first *Conselhos* had emerged as a result of bottom-up mobilization, it was this federal 'participation conditionality' which spurred a massive proliferation of deliberative health councils at the municipal level throughout the 1990s – with no fewer than 98.5 percent of municipalities having established a health *Conselho* by 1999 (Melo and Rezende, 2004: 46).[6]

Despite the strength of formal provision for user participation and *controle social*, a number of studies have drawn attention to the limitations of the *Conselho* system in ensuring accountability and pro-poor targeting of health spending. These failings have been attributed to the persistence of authoritarian social relations and the attempts by mayors to pack *Conselhos* with their own political clients (above all in smaller, more rural municipalities), as well as to the tendency of bureaucrats and health professionals to privilege 'technical' discourses, excluding traditional and popular knowledge from Councils' deliberations (Coelho *et al.*, 2002; Côrtes, 1998). As Arretche (2003) points out, a recurrent conclusion of these studies is that the scope for effective *controle social* is strongly dependent on the commitment of local politicians and technical staff to making participation work – in other words, on the kind of 'state-society convergence' which the *movimento sanitarista* initially fostered but whose operation at the local level has been extremely uneven across Brazil.

In recent years, as the SUS has rolled out a series of standardized packages for extending access to services, the emphasis of social movement and civil society mobilization has shifted towards demands for the recognition of social difference as a key element in securing genuine equity (Costa, 2004: 11). While indigenous peoples, historically treated as a special case, have since the late 1990s been the focus of a 'specific SUS subsystem' (discussed below), these demands have brought a broader range of actors – including the feminist, Afro-Brazilian and gay rights movements – into engagement with the SUS and its participation mechanisms.

Negotiating SUS implementation: sub-national governments and the private sector

A key element in the process of consolidation of the SUS was the relationship between the federal government, the source of the largest share of health system funding, and the states and municipalities. The latter were particularly important, given the system's emphasis on decentralization of service delivery to the municipal level. The municipalities were initially reluctant to take on the services, a reluctance which in addition to lack of capacity was attributed to uncertainty over whether the resources necessary for delivery would actually be provided and a desire to avoid the political onus of responsibility for poor-quality services (Costa, 2002: 60). This reluctance was eventually overcome by a combination of political pressure, fiscal incentives and the creation of transparent criteria and mechanisms for negotiating federal and state transfers, subsequently institutionalized in the 'bipartite' and 'tripartite' resource allocation fora. The result was a dramatic increase in municipal management of primary care (and in fewer cases of high-complexity services as well), with the proportion of municipalities taking decentralized responsibility for primary care increasing from 23.4 percent to 88.7 percent between 1994 and 1998 (Costa, 2002). By 2002, the proportion had risen to 99.6 percent, effectively completing the municipalization process for primary care (Arretche, 2004).

The SUS was similarly able to reach an accommodation with the growing private health care provision sector, though (as was the case with the sub-national governments) this accommodation was marked by periodic outbreaks of conflict over responsibilities and resources. The origin of this accommodation was not in the design of the health reform proposals championed by the *movimento sanitarista* – indeed, the 8th National Health Conference proposed the nationalization of the private health care and pharmaceutical industries – but rather in the messy compromise which emerged from struggles over the future shape of the health system in the 1987–1998 Constituent Assembly. Although the *movimento sanitarista* and its allies were successful in ensuring that the governing principles of the system were framed in universalistic, rights-based terms, the conservative *Centrão* bloc in the Assembly was able to insert Constitutional provisions which asserted the legitimacy of private-sector activity in health care at the same time as they affirmed the state's overall responsibility (Melo, 1993: 136). This subsequently underpinned the consolidation of a purchaser-provider relationship, with the SUS buying a substantial volume of services from private hospitals and clinics, thereby giving private providers a stake in the system. At the same time, it lent Constitutional legitimacy to the then-nascent private health insurance sector, which was able to embark on an energetic period of expansion in the 1990s – on the back of the windfall provided by middle-class flight from the increasingly overloaded public services – and which succeeded in remaining largely unregulated until the end of the decade.

The struggle to fund the SUS

The context within which user groups pressed their rights claims, and within which federal, state and municipal managers and private and public service providers struggled over resources, was one of rapidly increasing demand coupled with chronic underfunding. Health spending was on an upward trajectory in the early years of democratic transition, enabling initial moves towards decentralization and universalization of existing social insurance-funded health services to be piloted through a system known as SUDS. The Ministry of Health had already secured increases in its budget, succeeded in wresting control of social insurance funds away from the Social Security Ministry and replacing the SUDS with the fully fledged SUS. It now evolved from a marginal ministry into one of the government's most important spending departments (Costa, 2002; Melo, 1993;). This process had barely begun, however, when the 'neoliberal shock' of the Collor government (1990–1992) precipitated a dramatic decline (around 30 percent in real terms over two years) in federal health spending, which took almost five years to return to its 1989 level (Silva, 2003).

The crisis in morale among SUS service providers and in the public's confidence in the new system which followed could have provided an opening for policy entrepreneurs aligned with the ascendant 'neoliberal' tendency to dismantle the SUS and replace it with a more ideologically congenial system, such as the private insurance-based scheme adopted in Chile (Labra, 2001). Instead, the 1990s were marked by a series of efforts to generate additional resource flows for the SUS through political bargaining and the introduction of hypothecated taxes, and to earmark a specific share of government revenues to fund health services (Mansur, 2001).

In these efforts, community activists in the municipalities, *sanitarista* bureaucrats in the Ministry of Health and their allies in Congress received decisive support from an unexpected quarter: heavyweight politicians with little or no previous history of identification with the

SUS cause, nominated as Health Ministers by the privatizing, fiscally conservative Collor and Cardoso governments. When the first attempt to introduce hypothecated taxation (through the unpopular 'cheque tax' or IMF) proved short-lived, it was the vigorous lobbying of widely respected health minister Adib Jatene which ensured that it was replaced by a virtually identical 'provisional contribution' (the CPMF), which remains in force to this day. Jatene's most high-profile successor in the Ministry of Health, José Serra, was an effective exponent of political bargaining in defence of the SUS's share of federal government spending (Costa, 2002). His period in office, during the second Cardoso government, also saw the approval of a Constitutional Amendment earmarking a steadily rising share of federal, state and municipal revenues for spending on health services. This amendment had been proposed by members of the influential 'health caucus' in Congress (many of them veterans of the *movimento sanitarista*) in order to deal with the problem of austerity-minded finance ministers responding to increased hypothecated revenues by cutting the discretionary allocations for SUS funding (Mansur, 2001). Its approval, in September 2000, arguably represented the successful culmination of more than a decade of struggle to ensure adequate funding for the SUS model, in the teeth of economic and fiscal crisis and a macropolitical scenario dominated by the 'neoliberal' consensus.

Explaining the durability of the SUS model

Macropolitics?

Conventional explanations for the fact that the SUS model survived and remained hegemonic during this prolonged period of exposure to a highly adverse climate have emphasized macropolitical factors. These explanations tend to focus on one or more of the elements addressed in the previous section, particularly the existence of bargains with sub-national governments and the private sector and the agency of particular health ministers. We would argue, however, that while these elements do have some explanatory power each also contains serious limitations. Taken together, they are insufficient to account for the phenomenon of the SUS's political success.

The bargains struck with sub-national governments and the private sector were undoubtedly essential in enabling the SUS to get off the ground. However, as the discussion above has shown, the buy-in of the municipalities was achieved only with difficulty and at a relatively late stage of the system's development. Arretche attributes central importance to the fact that the SUS framework 'vested the Health Ministry with the authority to take the most important sectoral policy decisions' (2004: 22), but it was not until this framework had been in place for almost a decade that the institutional mechanisms for operationalizing the Ministry's decisions were sufficiently consolidated to create 'conditions for reducing uncertainty over [intergovernmental] transfers, giving credibility to the prospect that they would actually occur' (*ibid.*) and thus finally to ensure adherence at the municipal level. There was thus a hiatus of several years during which the support for the SUS model of sub-national political actors – both the municipal mayors and the politically powerful governors – was far from guaranteed, in which alternatives to this model could have taken hold.

Similarly, although some private providers had accepted the stake in the SUS that they were offered and others had profited from the largely unregulated growth of private health insurance, there were still frequent clashes between the vested interests of the private sector and those of the Ministry of Health. As SUS funding was squeezed and costs continued to rise, service providers engaged in frequent campaigns for increases in the Ministry's scale of fixed-rate service payments. As the federal government began to make its regulatory power felt towards the end of the 1990s, a part of the private sector which had been able to grow largely undisturbed by state action suddenly found itself facing sustained efforts to claw back the cost of care provided by the SUS to privately-insured patients. Private providers thus had plenty of incentives to abandon the SUS and support a shift to a fully or partially privatized system along the lines adopted elsewhere in Latin America – had such a shift ever been on the Brazilian political agenda.

The charismatic Health Ministers who championed hypothecated taxes and an increased share of government spending for the SUS were undoubtedly important political actors who made a significant contribution to the system's financial survival.[7] However, neither had the classic profile of a *sanitarista* 'true believer'. Jatene was a heart surgeon with a lucrative private practice, and Serra was an economist serving in a government which had enthusiastically adopted 'neoliberal' approaches in other policy areas. As Marcus Melo (2005) points out, the Cardoso government preserved the 'technical' profile of social-sector ministries such as education and health by excluding them from the bargains struck with conservative-clientelist allies. However, there was no lack of 'technical' arguments for Chilean- or Colombian-style privatizing reform (and no lack of financial and political support from the international financial institutions for those prepared to advocate such reform). Serra's key advisers were fellow economists brought in from outside, not the *sanitarista* bureaucrats entrenched in the Ministry. If Serra and Jatene championed the SUS rather than using their clout to push through alternative models, it was because there was political mileage to be gained from doing so. In other words, the SUS was politically potent enough to attract converts and fellow-travellers – which begs the question of why this should be the case.

One potential explanation is the strength of pressure from outside government, particularly from the social movement for health reform. It is undoubtedly true that the *movimento sanitarista* was one of the most influential political forces to emerge from the dictatorship period, and that its demands (crystallized in the recommendations of the 8th National Health Conference) provided the main inspiration for the provisions in the Constitution and the *Lei Orgânica da Saúde* which established the SUS. However, these successes, and the undoubted strength of grassroots activity in some localities (such as the East Zone of São Paulo) masked the movement's highly uneven levels of organization across the country and its surprising weakness in mass-mobilization; as both Melo (1993) and Weyland (1995) have pointed out, the response to the movement's effort to organize a mass petition in support of its proposals in the Constituent Assembly was less than overwhelming. Weyland argues that the movement fragmented and lost its momentum in the late 1980s, as clientelist reaction set in, many leading *sanitaristas* who had been drawn into SUS administration became absorbed in bureaucratic turf wars, and popular mobilization turned from demands for broad health system reform to emphasize localized claim-making. However, his pessimistic assessment of the movement's achievements, written in 1995, was belied by the decade-long trajectory of expansion and renewed confidence on which the SUS was even then embarking. If the original social movement base of the push for health system reform was uneven and soon fragmented, and if the *sanitarista* activists who penetrated the Health Ministry found themselves subordinated to political masters whose ideological origins were very different, how then did the SUS not only sustain itself but remain remarkably faithful to the reform principles upon which it had been founded?

Micropolitics?

We would argue that at least part of the answer to this question lies in the realm of micropolitics – specifically, the inclusionary practices associated with and symbolized by the participatory and deliberative institutions of the SUS. Above all, we aim to show in this chapter how these have functioned as spaces for the reproduction of SUS ideology and the recruitment of new adherents, operating at the interface between citizens and the state in a way which is distinct both from the 'invited spaces' (Cornwall, 2004) promoted by progressive bureaucrats in Fox's (1996) model of 'state-society convergence' and from the outside-the-state building of popular pressure which is the conventional model described in the social movement literature.

The SUS participation institutions, the *Conselhos* and *Conferências*, operate at the local, municipal, state and federal levels. While their density tends to be significantly higher in wealthier, more urbanized regions with a history of civil society organizing, they exist in some form or another in virtually every municipality in Brazil. This gives them an extraordinary capillary reach. Their deliberations have involved literally hundreds of thousands of citizens, many of whom had never before been given the chance to have a say in the governance of any of the services on which they depended. Their statutory status as *deliberativos* – which in Brazilian legal usage means 'empowered to make binding decisions' – may not always have translated into effective practices for securing accountability (as discussed below), but it has imbued them with a political weight far greater than the consultative 'invited spaces' which have proliferated in Brazil and elsewhere in recent decades (Cornwall, 2004).

The multilayered nature of the SUS's participation mechanisms has also provided opportunities for engagement to a huge variety of different actors at different levels, from grassroots Catholic Church health workers in rural municipalities to regional feminist health networks to national health policy specialists. The deliberative-democratic spaces of the SUS are linked in turn with the institutions of representative democracy through the *bancada da saúde*, a Congressional caucus whose cross-party composition has helped to ensure that the 'SUS project' does not fall victim to changes in the political fortunes of particular parties, and which remains one of the most significant forces to be reckoned with in the national legislature (Duncan Semple, pers. comm.).

These participatory institutions have also provided a focus for successive waves of emerging social movements to engage with the SUS. The influence of the Popular Health Movement may have waned, but others have taken its place. The feminist health movement has secured a significant voice in the shaping of the SUS at the regional and national levels. Since the transfer of responsibility for indigenous health care to the SUS in the late 1990s (see below), indigenous peoples' organizations have become increasingly visible in health policymaking, culminating in the reorganization of the National Health Council to include indigenous representatives. Catalysed by debates over the national HIV/AIDS policy, sexuality rights groups have increasingly moved centrestage. Growing recognition of the need to address the health issues of Afro-Brazilians (Maio and Monteiro, 2005; Oliveira, 2002) has accompanied an increased presence of the *movimento negro* in SUS participation fora in recent years. Each of these movements has identified the SUS as a key site of struggle for its rights claims, and has pursued these claims by invoking SUS principles.

This process of identification has been facilitated by the longstanding preeminence of a particular discourse of citizenship – *cidadania* – in Brazilian rights-claiming mobilizations. As we have discussed elsewhere,[8] *cidadania* invokes a notion of citizenship which incorporates both universal rights and active participation. Activists interviewed during the case study research repeatedly cited the SUS – founded on a Constitutional affirmation of the universal right to health and endowed with an extraordinary breadth and depth of opportunities for citizen participation – as the exemplar of a policy framework which promoted both aspects of *cidadania*.[9]

The cumulative effect of these multiple inclusionary processes – bringing previously excluded citizens into local-level spaces and new waves of social movements into higher-level engagement – has been a continual deepening and broadening of the range of actors committed to the 'SUS project'. Unlike the *movimento sanitarista*, this is not a recognizable 'movement' with a single platform and identifiable leadership group. Though it includes some formal networks, and a classic semi-formal political coalition in the shape of the *bancada da saúde*, it is bound together by shared visions, values and discourses rather than by a coherently articulated set of strategic goals. We would argue that this diverse collection of actors forms a potent 'epistemic community' (Haas, 1992), and that its power operates at the discursive and ideological level to sustain the political momentum for rights-based health reform in Brazil.

Crucially, this is an 'epistemic community' which draws its strength from the number and social diversity of its adherents rather than solely from their location in key decision-making and opinion-forming positions. It thus contrasts with the more elite-centred examples studied by Haas, and with the majority of the 'policy networks' whose importance is stressed by McCourt and Bebbington (Chapter 1). In many ways, it could be considered more akin to a social movement than a policy network – were it not for the fact that its key sites are located not outside the state but firmly embedded within the public policymaking apparatus.

It is the participatory institutions of the SUS which serve as the locus for the continual reproduction of rights-based health reform ideology and the recruitment of new members of the 'epistemic community'. These institutions became consolidated just as the *movimento sanitarista* had begun to fragment, and in the intervening years they have provided a constantly growing number of Brazilian citizens and civil society groups with the sites for mobilization, skills-development and debate over common platforms traditionally associated with social movements. At the same time, they have enabled potentially sympathetic policymakers who may otherwise have had few opportunities to engage in policy debate with a diverse array of citizen representatives both to influence and to be influenced by them. Their contribution to this process helps to explain why the *Conselhos* and *Conferências* have remained central to the SUS model despite their manifest limitations in achieving the purposes of accountability and policy formation for which they were supposedly created. In the next section, we explore this further by examining the dynamics and contradictions of three very different cases of participation in the SUS.

Sustaining the SUS through inclusionary practices

Case 1: Cabo de Santo Agostinho Municipal Health Council

In Cabo de Santo Agostinho, a medium-sized municipality in the north-eastern state of Pernambuco, the Municipal Health Council (*Conselho Municipal de Saúde*, or CMS) had barely been created, in 1994, when a progressive municipal government fell to an incoming right-wing administration. Their ostensible lack of commitment for following through the constitutional promise of democratizing the governance of health care served to cement alliances between a diversity of social actors. A popular front was formed, bringing together the women's movement, represented by a vocal and well-connected feminist NGO with a regional presence, the *Centro das Mulheres do Cabo*, activists from groups associated with progressive elements within the Catholic and Protestant churches, labour unions, and a natural medicine NGO who had long played a part in debates about public health in the municipality (Cordeiro *et al.*, 2004). Their efforts were rewarded in 1997, when a leftist (*Partido Popular Socialista*) municipal government took power and brought in a radical health reformer and veteran of the *movimento sanitarista*, Cláudio Duarte, who set about institutionalizing the municipal SUS and breathing new life into the health council.

Interviews with Duarte and his successors revealed a shared vision in which *controle social* came to embrace more than the promise of accountability and the pragmatic gains of health service user feedback. It came to represent to them a process of democratization through which user involvement in the council stimulated the emergence of new civil society leaders and the enlistment and engagement of social movements and neighbourhood associations in the SUS project. But this went beyond a tale of alliances forged between progressive elements of 'the state' and 'civil society' (cf. Fox, 1996); the institutions of the health council and municipal health conference provided sites for a more diffuse process of constructing what Duarte called '*convivência construtiva*' – constructive coexistence – between heterogeneously positioned actors and networks spanning the state and society, but also within and across those positioned within diverse state and societal institutions.

Senior managers spoke of how the council provided a bridge into the community: as one put it, the councils are an opportunity for government to learn from the 'collective intelligence of society' by bringing together different visions of how services might be managed and implemented. 'It's an opportunity', she said, 'for people to grow, to deepen democracy, to create a debate – in this city, where we have such diversity'. From the perspective of some *sanitarista* senior managers, engaging 'civil society' in the council was as much about democratizing society, as the role that 'civil society' might have in democratizing the state. One spoke of how conferences opened up opportunities for 'new faces, new people' to engage with the state, going beyond the 'usual suspects'; others highlighted the democratizing dimensions of renewal of the council's membership (Cornwall, 2006).

As we argue in this paper, the participatory elements of the SUS project go beyond alliance-building to promote the construction of an 'epistemic community'. Part of this process, senior health officials suggested, involves the co-construction of a vision for the delivery of health services that socializes an appreciation of the importance of preventive medicine and the provision of primary care services. They emphasized the educative dimensions of participation, relaying tales of how health user representatives had shifted from initial demands for ambulances and acute services towards a greater appreciation of the gains that could be made through the expansion of primary care. These gains have been tangible; improvements in health indices have become political capital. Especially significant is the sharp drop in infant mortality from 47/1000 in 1998 to 16/1000 by 2003 with a further fall in the last three years to 10.2/1000.[10] These figures attest, in no small part, to the success of the federal government's primary health care programme, the *Programa Saúde da Família* (PSF). But the PSF's success is not only in improving health outcomes. It is also part of the story of strengthening *controle social.*

Institutionalizing the SUS in Cabo has brought actors into the arena of deliberation over health policy who might otherwise never have had an opportunity to engage in such debates. Among them are the auxiliary nurses and community health workers engaged through the expansion of the PSF programme in the municipality. For health workers, especially those at the lower end of the hierarchy, membership of the council has brought new confidence in their capabilities and renewed commitment to their work. This commitment, and health workers' part in enhancing *controle social,* have been observed by Tendler (1997) for the nearby north-eastern state of Ceará. Interviews in Cabo suggested that this was not only because of their location at the interface with the community, but also their own identifications as citizens and with political parties. Health workers' agency is compromised by the fragility of their employment status as contract workers and government employees, and the difficulties of organizing as health workers across the hierarchies of the medical system (Cordeiro, Cornwall and Delgado, 2004). Yet the active engagement of health workers in the council's everyday work, as well as in promoting and seeking to sustain efforts to promote local health councils in the municipality, and with this a capillary approach to democratizing the governance of health services, reshapes relations not only at the interface between state and society, but within the health system itself. As a primary care worker noted, these spaces create opportunities to 'bring together different worlds'; they also permit those who are delivering services to get a sense of the world of their managers, and gain opportunities to debate and influence the implementation of policy.

Health service user representatives on the council are overwhelmingly from the lower ends of the class spectrum; many had no previous experience of similar institutions, or indeed responsibilities such as those they come to assume as health councillors (Cornwall, 2006). For some, involvement in the council came from direct experience of the deficiencies of the health system; for others, serving as representatives of established social actors provided a way of extending influence pursued through other channels. The sheer heterogeneity of Cabo's universe of social actors militates against any simplistic notion of 'civil society' as watchdog, or indeed as in itself a motor of democratization. Many of these organizations are enmeshed in complex dependencies with the state, whether through the receipt of subsidies or contracts with the government, or party-political networks. Their autonomy is compromised by these linkages; yet they also afford the possibilities for the co-construction of joint initiatives, such as the improvement of women's health services or the promotion of herbal medicine in primary care. The *Conselho* serves as a site of articulation between the disparate interest groups represented by 'civil society', brought together around a shared identification with the SUS project.

The monthly meetings of the health council provide little opportunity for the kind of deliberation, problem-solving and consensus-building described by deliberative democrats (Cohen and Sabel, 1997; Fung and Wright, 2003). More often, they consist of didactic accounts of municipal plans and programmes interspersed with heated arguments over access to information on spending. Discussions tend to be dominated by the more articulate and experienced few; many civil society representatives, especially those who are new to this arena, remain silent onlookers. Drawn out contestations animated more by party-political wrangles than by substantive concerns over health policy – on which there was rarely disagreement, let alone discussion – captured much of the energy of the council over the period 2003–2005. It was these contestations, and the possibility of confronting the municipal government, exacting answerability and expanding the remit of the council as a political space, that lent the council its vigour, even if it produced its share of frustrations. The performative dimensions of contests within the council arguably have an important symbolic function, representing the very democratizing vision that animates the SUS project at the same time as embodying some of its contradictions. In so doing, they come to represent new dimensions of citizenship practice and, with that, the glimmer of the promise that the architects of the system of *controle social* had within their sights.

Case 2: Rio Negro Special Indigenous Health District

Indigenous peoples have historically been treated as a 'special case' in Brazilian policymaking. Throughout Brazil's history, the state's approach to the indigenous population has veered between the genocidal and the paternalistic, and until the 1988 Constitution 'Indians' were officially classified as 'wards of the state'. The legacy of massive mortality (both from violence and from epidemics) among indigenous groups experiencing contact with non-indigenous society projected an image of unique vulnerability. This helps to explain why even after the Ministry of Health wrested responsibility for indigenous health services away from FUNAI (the Justice Ministry department responsible for indigenous affairs) in the late 1990s, the chosen delivery mechanism for these services was a 'specific SUS subsystem' sitting alongside the mainstream municipality-based SUS.

The design of this subsystem, based on 'Special Indigenous Health Districts' (DSEIs) which in following ethnic rather than political boundaries crossed the borders between municipalities and even states, was strongly influenced by an emerging alliance between *sanitarista* health professionals and indigenous leaders. This alliance began to take shape during the mobilization to secure health and cultural rights in the Constitution, and was consolidated by the 1993 National Conference on Health Care for Indigenous Peoples (Garnelo *et al.*, 2003). Initially blocked by resistance from FUNAI, the DSEI model finally began to be implemented some five years after the Conference, by which time a series of highly publicized epidemics among the Yanomami and other indigenous groups had made the national and international pressure for change irresistible.

Once it had taken over responsibility for indigenous health care, the Ministry of Health found itself with a problem: having decentralized most of its functions to the municipalities, it lacked the capacity to implement the DSEIs itself. The Ministry delegated responsibility to its one remaining executive agency, the National Health Foundation (FUNASA), which – faced by an IMF-inspired ban on hiring new staff of its own – promptly set about outsourcing the work of the DSEIs. Although (as discussed above) government financing of non-state provision is a well-established element of the SUS, this outsourcing process, which included contracts with municipalities, universities, Church agencies, NGOs and even some of the indigenous movements themselves, was arguably the most far-reaching such process to occur in any area of the health system. As with the mainstream SUS, accountability was supposed to be ensured by a series of local and DSEI-level *Conselhos* with guaranteed (indigenous) user participation. However, the widely differing levels of political organization among indigenous peoples and the bewildering array of different service providers made it hard to establish clear accountability relations – especially in the DSEIs where indigenous movements themselves had taken on service-delivery contracts and therefore sat on both the 'user' and the 'provider' sides of the table.

This was the case, for example, in the Rio Negro DSEI, one of the largest in the subsystem, responsible for some 30,000 members of 22 different indigenous groups living in three municipalities in the far northwest of the Brazilian Amazon. In the Rio Negro, the regional indigenous peoples' federation FOIRN (*Federação das Organizações Indígenas do Rio Negro*) took on responsibility for service delivery after a breakdown in relations between FUNASA and the collection of mainly NGO service providers with which it had initially contracted. Despite a number of implementation problems (chiefly caused by FUNASA's tendency to delay funding transfers at critical times, the reason for the collapse of the original outsourcing arrangements), the FOIRN-FUNASA partnership managed to extend coverage and bring about some improvements in health indicators among the indigenous peoples of the region. This relative success (particularly significant in the light of the disastrous experiences of indigenous movements who took over DSEIs elsewhere in the Amazon) boosted FOIRN's credibility within the region and further afield.

The federation was also able to secure a majority in the District *Conselho*, and to use FUNASA resources to strengthen its political mobilization work by establishing a specific *controle social* department in the DSEI, staffed by FOIRN-affiliated indigenous leaders. These leaders travelled extensively around the DSEI's vast territory, relaying news, convening local health council meetings, collecting complaints and mediating in disputes between health workers and the local population. For service users, they became the most familiar and accessible face of the DSEI, with an authority which was perceived as greater than that of the elected *Conselheiros* – since their link with health district management ensured that their remit extended to the non-indigenous professionals, who had strenuously resisted attempts to ensure oversight of their work by user representatives.

Given this remarkable level of indigenous dominance of the institutions of both service delivery and participation, it is at first sight perplexing that the Rio Negro DSEI remained resolutely 'un-indigenous' in its practices. *Conselho* meetings were dominated by endless discussion of financial and administrative issues, movement leaders spent their time struggling to meet the bureaucratic demands of FUNASA, non-indigenous health professionals hired in from elsewhere in Brazil were sent into the villages without any anthropological training or familiarization with indigenous culture and the agenda for incorporating traditional medicine that had been framed by a group of shamanic practitioners and their NGO allies made little headway.[11] Instead of focusing on adapting the DSEI's practices to ensure a better fit with the cultural realities of the region, the *controle social* department emphasized educating service users in the villages on the complexities of District management and ensuring adherence to the centrally-ordained schedule for formal user participation.

However, interviews with indigenous leaders revealed a perception that the political gains for FOIRN outweighed these failings. One former FOIRN health representative stated that 'in the Rio Negro the District has strengthened our movement... for the other movements, it seems like health work was a separate thing, which couldn't be combined with political work, but FOIRN has developed health work and political work together'. The *controle social* department exemplified this, reproducing FOIRN's political legitimacy by representing and reaffirming its status as manager of the DSEI, a powerful institution whose power derived from its links to the 'white' health system. The movement, whose historical position in defence of cultural rights, diversity and respect for traditional knowledge stood in fundamental contrast to the top-down, one-size-fits-all, biomedicine-centred *sanitarista* ideology, discovered that buying into the 'SUS project' could pay significant political dividends. Even as the participatory institutions of the DSEI failed to enable users to hold service providers to account or to shape an alternative vision of culturally-adapted services, they provided a space for leaders to challenge the racist stereotype of indigenous incompetence and assert their credentials for membership of the SUS 'epistemic community'.

Case 3: the 2003 National Health Conference

The 12th National Health Conference of December 2003 was part of the sequence of regular large-scale discussion fora mandated by the SUS participation framework to deliberate on the strategic direction of health policy. The system of *Conferências* includes periodic meetings at every level from the local to the national, as well as sector-specific conferences discussing everything from oral health to medical technology. The 'creation myth' of the SUS was rooted in the historic 8th National Health Conference of 1986, and subsequent conferences have frequently been used to reinject political momentum into the 'SUS project'. Taking place in Brasília a year after the election to the Presidency of Luís Inácio Lula da Silva of the Workers' Party (PT), the

2003 National Conference was the focus of considerable expectations, heightened still further by the new Health Minister's promise that the forthcoming National Health Plan would be based on its conclusions.

The Conference brought together some 5000 delegates, from all over Brazil, in an enormous and ambitious deliberative process. It built on preparatory events at municipal and state levels that garnered the views of some 300,000 people and elected delegates to represent them at the national level. The social diversity of the delegates, drawn from all regions and races and with a plurality of working-class women among the 'service user' representatives, mirrored the inclusionary message of SUS ideology. Standing in the lunch queue, surveying the thousands of people around her, a young black woman from Ceará beamed with pride and proclaimed 'All of Brazil is here. We are all here. We are Brazil.' Unabashedly Utopian rhetoric and appeals to SUS mythology were omnipresent at the Conference. It was officially named the *Conferência Sérgio Arouca*, in memory of the Communist politician (and FIOCRUZ-based *sanitarista*) who had been a prime mover of the 8th Conference and of the Constitutional provisions for the SUS. The Health Ministry's recently nominated Secretary for Participatory Management spoke with visible emotion of his memories of Arouca as a comrade-in-arms during early struggles to promote a *sanitarista* agenda within the Rio de Janeiro medical association. The Conference's official theme was 'the health we have, the SUS we want', and above the podium in the hall where plenary sessions took place was a banner which proclaimed 'here it is permitted to dream'.

The deliberations of the Conference, which took place over four days, incorporated varied 'democratic practices'. The closest to the deliberative-democratic ideal were the small-group sessions, where participants were randomly allocated to one of almost 100 different groups according to criteria which were designed to ensure that each group's composition approximated the mix of regional origins and institutional affiliations of the wider Conference. They debated the draft resolutions line by line, with computer operators on hand to provide real-time online registration of proposed amendments using software specially developed by the Ministry of Health.

The resolutions and proposed amendments then passed to the plenary itself, where the solemn deliberations of the small groups gave way to raucous confrontations and shop floor-style votes in which delegates enthusiastically waved their badges in the air in response to calls for a show of hands. One of the most strenuously contested of these confrontations was between the feminist health movement and the Catholic Church's Health Pastoral over a resolution declaring abortion a key public health issue, which ended with the resolution being voted down by a massive mobilization of grassroots health worker delegates. Many of these workers were women from remote rural municipalities who had been taken on by the SUS Community Health Agent programme after first being recruited by the Church's network of child health monitors, and for them commitment to the SUS public health ideology sat alongside – and was occasionally eclipsed by – a strongly held Catholic faith. The feminist leaders, veterans of mobilizations for reproductive rights from Brasília to Beijing, ruefully acknowledged that they had neglected to cultivate grassroots networks capable of matching the power of the Church and stated their determination to remedy this – confirming the importance of the SUS participation spaces as sites of struggle among different social forces, not merely between 'civil society' and 'the state'.

Meanwhile, other political practices were in evidence with energetic caucusing and lobbying around the fringes of the plenary. In a vast country where internet-based networking is an unattainable dream for many grassroots activists, the Conferences represent a rare opportunity for different movements to reconnect their scattered regional chapters and reenergize their sense of common purpose. At the 2003 Conference the Hansen's Disease (Leprosy) movement MORHAN, many of whose grassroots workers are based in remote rural communities in the Amazon, capitalized on the presence of one of its leaders on the Conference's organizing committee to secure national visibility for a disease all too often obscured by stigma and shame. Another highly visible presence in the Conference was the *Movimento Negro*. Relative newcomers to the SUS 'epistemic community', the movement's activists made their presence felt in several sessions, as they rode a wave of interest in the health of the black population that had been catalysed by high-profile academic reports on the issue and the Lula government's creation of a special secretariat for race equality (Maio and Monteiro, 2005). Despite the pro-Lula sentiment which was evident among the vast majority of delegates, the alliances built at the Conference reflected movement identities rather than party-political ones. The President himself was rapturously received, but an attempt to interrupt the Conference for a lengthy bout of official propagandizing on the virtues of the PT government was drowned out by shouts of '*Plenária! Plenária!*' from delegates determined to continue the plenary debates.

The Conference was both a triumph and, some would now reflect, a charade. Its policy impact was questionable, not least because of the sweeping ambition of its declared aims: a Conference resolution to ban SUS payment for private provision, for example, was swiftly declared unimplementable without a Constitutional amendment. The failure (despite a concluding plenary session which went on late into the night) to vote on some contentious issues made it impossible to finalize an official Conference Report until a tortuous process of regional ratification meetings had reached its conclusion almost a year after the Conference itself. This, in turn, made full incorporation of the Conference's recommendations into the National Health Plan impossible – which may or may not have suited the policymakers who thereby acquired greater freedom to shape the Plan as they saw fit.

For all these failings, however, the political impact of the *Conferência Sérgio Arouca* was undeniable. The many movements which already identified with the SUS were able to reenergize their grassroots support, while at the same time new movements found a space in which to frame their health rights struggles under the SUS umbrella. The formidable mobilization power of the Conference, witnessed by the President and other senior government figures who visited the plenary sessions, provided a valuable boost to the credibility of the Ministry of Health. Fronted by a Minister considered to lack the political firepower of predecessors such as Jatene and Serra, and locked in a struggle over SUS financing with yet another austerity-minded Treasury team, the Ministry once more saw its macropolitical bargaining power boosted by the SUS 'epistemic community' – which in turn had been able to reproduce itself and continue to grow in the myriad micropolitical spaces which made up the *Conferência* process.

Conclusions

These three very different cases all illustrate the multifaceted role of SUS participation processes in sustaining, deepening and broadening the commitment to rights-based health reform in Brazil. The Cabo de Santo Agostinho Municipal Health Council may have made only hesitant progress towards genuinely strategic discussion of service priorities, but the engagement of diverse social actors, including health workers, in struggles to realize the promise of *controle social* speaks to the broader democratizing vision of the SUS project. The Rio Negro Special Indigenous Health District's combination of community participation structures with outsourcing of services to indigenous movement organizations may have failed to fulfil the system's promise of local control and cultural sensitivity, but it secured the adherence of a social movement which had originally been built on very different values to those of the SUS. The National Health Conference may have failed to agree a coherent platform capable of shaping the health policy of the new government, but it mobilized a huge range of participants and perspectives and provided a space for new movements to engage with the SUS and align their demands with its founding principles. In each example, the SUS participation architecture failed partially or completely to fulfil its *governance* functions of promoting accountability and shaping policy. At the same time, the inclusionary practices associated with this architecture proved extraordinarily successful in the specific *political* function of encouraging the adherence of different actors to the SUS 'epistemic community'.

These practices have also helped to build a sense of inclusion and citizenship whose wider importance for Brazil's complex and tortuous progress towards democratization should not be underestimated. In her comparative study of health system development in Brazil and Chile, Labra (2001: 374) singles out the contrast between the 'insulated' Chilean system and the 'phenomenon' of participation in the *Conselhos* of the SUS. In Chile, reformist technocrats have achieved improvements in health indicators, but in the absence of broad and deep links with other social forces, progress towards genuine equity remains dependent on the struggle for democratization in the formal party-political arena. In Brazil, Labra argues, participation in the health system itself contributes to broader democratization: 'the SUS is here to stay and is slowly being internalized at all levels and by all sectors in the country, spreading the sense of democracy as a value that must be carefully preserved' (*ibid.*). The same author develops this argument further in reporting the findings of a study of participation in health councils in the Rio de Janeiro metropolitan area, identifying a 'virtuous circle' linking participation, the growth of social capital and broader democratization (Labra and Figueiredo, 2002: 546). In the terms defined by McCourt and Bebbington, the SUS can thus clearly be identified as a 'development success' which strengthens the human capabilities of poorer groups not only through improved access to health services but also through increased access to and capacity for the practice of democratic citizenship.

What broader lessons can be drawn from Brazil's experiences with deliberative and inclusionary practices in the health sector? A key element is certainly the significance of the ideological commitment to public involvement and accountability that was the clarion call of the *sanitarista* movement. This commitment remains embedded in the health service through those who engaged with the movement and with radical democratic politics in the post-dictatorship era. Rather than being restricted to the pro-poor agency of elite reformists, however, it has been institutionalized in legal and constitutional frameworks that guarantee participation, through which the more than 5000 health management councils came to be created and which guarantee the engagement of organized civil society in these institutions at each of the three tiers of government. This engagement, in turn, is able to catalyse the recruitment of new groups who become committed (each for their own reasons) to sustaining the system even as they struggle over resources and priorities within it. This combination has served to brand the SUS as a paradigmatic arena for the consolidation of democratic citizenship, which has both enhanced its survival prospects and extended its influence into other areas of politics and society. The SUS experience demonstrates that – far from being short-lived and fragile Utopian projects – given these enabling elements, rights-based alternatives to neoliberal health system reform can display remarkable political depth and durability, even in harshly adverse macropolitical circumstances.

Notes

1 The case study material in this chapter derives from work carried out by the authors with Sílvia Cordeiro, Nelson Giordano Delgado, Renato Athias and Raimundo Nonato during the Olhar Crítico project, funded by the UK Department for International Development (DFID) Brazil office and coordinated by Sue Fleming of DFID Brazil and Jorge Romano of ActionAid Brasil. The authors would like to thank the Centro das Mulheres do Cabo, Associação Saúde Limites, the Federação das Organizações Indígenas do Rio Negro and the organizers of the 12th Conferência Nacional de Saúde (especially Artur Custódio and Crescêncio Antunes Silveira Neto) for their assistance with the case study research. They would also like to thank the editors of this volume, Marcus André Melo, Newton Sérgio Lopes Lemos, Jason Lakin and other participants in the seminars on 'Explaining Brazil's policy successes' (at the Institute of Development Studies, University of Sussex, July 2005) and 'Politics and health policy in Brazil, Mexico and the UK' (at the Centre for Brazilian Studies, Oxford University, December 2005) for their insightful comments on earlier versions of the text.

2 See the debate in Ciência e Saúde Coletiva summarized by Côrtes (1998) and the review of critical perspectives in Coelho *et al.*, 2002.

3 Both 'neoliberal' and 'rights-based' are, of course, slippery and contested terms. Here we use the former as shorthand for the privatizing, state-shrinking agenda for policy reform in Latin America famously summarized as the 'Washington Consensus' by Williamson (1990), and the latter as shorthand for an agenda which emphasizes citizenship, participation and accountability of, by and to the historically marginalized or excluded,

which has tended to emphasize the centrality of state responsibility for rights realization (cf. Cornwall, 2000; DFID, 2000; Gaventa, 2002).

4 That is, those with a household per capita income at or below the monthly minimum wage.

5 Which increased from US$2.4 bn to US$16 bn between 1989 and 1998 (Mendes, 1998).

6 This national-level pattern mirrors the state-level findings of Tendler and Freedheim (1994), who noted the importance of the incentives and directives put in place by the Ceará state government in promoting citizen participation and municipal adherence to a pro-poor health policy.

7 Though this contribution may have been overestimated by authors such as Costa (2002), who concludes his review of health reforms in the 1990s with a paean of praise for Serra; as Silva (2003) demonstrates, federal health spending was already on an upward trajectory before the periods in office of both Jatene and Serra.

8 See Cornwall, Romano and Shankland forthcoming.

9 As Evelina Dagnino (2005) has eloquently argued, 'neoliberal' versions of *cidadania* (which emphasize self-help and targeted, 'safety-net' provision of public services) also assume active civil society participation (in the shape of philanthropic service provision). While this has stripped social movements and the political Left of their monopoly of the use of the term, it also serves to neutralize conservative reaction aimed at denying the validity of movements' invoking *cidadania* as the basis for claims.

10 *Source*: http://www.cprh.pe.gov.br/downloads/pnma2/projeto-orla-cabo/3.1analise-situacional.pdf; and Cabo de Santo Agostinho Municipal Government Health Plan 2006–9.

11 For a more detailed discussion, see Shankland and Athias 2007 and Athias *et al.*, 2004.

8

The 'Nampula Model': A Mozambique Case of Successful Participatory Planning and Financing

David Jackson

Introduction

In 1996 a local planning, financing and governance model was conceived in Nampula province, northern Mozambique. Within ten years it was being hailed as a success by Mozambique's Prime Minister, by the donors who supported it and by academics who studied it (Galli, 2003; Roll, 2004; Weimer, Cabral, and Jackson, 2004). It had influenced national legislation, and attempts to replicate it under World Bank auspices had begun. Yet several of its features remained unclear. There was disagreement about what kind of experiment it was; it occurred amidst centralizing as well as decentralizing initiatives in central government; and the replication attempts have had patchy success. Thus the reports of success should not be taken at face value. We stress this obvious point because we approach the initiative from an insider's perspective – the author was involved in its implementation – with all the usual limitations that entails.

In this chapter we outline the historical background before describing the content of what we will call the Nampula model. We will go on to look at how the formation of an informal political alliance contributed considerably to the reform outcome.

Independence and after: politics over the heads of the provinces

Bypassing the countryside

It is a feature of rural Nampula's experience of the struggle for independence from Portugal that, like other rural parts of Mozambique, political developments passed it by. The guerrilla fighters of FRELIMO (Mozambican National Liberation Front) which came to power in 1974 came largely from the northern Christian Maconde tribe, whilst the leadership was chiefly composed of a small group of socialist revolutionaries from the southern Shangana and Ronga ethnic groups, also mainly Christian. Nampula, along with the other populous northern and central provinces of Zambezia, Sofala and Manica, was barely involved in the armed struggle.

The 1992 peace agreement between FRELIMO and RENAMO (Mozambican National Resistance) which ended the 1980–1992 civil war, together with the 1990 constitutional reform which preceded it, are often taken as the starting point for Mozambique's economic recovery and governance reforms, and they are an important backdrop to Nampula's reforms. FRELIMO's legitimacy after 1992 depended on implicit agreements at central, not provincial level with three groups:

- an agreement with international donors that reforms would be based on the prevailing economic, and 'good governance' orthodoxy (it is important to note that Mozambique has depended heavily on aid in the last 15 years);
- an agreement with the government and the urban intelligentsia and civil society that there would be a free press and a secular society;
- an agreement that RENAMO's Alfonso Dlhakama would become 'official' leader of the opposition, supported by his parliamentary deputies. Given RENAMO's system of hierarchical patronage, this meant that they became dysfunctional as a peacetime opposition political force (Weimer, 1999).

In short, the picture is of a Mozambique in which large parts of the rural population were not involved in the independence struggle, and sometimes bypassed in the key post-independence developments. This picture is consistent with the anthropological literature (Harrison, 1998; West, 2005).

Nampula before the peace agreement

Let us now look in more detail at Nampula itself, where the relationship between state and society is conditioned by the historical experience of the dominant Macua ethnic group.

Representing about 30 percent of the population of Mozambique as a whole, they are the largest single ethno-linguistic grouping, centred on

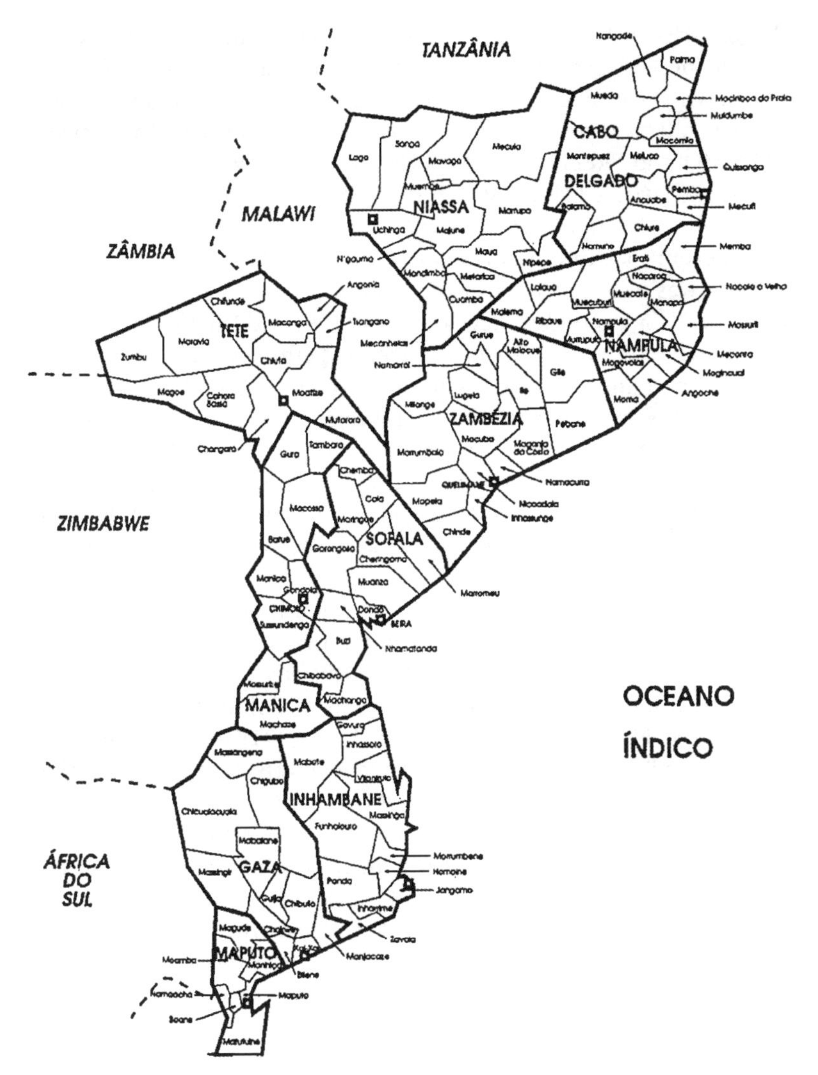

Figure 8.1 Administrative division of Mozambique into provinces and districts

Nampula but covering a contiguous area reaching into the neighbouring provinces of Zambezia, Cabo Delgado and Niassa. Unlike the southern empires of Gungunhana and Monomatapa, the Macua claim never to have been defeated by the Portuguese. They maintained their cultural coherence without confronting the colonial power head-on

(Viegas, 1999). To some extent they adopted a similar strategy in the face of the FRELIMO governors and administrators, mostly from the south, who arrived following independence in 1974 (Harrison, 1998).

Party allegiance in Nampula was split almost equally between RENAMO and FRELIMO in the 1994 and 1999 elections. The inland Christians favoured FRELIMO whilst the Islamic areas towards the coast predominately supported RENAMO. In the latter areas, the district government's legitimacy was weak (Viegas, 1999).

But it was not very much stronger even in some FRELIMO-supporting areas. Just as political developments bypassed the rural areas, they also bypassed or even deliberately sidelined ethnic groups – the 'tribes'. This was part and parcel of the postcolonial nation-building project of the African state in which ethnic and regional identities were seen as threats to national coherence: 'Kill the tribe to build the nation,' as Mozambique's first independence president said (Machel, 1985). Large minorities became alienated from the political process. The Ndebele in Zimbabwe are a well-known and blatant example, and the Macua in Mozambique are another.

In the period before the 1992 peace accords the state's legitimacy was further undermined by the proliferating aid agencies that were dismissive of both the 'unaccountable' district government and the 'unrepresentative' local traditional structures. Some of them were also opposed to FRELIMO's ideology (Hanlon, 1991). In the absence of effective civil society structures, aid agencies attempted to create their own, typically using a Participatory Rural Appraisal methodology (see Chambers, 1994) to develop links with local communities. Since the state's role was negligible, government had no incentive to maintain whatever the aid agency created, and the community had no incentive to engage with the state (Jackson, 2002). Even when aid agencies did work with the district governments in addition to their direct work with communities, there was little benefit in terms of the role of the district within the overall state hierarchy. Rather than giving districts a reason to listen to community voice, districts were listening to their new external 'friends', and through them increasing their operational capacity and powers of patronage.

The 'Nampula model'

The origins of the Nampula model

With the peace agreement in prospect, in 1991 the government began to plan for the redevelopment of territory that had been beyond its reach for a decade. The National Reconstruction Plan (*Plano Nacional de Reconstrução – PRN*) involved provincial teams combing the still dangerous countryside to log details of destroyed and damaged infrastructure, producing a portfolio of potential investment projects and fostering an *esprit de corps* amongst provincial civil servants. Many staff had been trained in Cuba and the Eastern bloc, and now had an opportunity to put their *dirigiste* development planning skills to use. The PRN portfolio was the basis for the rolling Three Year Public Investment Plan (*Plano Trienal de Investimento Público – PTIP)* most of which was financed by central government.

From 1994 limited PTIP resources were made available to provincial governments. This allowed Nampula's Provincial Directorate of Planning and Finance (*Direcção Provincial de Plano e Finanças – DPPF)* influence over the public investment proposals from provincial line agencies (health, education etc.) prior to their submission to the Ministry of Planning and Finance (*Ministério do Plano e Finanças – MPF*) in Maputo. Once approved by national parliament, DPPF took the lead in managing the money. By 1997 Nampula province was managing a portfolio of small public investments worth $1 million per annum, allowing for meaningful expenditure for the first time, and providing a sense of power and purpose to the previously cash-strapped provincial government.

While in other provinces the money was divided up between the provincial representations of central government ministries, Nampula split some of its allocation amongst district administrators, and persuaded the provincial directorates to invest in certain priority districts. This was motivated by PRN evidence that some districts had lost more government buildings than others, and by a desire to compensate those districts that lacked aid agency 'friends'. In essence, this was the beginning of the 'Nampula model'.

During 1995 and 1996 a group of actors began to coalesce around a provincial development agenda which focused on the local economy and local Macua society. The Coalition (as we shall call it) comprised:

- the political leadership, Provincial civil servants and the Netherlands government;
- two donor-funded technical advisors, one of whom had lived in the province for a number of years developing links with Macua historians and intellectuals, while the other (the author of this chapter) had worked in local government in the United Kingdom during the 1980s.

Through an informal process the Coalition developed a political agenda that stressed the need to establish government control and legitimacy in rural areas dominated by RENAMO by demonstrating an ability to respond to local needs and by fostering regional identity as a unifying factor. The Coalition also saw the underused potential of the province's strategic assets: the rail corridor between the Indian Ocean and Malawi, and the export crops of cotton, tobacco and maize (Jackson, 2001). The Nampula district planning and financing model emerged as part of this agenda.

We will return to the Coalition and its style of operation later. We turn now to the technical detail of the Nampula model and the evidence for its success.

Turning the hierarchy on its head

To understand the model, we need to appreciate the structure of local governance in Mozambique. The 1990 constitutional reform and the 1992 peace agreement, far-reaching in other respects, did not change local administration in most of the country. Although a multi-party system was installed, the fact that FRELIMO held power ensured that the party-state relationship remained, albeit in a weaker form.

Mozambique was divided into ten provinces and 128 districts in a hierarchical structure. Central ministries had provincial directorates. Likewise, provinces had district directorates subordinate to their respective provincial directorates. Provincial governors were the representatives of the central state, and provincial directorates were subordinate to them. Governors appointed district administrators responsible for political leadership and coordination of district directorates. The provincial and district 'governments' were simply the collective of the directorate heads, chaired by the governor or the administrator respectively. The district administrator had a small executive known as the 'district administration', which was distinct from the wider district government, but there was no local government as classically understood: all expenditure came from the central state budget approved by national parliament.

This was a system of deconcentration and dual subordination in which each institution was accountable to its ministerial hierarchy and its local political boss. All accountability was upwards, rather than downwards to lower-level institutions, let alone citizens.

The aim in Nampula was to transform this collection of disparate and unaccountable district agencies into a cohesive local governance unit. The role of the district administrator changed from party

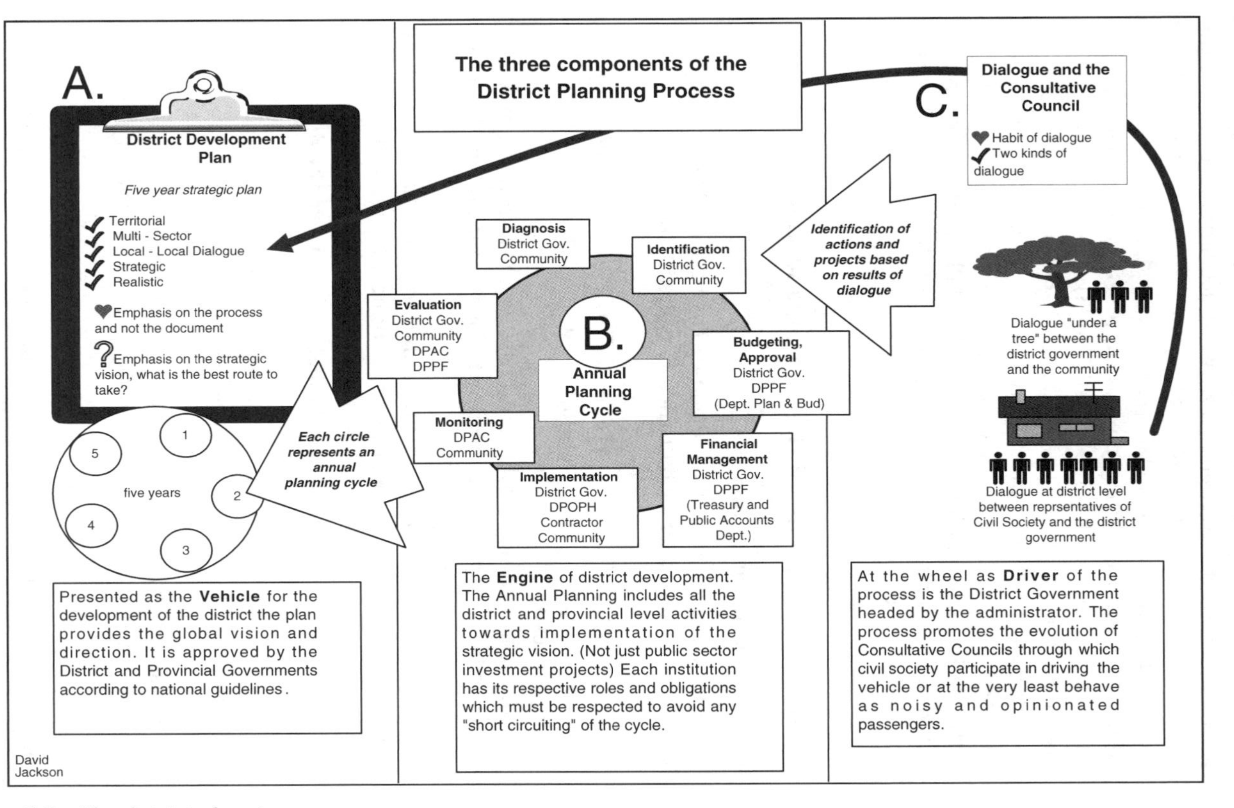

Figure 8.2 The district planning process

apparatchik to proactive agent of development. By introducing resources, representation and downward accountability in the districts the province – district hierarchy was turned on its head. The new 'developmental districts' were supposed to promote efficient public expenditure management, improved service delivery and economic growth (DPPF, 1999; Galli, 2003). The vehicle for all this was a development project (*Projecto da Planificação e Financiamento Descentralizado* – PPFD) implemented by the DPPF. Later on we shall examine how members of the Coalition interacted with aid agencies in the design and implementation of the PPFD. First, however, we shall briefly describe the three components of the model in its initial formulation in 1999 (DPPF, 1999).

The three components of the Nampula model

Strategic district planning

A District Development Plan (*Plano de Distrital de Desenvolvimento* – PDD) was developed for each district. It aspired to be:

- *strategic*, with a long-term vision of district development (this was the most important innovation, providing a rationale for the planning process);
- *local*, looking for local solutions rather than waiting for provincial ones to trickle down, and covering the whole territory of the district rather than isolated pockets;
- *multi-sectoral*, focusing on themes rather than institutional responsibilities (thus, for example, the theme of health involved education, water and agriculture as well as the health directorate itself);
- *partnership-oriented*, emphasizing dialogue between the district government and civil society;
- *realistic*, in the sense that nothing should appear in the plan without realism about how it would be achieved (DPPF, 1999).

The Plans were based on central government guidelines (MPF/MAE, 1998), but they had an even earlier origin in the Coalition's determination to develop a local focus for provincial development. That determination was refined by the present author's view that local planning would degenerate into a collection of small isolated infrastructure projects unless it was conducted within a local strategic framework. A strategic vision- and mission-setting methodology was used to supply that framework (Jackson, 2001; see also Leach and Collinge, 1998 for an account of the strategic methodology).

Annual planning, budgeting and procurement

The PDD strategy was implemented through annual planning and budgeting with the help of District Development Funds (*Fundos de Desenvolvimento Distrital* – FDD). Strictly speaking, the FDD represented the allocation of a provincial budget line to the district government. As mentioned above, both district and provincial institutions belonged to the same hierarchical structures within a deconcentrated local administration system. There was no devolved autonomy and no local government as classically understood; all expenditure belonged to the central state budget approved by parliament.

In addition the district sought to leverage other state and non-state actors in support of its strategy (DPPF, 1999). Later, districts began to use their revenue (both retained fees and taxes which they were obliged to pass to the central treasury) to produce an annual plan with an income and expenditure budget (*Plano Económico e Social / Orçamento Distrital* – PESOD). The PESOD aimed to capture all government and non-governmental financial flows and activities within the district, whether programmed by the district institutions or not (DPPF, 2005).

The general-purpose nature of the FDD allocation allowed the district to plan, and to apply performance-based and output-based budgeting techniques. It also allowed for innovative financial relationships between the DPPF, the provincial directorates and the district government, all within the broad structure of the deconcentrated state system. The district could rely exclusively on its own resources, or co-finance activities with other actors. The involvement of aid agencies in strategy development meant that they were willing to submit their expenditure programming to the district planning process.

A further innovation was the involvement of the district in procurement, hitherto the domain of the province. The district administrator signed construction contracts, and the Provincial Directorate of Public Works assisted in tendering and contract management. This was a practical expression of the attempt to turn the existing hierarchy on its head, with the district becoming an empowered 'client' and the province acting as its facilitating 'agent' (DPPF, 2000).

The annual planning and budgeting cycle had two sources:

- an earlier 'Support to Local Grassroots Initiatives' project was incorporated into the PPFD. It ran from 1995–1998, and used a

combination of Participatory Rural Appraisals and the problem tree (ZOPP) methodology developed by the German development agency GTZ;
- a portfolio of Local Development Funds financed by the United Nations Capital Development Fund (UNCDF; they had also financed the earlier Grassroots project) in which decentralization was promoted through a policy dialogue with governments, and through a development fund to pilot fiscal transfers to lower levels of local administration (Romeo, 1999, 2000; Shotton, 2000).

However, it is important to note that the international methodologies taken from those two sources were adapted to align them with the Mozambican planning and budgeting system. Moreover, project professional staff contributed significantly in their areas of expertise, for example in local procurement and contract management, and local public expenditure management (DPPF, 2005; MPF/MAE, 2002).

District consultative councils

The PDD strategy was approved by consultative councils (*Conselhos Consultivos Distritais* – CCD) that were chaired by the district administrator. They included representatives from the traditional leadership structures, from RENAMO and FRELIMO, Christian and Islamic faiths, aid agencies, district government staff, other government agencies and anybody else that the administrator chose to invite. It was the first time that all of these groups had met under one roof.

The CCDs were organized on an 'interest group' basis, meaning that issues were discussed by sub-groups such as 'political parties' or 'religious bodies' (thus forcing RENAMO and FRELIMO to talk to each other), and then the consensus of these sub-groups was presented to the plenary. The CCD approved the district development plan strategy and the annual plan.

The CCDs were intended to make up for the absence of any form of representative assembly in the districts, and to establish the district government as both agent of development and legitimate political structure. Thus they were seen as an experimental first step in local democratic governance.

In a sense, the CCD approach to participation represented a critical application of Participatory Rural Appraisal (PRA). During 1998 and 1999 Mozambican staff were given free rein to organize the 'participatory' aspects of the programme to fit the local political and social context, somewhat to the chagrin of the donors (Pijnenburg, 2004). A process of internal discussions led to modification of the practices inherited from the earlier project. Its participatory appraisals had been one-off, time-consuming exercises that involved a wide range of techniques, which were often only used as a programming tool for deciding what infrastructure to build, even though the techniques themselves were designed for wider diagnosis. Instead, the PRA methods were applied by district governments as a way of institutionalizing an ongoing dialogue with the community.

The outcomes: economic benefits and institutionalization

Economic outcomes

Between 1996 and 2006 over $10 million was spent on roughly 250 small-scale district infrastructural investments through the PPFD. They fell into three categories: construction and rehabilitation of markets and administration buildings, and also of 18 schools and 16 health posts; 25 road improvements; and construction of 173 wells and boreholes (UNCDF, 2006). These investments were over and above the state budget PTIP allocation. Admittedly, greater sums of donor money were disbursed outside the PPFD framework than within it, even in terms of small-scale infrastructure. But for a provincial population of over 3 million it was still a significant scale of activity.

Most of the detailed impact studies have focused on the district of Mecuburi, because it was one of the first to be involved in the initiative, and because it had a good technical and administrative capacity which allowed the methodologies to take root quickly (ECIAfrica, 2004: 46). In addition, its social homogeneity and its strong and united traditional clan leadership facilitated the establishment of the Consultative Council.

A study based on a survey of 200 households in Mecuburi and separate group discussions found that investments had had a clear pro-poor impact and positive economic externalities. Admittedly, some activities such as the construction of roads had benefited richer households (the study notes that the 'pro-poor' orientation of an investment was not used as a criterion in Nampula, where the emphasis was rather on ensuring that investments were integrated with local development strategies). But the authors conclude that

> Taken together, these findings from the survey, as well as the overwhelmingly high levels of satisfaction expressed by the beneficiaries,

> must support a conclusion that in Nampula the improvements of access to infrastructure are exerting a strongly pro-poor impact in the local area ... Although direct links between positive poverty impacts and participatory processes cannot be firmly established, there is important suggestive evidence that participatory processes are enhancing social capital in these localities which over time will further have a positive impact for poverty reductions. (ECIAfrica, 2004: 64)

A second study (Roll, 2004) paints a positive picture of economic development based on anecdotal and statistical evidence on the improvement in household income between the author's visit in 2003 and the end of the civil war ten years earlier. However, it is unable to establish a direct link between growth and the Nampula initiative. Mozambican growth during that period averaged 7 percent per year (IMF data), and Nampula benefited from the revival of the market for its traditional cash crops (cotton, tobacco, maize) and the introduction of some new ones, such as sesame seeds. The period saw an increase in exports to Malawi and the emergence of a new generation of wholesale buyers (Afro-Mozambicans and Europeans, who competed with the established Indo-Mozambican families). These developments were not directly related to the PPFD project.

Overall, these studies (see also Galli, 2003 and Weimer *et al.*, 2004) suggest that the PPFD did have an economic impact, but the impact is hard to separate from the impact of other developments.

Political outcomes

Focusing on economic benefits, as we have just done, begs the important question of what kind of initiative the 'Nampula model' really was. For the success of the Nampula experience, such as it was, does not reside exclusively or even mainly in its economic impact: a *political* impact was also sought. From some donors' point of view, their support had the primary intention of stimulating a policy dialogue in order to demonstrate the value of decentralization as an instrument for wider development goals (Romeo, 1999). From the Coalition's point of view, the initiative was a way of establishing government legitimacy in the districts. Both donors and Coalition shared the objective of promoting greater financial autonomy for provinces and districts.

There was a degree of tension between the economic and political objectives. The project had to take account of UNCDF corporate indicators that required tangible development outputs as part of an international portfolio of Local Development Funds, and so economic impact took precedence in the PPFD log frame. A 2004 evaluation duly criticized the project logical framework for understating the political objectives, which it saw as the overriding ones (Borowczak *et al.*, 2004).

Roll invokes Houtzager's (2003) 'polity approach', in which we shift our attention

> from the decentralized and autarkic engagements of civil society and market actors towards the political arena and the institutions of representative and deliberative democracy...The polity approach focuses on how societal and state actors are constituted, how they develop a differential capacity to act and form alliances, and how they cooperate and compete across the public-private divide to produce purposeful change. The capacity and nature of both state and societal actors are understood as the outcome of a two-way exchange that is shaped in substantial ways by the institutional terrain in which it takes place. (Houtzager, 2003: 2)

For Roll, the consultative councils exemplify what he calls the 'politics of proximity' in the way that they have connected state and non-state agents, thereby legitimizing the district government. His finding is supported by the ECIAfrica report, in which their citizen respondents were satisfied with both the investments provided by the PPFD and with their representatives' participation in the investment decisions.

While most of the studies are generally positive, Pijnenburg (2004) is more sceptical. He suggests that the consultative councils had the effect of reinforcing the local elite rather than challenging it. His evidence includes the hierarchical way in which meetings and the public banquet that often followed them were conducted, even in terms of who sat where. Bringing stakeholders together was of greater use to the administrators than to the people. For Pijnenburg, the Nampula model represents little more than mouthing of the participatory discourse by the project management and their allies in provincial government, for own selfish reasons. He describes the role of the PPFD project manager (who happens to be the author of this chapter) as providing a buffer between the donors and the Coalition, keeping the donors happy whilst working with the Coalition in its own terms. However, his account is contradicted by the more positive opinions of citizens themselves.

Perhaps, though, we should stress the complementarity of the economic and political objectives rather than labour the opposition between them. According to the ECIAfrica study:

> Although direct links between positive poverty impacts and participatory processes cannot be firmly established, there is important suggestive evidence that participatory processes are enhancing social capital in these localities which over time will further have a positive impact for poverty reduction. (2004: 64)

Durability

It is worth drawing attention to the fact that the Nampula model at the time of writing had just crossed the ten-year 'durability' threshold that was one of McCourt and Bebbington's characteristics of development success (see Chapter 1). Moreover, while there has been no change of government in Mozambique during this period (another of McCourt and Bebbington's *desiderata*), there have been two general elections, a new President and, most significantly, new personnel in key local positions. The provincial governor, DPPF Director and many other figures referred to in this chapter have all moved on during the ten years. In fact the Nampula model has survived three different provincial governors and changes of donor agency and donor-appointed staff.

For Roll, the durability of the Nampula experience owes much to its ownership by the provincial government and the way in which the latter has used it as part of its strategy for governing the province. The model's longevity has probably also contributed to its incorporation into national legislation, in the form of the Local State Bodies law and regulations (MAE, 2003) and the direct budgetary allocations from the state budget to the districts which began in 2006.

Outcomes of the Nampula model: a summary

We can summarize our review of the Nampula experience as follows:

1. There has undoubtedly been significant economic development and an increase in household income in Nampula province during the period 1992–2006, but it is hard to isolate the PPFD contribution, especially as there were many other infrastructure programmes operating in the province at the same time.
2. It seems fair to conclude that the PPFD and the participatory process that went with it have helped to legitimize the local state in the eyes

of Nampula's citizens, a worthwhile achievement in view of Nampula's exclusion from the mainstream dating from the colonial period right up to the peace agreement in 1992. That, however, is not to say that Houtzager's ambitious 'polity approach' has fully materialized in Nampula.
3. The 'Nampula model' has crossed the ten-year 'durability' threshold.
4. It has been taken up at national level in legislation and practice.

It is on the basis of those conclusions, and having made all the necessary qualifications, that we claim Nampula as a development success. To understand how it happened, we turn now to the intra-bureaucratic politics of reform, where success was chiefly located.

The political economy of success

The Nampula 'coalition': origins and teething troubles

Our review suggested that although we have some evidence of an increase in household income, it is in the political dimension that success has been most striking. This section will look at how the new planning and budgeting methodologies were institutionalized, leading to an increase in administrative autonomy and in resources available to lower levels in the state system. We will argue that success was the outcome of the formation and operation of an informal policy coalition which developed a strategy to influence and then exploit central government guidelines and donor resources in order to implement a local governance policy; one which, ironically, 'bit the hand that fed' by confounding the expectations of donors and some government officials about what such a policy should look like.

The first point to note is that the PDDs were produced according to District Planning guidelines published by government in 1998, which created a vital institutional space for the Nampula model. In our opening section we outlined the provincial development agenda and the Coalition that developed around it in the early 1990s. To endure, the agenda needed to be rooted in the existing state structure. In 1995 the provincial governor and the DPPF were already sticking their necks out as far as they could go through the PTIP allocations they were making to the districts. There was a real risk that the provincial directorates, which were not at all keen to see provincial money go down to the districts, would overturn the initiative. The Coalition countered this by first creating an institutional space that would allow the provincial government to apply a district policy, and then using that space to implement a district planning project.

The institutional space was created by a national study of district planning. Commissioned by the Ministry of Planning and Finance in Maputo but shaped by members of the Coalition, it looked at examples of district planning supported by aid agencies around the country, with a view to recommending how the government could coordinate them (MPF/DNPO, 1997). It concluded that there should be national guidelines for PDDs, including those developed with the support of aid agencies. The same team went on to produce the 1998 guidelines with a view to piloting them in Nampula. Although they had no legal force, they gave Nampula a licence to proceed. Nampula produced its own practical guide that was used immediately by the PPFD, which duly began operations in January 1998.

The PPFD itself represented the second phase of the strategy, and inaugurated the collaboration between the Coalition and UNCDF. The preexisting UNCDF 'Support to Local Grassroots Initiatives' project was expanded with Dutch co-financing and transformed into the PPFD, an instrument through which the Coalition would implement its programme. The Project therefore had four simultaneous functions. It was the vehicle for the Coalition agenda; it was piloting guidelines for national government; it was part of UNCDF's international portfolio of local development funds operated from New York; and it was part of the Netherlands Government programme in Nampula province. Pijnenburg was right to emphasize the art of balancing these contradictory functions.

This genesis of the PPFD took place over a period of years and involved numerous meetings, memos, arguments and discussions. The Coalition developed a strong bond, making alliances with some national officials, including, crucially, the Deputy National Director for Planning and Budgeting. Such nuances of coalition-building are below the radar of project evaluations. Indeed early reports were extremely sceptical. Condy and Negrao (1999) were scornful of the idea that the PPFD could 'pilot' the district planning methodology when there was no national commitment to legislate for or resource the district plans. They also believed that the guidelines had little significance within either central or provincial government. Yet for all their legislative frailty, the guidelines were a crucial part of institutionalization.

The PPFD was almost strangled at birth by the introduction of the 'Sector Wide Approach' from 1997 onwards. In this new form of donor support, donors and government pooled funds and jointly developed programmes for each ministry, in particular ministries involved in poverty alleviation and the emergent Poverty Reduction Strategy Paper. This reduced the discretionary element of the provincial PTIP, because resources for Health, Agriculture, Education, Water and Roads were no longer influenced by the DPPF (DPPF, 2000). The Netherlands government, one of the main proponents of the sector approach (Netherlands Ministry of Foreign Affairs, 2000), closed down its Nampula programme abruptly.

Unlike the early 1990s, the late 1990s were a period of centralization of expenditure and a downgrading of the role of the provinces in planning and budgeting. In spite of this negative national policy environment, PPFD continued to create a 'reality on the ground' within the circumscribed institutional space it had created.

Implementation: the anti-project

We now come to the way in which the PPFD operational philosophy facilitated district ownership, a significant aspect of Nampula's success. We have established how the Coalition ensured provincial ownership. However, in order to achieve the Coalition's objectives it was important for the district governments and rural communities to perceive the process as a government one rather than an externally induced project. A 'project' would have triggered all the negative reactions that we described in the opening section.

The PPFD in effect implemented a local polity approach where the district government, coming under community pressure, put its own pressure on the province. This is what legitimizing the local state was supposed to mean: not acting with impunity, but operating in a local political space where it became the accepted forum for local decisions (DPPF, 1999).

The PPFD had to become an anti-project. This was difficult because many district administrators were hoping for a new 'external friend', and PPFD project staff themselves had been used to playing that role in previous incarnations.

The PPFD therefore reconfigured itself. Project staff were inducted into the new methodology and seamlessly merged into the provincial government administrative machinery and line management. The previous UNCDF project office was closed and staff were distributed around the DPPF departments. A mechanism was found to mask the donor funds and mix them with government budgets. The approach dispensed with the all-powerful 'Project Implementation Unit' and instead put government institutions to work implementing the annual cycle of planning and budgeting. This involved putting institutions in touch with each other, giving them genuine responsibility and creating a web of connections between district and provincial levels. The PPFD itself aimed to have as little concrete existence as possible, and in cases of dispute left no room for arbitrary largesse or appeals to an omnipotent project coordinator (see Jackson and Lambo, 2003).

Thus provincial institutions became facilitators to the districts. The province was divided into regions and a mixed group of civil servants, PPFD staff and aid agency staff made up the technical training teams for each region. Yet care was taken to ensure that the relationships between the provincial and district governments followed established protocols. In the context of post-conflict recovery this allowed weakened institutions to find their feet and recover their confidence. However it also meant that decision-making was slow and frustrating (DPPF/PPFD, 1999).

Operating as an 'anti-project' required a sustained effort over a period of many years. UNCDF, trying to raise its profile internationally, did not take kindly to having it lowered locally, although in time it came to appreciate the positive results and the publicity they generated. UNCDF and the Coalition remained partners in a rocky marriage, often bickering but staying together for the sake of their child, the PPFD.

Making the model work: the nuances of success

It was not enough to create 'institutional space' and to design a planning framework: the framework had to be made to operate. The initial experience was mixed. In Muecate district, for example, the first consultative council meeting in 1998 was a landmark event which persuaded the local 'traditional' leadership to throw its weight behind the PPFD (DPPF, 1998). By contrast, in Mogincual district, a district where free food aid had reinforced a supplicant posture, the few people who turned up for the first meeting in 1999 were looking for a 'project' that they would get something from. When the 'traditional' leadership found out that the meeting was under the auspices of the district government and not an aid agency they stormed out, demanding payment for their wasted journey. The meeting ended in chaos (Belo, 1999).

The attitude of the district administrators was a key factor in the implementation of the programme, and the PPFD developed an index, perhaps tendentiously, to measure their commitment to Coalition objectives (Bardill, 2000). Some administrators were sympathetic, but others were still looking for a project 'friend'.

An important concrete but also symbolic event was the construction of a police station, complete with cells, in Malema district. The local community had identified security as its key priority, but doubted whether the PPFD would be able to fund this sort of infrastructure. After consultations, the Coalition decided that the integrity of the district planning model required all forms of public expenditure to be eligible. On this occasion the representative of the Netherlands government (a Coalition insider) was privy to the decision, whereas UNCDF in Maputo and New York were kept in the dark until after the decision had been taken. State security was outside UNCDF's mandate, and it would have been likely to object. This event helped to cement the understanding that district planning was a local process, not an external 'project' (Olaia, 2003).

A further development was the 'franchising' of the district planning methodology to the aid agencies Concern (Ireland) and SNV (Netherlands). An arrangement was reached whereby the agencies assumed some responsibility for financing and supporting the model in the districts where they operated. They concentrated on community development, which was to be manifested through a strengthening of the consultative council and its ability to put pressure on the district government.

But this arrangement never worked perfectly. For example, SNV brought its own community development model, of Local Development Committees (*Comités de Desenvolvimento Local* – CDL). These operated at a village level, below the level of representation used in the consultative councils. During the simultaneous mid-term evaluation of the UNCDF and SNV programmes, arguments developed about the merits of the two agencies' approaches (Bardill, 2000).

The Coalition agenda also attracted the interest of the central authorities. From 2000, the province began to receive a stream of high-ranking visits. The Mecuburi district administrator presented the model to a national meeting of district administrators in mid-2000 at which the prime minister publicly endorsed the approach. These events created some tension between UNCDF, keen to advertise 'its' project, and the Coalition, which preferred to stress national ownership, believing that Government would be more likely to base reforms on an indigenous initiative than on a donor project.

Two months later the Council of Ministers held its first ever meeting outside the capital in Angoche, a Nampula district strongly supportive of RENAMO and the scene of renewed violent conflict earlier in the year. The only item on the agenda was the PDD. The President opened his address by stating that they were meeting in Angoche to show that Mozambique was one and that the writ of national government ran throughout the country. At the same time, he offered the district planning process as a token of the government's sincerity and its peaceful intentions (Jackson, 2002).

Later the same year the World Bank was invited to finance the mainstreaming of the model, and in 2002 UNCDF extended its support to neighbouring Cabo Delgado province. In 2003, the Local State Bodies law was passed, incorporating the three components of the Nampula model (MAE, 2003). Ministers and officials freely acknowledge the role of Nampula in shaping this legislation, which provides for a district plan and budget and for Consultative Councils (now called District Councils – though they have little executive power) and an enhanced role for the administrator and provincial governor in coordinating district development. The 2006 state budget included the first multipurpose capital allocations (approximately US$300,000) for each district, amounting to 3 percent of the national investment budget, alongside 3 percent for each province. These resources were found by reducing the value of government contributions to some sector programmes and were to be available directly to the districts in addition to donor resources, in effect replicating nationally the Nampula DPPF experiment of ten years earlier.

Yet while government eventually adopted the Nampula model, donors found it difficult to do likewise. In late 2000 it was proposed that the World Bank and UNCDF would provide funds to the Ministry of Planning and Finance to enable a national programme based on the model. This did not happen. A donor review in 2006 exploring the possibility of a national joint donor programme had produced few concrete results at the time of writing. There appeared to be donor coordination problems of a kind that many readers will recognize.

For instance, the World Bank, whose procurement and financing regulations militated against subsuming Bank funds in a government initiative, opted for a separate funding mechanism, where the different components of the model were put out through separate international tenders. The inevitable problem of district ownership that this created was compounded by mixed signals from government. The Minister of Planning and Finance asked the Bank to focus on the largely RENAMO supporting provinces of Tete, Manica, Sofala and Zambezia and to move fast. But building up district governance is a slow and painstaking process, as we have seen.

In Cabo Delgado province, meanwhile, it took time for local ownership of the project that UNCDF started in 2003 to build up. Collaboration between UNCDF and the World Bank was positive and friendly, but there were ownership issues here as well. The Nampula and Cabo Delgado PPFD was still part of the UNCDF international portfolio, monitored according to a patented software system, the source code for which was not openly available. This made it difficult for government and other donors jointly to monitor the same indicators in all provinces.

Conclusion: policy alliances and the political economy of reform

Summing up, it seems reasonable to state that the Nampula model has been successful in institutionalizing a significant reform of the planning and budgeting system. Admittedly, the initiative stopped short of full devolution to autonomous local governments. At the time of writing, the state system outside Mozambique's 33 municipalities was still deconcentrated rather than decentralized. Resource allocation was still largely based on sector ministries, and donors were still supporting sector programmes, tying up funds in centralized ministry hierarchies. But through consistency and sheer patience in applying a strategy in the face of fickle donor and government agendas, the model generated significant economic and (still more) political benefits, and achieved greater local flexibility and delegation of responsibilities.

What contribution has our study made to our understanding of development success in general? We suggest that it shows how a political economy of project implementation, focusing, in the Nampula case, on the operation of a heterogeneous policy coalition, can help explain policy outcomes through identifying factors that lie beyond the conventional 'log frame' project evaluation approach. Our account of the political economy is touched on in two academic studies of Nampula, namely Pijnenburg's and Roll's, but it is completely missing from the formal project evaluations that we have referenced (Bardill; Condy and Negrao; Borowczak *et al;* and ECIAfrica). The Malema police station episode and similar events were crucial in establishing meaningful ownership by the public administration bureaucracy, yet they were beyond the reach of formal evaluations. Paradoxically, the mechanical replication of the model was making it less likely that the replicating provinces could find the space to demonstrate independence and generate ownership.

The Nampula experiment also highlights the complexity of public purposes, and of public servants' motivation (Tendler, 1997). It began as an attempt to reestablish government legitimacy in a war-torn and divided province, at a time of great change and hope. The attempts to replicate the model took place in a different, more stable Mozambique. The focus was now on the relative efficiency of local state bodies in providing infrastructure and services. Local levels of the state may be more efficient, but we cannot inspire local civil servants with such dry economic arguments. With some observers arguing that there is less of the idealism that was present a decade earlier (such as Hanlon, 2001; 2002), offering local public servants something to rekindle that idealism will be vital.

Words like 'teambuilding', 'good governance' and 'ownership' only gain substance when they are accompanied by real exercise of power. In the case of Nampula, people dedicated to the development of that green and bountiful province exercised that power. They represent the real force behind the Nampula success, and this chapter is dedicated to them.

9
Explaining (and Obtaining) Development Success

Anthony Bebbington and Willy McCourt

In this final chapter we draw lessons from the seven cases that our contributors have presented, and whose main elements are summarized in Table 9.1. We discuss what they suggest about the nature and explanation of development policy success in terms of the framework which we developed in Chapter 1 and with reference to broader debates in the literature. As noted in Chapter 1, our research strategy and choice of cases mean that our conclusions will be tentative ones. We will open up avenues for further research at the same time that we close down our present enquiry.

The nature and durability of success

What kind of success?

In our introductory chapter we suggested that how we define development success depends on how we define development itself. Our 'normative' definition was 'the enhancement of human capabilities, in particular for the people who have the greatest capability deficits'. Such capability enhancement, we said, could occur through direct investment in financial, physical, social or human capital, or through improvements in the environment in which these assets are developed and used; improvements that could occur through initiatives as diverse as peace-building, macroeconomic reform and good governance programmes. We were interested in both economic and social development, but with the proviso that the development should be (in the jargon current at the time of writing) 'pro-poor'. Although we went on to refer to the traditional and contrasting public policy assumption that development might also be whatever a legitimate public actor said

Table 9.1 Summary of case findings

CHAPTER	COUNTRY/ REGION	NATURE OF POLICY	DURATION (all policies extant except where stated)	EVIDENCE OF SUCCESS	SUCCESS FACTORS
2. Melo	Brazil	Cash transfer to poor families	First municipal programme started 1994; federal programme started 1997 and survived change of government	95 percent of municipalities participating; 34 million people benefiting from annual transfer of US$2.2 billion	Functional electoral competition Design and political incentives Early social mobilization Leadership
3. Hofman *et al.*	Indonesia	Macroeconomic policy	1967–1997, coterminous with Soeharto regime	Average GDP growth of 7 percent p.a. 1967–1997; poverty down from 60 percent to 11 percent of population	Positive investment climate; Competent, insulated technocrats; Policy design; Pragmatism and flexibility; Donors
4. Grindle	Latin America	Industry and education	1965–80 (import substitution); 1950–1980s (access to education)	4.4–9 percent annual growth 1965–80, illiteracy 42→15 percent 1950–90; success of current policies remains unclear	Policy design Leadership to dislodge vested interests
5. Hulme and Moore	Bangladesh	Microfinance	Government ordinance for Grameen Bank in 1984; survived changes of government	1200+ MFIs, with good repayment rates; 13 million poor households benefiting; gender orientation empowering women	Innovation Policy specification Implementation factors Leadership and social energy

Table 9.1 Summary of case findings – *continued*

CHAPTER	COUNTRY/ REGION	NATURE OF POLICY	DURATION (all policies extant except where stated)	EVIDENCE OF SUCCESS	SUCCESS FACTORS
6. Mitlin	Chile, Philippines, South Africa	Housing	Scale operation began in mid-1980s (Chile), 1982–1998 (Mexico); programmes survived regime change in Chile and Philippines	Operation at 'scale'; up to 1.4 million beneficiaries (South Africa); enhanced ability of poor people to contest for power	Building a policy alliance without elite capture Empowerment of urban poor groups and allies
7. Shankland & Cornwall	Brazil	Health	SUS enshrined in 1988 constitution; survived changes of government	Universal, publicly funded health provision; dramatic improvement in basic health indicators	Popular participation prevents elite capture of policy alliance Pro-rights based health system policy networks/ epistemic communities
8. Jackson	Mozambique	Participatory planning	PPFD started in 1996; survived two elections and key personnel changes	Some economic improvement; increased state legitimacy	Policy coalition

it was, in fact all our contributors have written in the spirit of our normative definition.

That is markedly the case with a chapter like Alex Shankland and Andrea Cornwall's, which contrasts Brazil's health reforms with the neoliberal policies prevalent elsewhere in Latin America, and implicitly also with Hulme and Moore, Mitlin and Jackson's chapters. It is also true of Merilee Grindle's chapter. One of her criticisms of Latin America's state-centred education policies in the post-war period is that while they increased access to education for everyone, education was still inequitably provided, with poor children less likely to finish schooling, and the rural poor least of all. Likewise, if she ultimately reserves judgement on whether the new industry and education policies have been a success, that is largely because we lack evidence that they have led to broad-based growth or improved schooling for poor children.

The normative view also informs the analysis of Bert Hofman, Ella R. Gudwin and Kian Wie Thee, which again at first glance might appear indifferent to the distributional effects of growth. Earlier accounts of good economic performance in East and South-East Asia departed from prevailing free market orthodoxy mainly in stressing the positive role that government and government institutions had played in regulating the market (Wade, 1990; World Bank, 1993a). Hofman and his colleagues, however, say that what government got right more than anything else in the period before the 'crash' of 1997 was that it secured high growth that was also highly pro-poor.

Thus our normative view of development success seems to have survived the shock of contact with reality as represented by our seven cases. But of course even if our contributors agree roughly on what constitutes success – which might reflect an early 21st century consensus on the purpose of development that is no more permanent than the late 20th century 'Washington consensus' that preceded it – the policies that they have chosen as their examples of success differ widely, as we intended that they would. Let us see whether the evidence that our contributors offer gives us any grounds for comparing explanations for the success of these very different policies.

Evidence of success

In order to generalize about success, we must first show that success did indeed occur. In Chapter 1 we said that we were looking for cases which had the following features:

- They would target *the enhancement of human capabilities, in particular for the people who have the greatest capability deficits.*

- They should do so on a large scale: this might entail *scale-up* from an initial policy experiment.
- The policies would have been implemented over at least ten years, and preferably across at least one change of government: *policy duration* was important.
- They would preferably have succeeded *against the odds*; that is, at the point of inception a reasonable observer would have predicted that success was unlikely.

We list our contributors' evidence in the above order, starting with two forms of evidence of enhancement of human capabilities (readers may want to refer again to Table 9.1, where most of this evidence is summarized).

1. *Impact on income or other human development indicators*, arguably the most important form of evidence. While we must of course allow for the usual problem of demonstrating a causal relationship between a policy and a particular outcome – something that David Hulme and Karen Moore deal with thoroughly, and that David Jackson also discusses – our authors, experts in their respective policy domains, are confident that some such causal link exists. While some of them may have hoped for greater impacts (Diana Mitlin's discussion comes to mind), the chapters do suggest that improvements in indicators of health, shelter, income, nutrition and other outcomes can be attributed to the policies they discuss.
2. *Social and political impact*. Although Hulme and Moore present evidence of the economic impact of microfinance, they also say that 'it often seems as if this fundamentally economic approach has performed best in the social domain', particularly in women's empowerment. Similarly, Jackson argues that the most important success of the Nampula experiment has been in the political sphere, in the way in which the experiment has enhanced the legitimacy of the state in a country which is still recovering from a long civil war and in a province which had been bypassed by both the independence struggle and the initial policies of the FRELIMO government. The implicit arguments here are that there are important individual social benefits such as increased confidence and participation which human development indicators fail to capture, and that there are also collective political benefits which are different from the sum of the benefits to individuals.
3. *'Scale-up'*: an indication that initiatives that began life in a policy test tube were 'rolled out' on a large scale. Cash transfers in Brazil

existed only in Senator Eduardo Suplicy's fertile imagination in the late 1980s, but by 2002 95 percent of municipalities had such a scheme (Chapter 2). The Grameen Bank in Bangladesh began as a student action research project in 1976, but by 2002 there were 1200 microfinance institutions, reaching 13 million poor households (Chapter 5). Only Nampula's participatory planning experiment in Mozambique has still not been successfully scaled up to national level, despite donor-sponsored attempts, and despite its embedding in Nampula province itself (Chapter 8).

4. *Policy duration.* We stipulated in Chapter 1 that a successful policy would be one that survived for at least ten years and, in a competitive democracy, preferably also a change of government. This was the only element of our view of development success to which all our contributors responded. All of their chosen policies had delivered benefits for over a decade. Latin America's import-substitution policies may have become 'exhausted', but Grindle points out that this was only after they had generated sustained growth for at least the 1965–1980 period, an achievement that neoliberal critics of those policies tend to overlook: the policies were 'good' before they went 'bad'. In some of the cases policies also outlasted the government that introduced them (income transfer programmes and health policy in Brazil, housing programmes in Chile and the Philippines).
5. *Success against the odds.* (We could not find an economical way of presenting this evidence in Table 9.1.) We do not have evidence here in all our cases. Growth in Indonesia up to 1997 was not more impressive than in the other 'Newly Industrializing Countries' of East Asia, and, from the vantage point of the present, less impressive than in South Korea or even neighbouring Malaysia. From the same vantage point, recent industrial development in Argentina, one of the Latin American countries that Grindle discusses, has proceeded in fits and starts, with the crisis that reached its climax in December 2001 still a recent and painful memory.

   But we do have fairly clear evidence in three of our cases. When Henry Kissinger infamously called Bangladesh a 'basket case' in December 1971, would anyone outside the country have expected that this supposedly supine recipient of rich world handouts would be the source of that burst of 'social energy' which created the microfinance movement only five years later? Similarly, though less dramatically, Brazil's National Health System, the SUS, swam against the neoliberal current in Latin America which saw neighbouring

Chile introduce private insurance-based health provision, and it came out of the 'neoliberal shock' of the Collor government stronger than when it went in. On a smaller scale, participatory planning took root in a relatively remote province of Mozambique which had been neglected by the capital both before and just after independence.

Policy durability: rent seeking or social learning?

The way in which our case policies endured is as interesting as the sheer fact of endurance. Our initial naïve assumption about durability was that it would not be possible to have too much of a good thing; that as long as a good policy lasted, it would continue to produce reliable benefits. We did indeed have three fairly unambiguous examples of that, in the continuing development of microfinance in Bangladesh, and the maintenance of public health provision in Brazil and of a participatory planning model in Nampula province, Mozambique (Chapters 5, 7 and 8). Even there, however, we underestimated the effort that goes into maintaining a good policy, and also the potential for good policies to 'go bad', in Grindle's words. Microfinance was sustained by innovation in microfinance products, the result of a virtuous circle of social learning in which implementation generated feedback, which was used in turn to refine the policy. In Brazil and Mozambique, policies were sustained by policy coalitions. Even when the Brazilian coalition was placed on a firm institutional footing, it still had to be nurtured through health councils and conferences. In Mozambique, where the coalition's institutional footing was still wobbly at the time of writing, internal bonding activities and cultivating local and national relationships have steadied it somewhat.

Thus health policy in Brazil and participatory planning in Nampula are examples of policies that have stayed on course. But that is not true of all our cases. Mitlin (Chapter 6) shows that the nature of the coalitions that assembled around pro-poor housing policy in Chile, the Philippines and South Africa compromised policy objectives from the outset. The private construction companies which it was felt necessary to involve skewed housing policy towards the provision of finished housing units, and away from a 'sites and services' approach which would have served poor people better, because supporting residents' own efforts is far more likely to meet broader needs, including the enhancement of residents' collective capacity, than providing finished units on a plate, as it were. This is not only because of the inherently higher cost of finished units, sometimes inflated by the construction industry lobbying for rules requiring minimum standards that increase the unit cost. Politicians, for their part, were prone to using housing for political advantage, at the expense of allocation decisions based on need rather than clientelism.

Innovation and social learning through feedback, and the positive and negative roles that policy coalitions might play: these were all envisaged in our original framework, although the case chapters have fleshed out their ramifications in important ways. Jackson's personal account, for example, makes it painfully clear what a tortuous affair assembling and maintaining a coalition can be. But we failed to anticipate Grindle's insight, which Hofman *et al.*'s exposition of Indonesia's macroeconomic policy reinforces, that policies that started out 'good' might end up going 'bad'. This happens when the policy diverges from the policy need it was meant to serve. It is a sure sign that the policy has been captured, whether by the original beneficiaries who are no longer worthy ones (such as industrialists whose 'infant industries' should be well able to stand on their own two feet) or – what Grindle highlights – by interest groups that the policy itself has created (teachers' unions which resist a reorientation of education policy from access to quality), or alternatively by frankly parasitical interests (Indonesia's crony capitalists).

Up to this point Grindle's insight is consistent, as she recognizes, with the rent-seeking literature's pessimistic view that policy capture is inevitable, as it is economically rational for interested parties to capture it. The rent-seeking literature deals with the problem by calling for a reduction in state activity in order to diminish the potential for rents (Krueger, 1974; Tullock, 1967, 2005). However, Grindle reports that it has been possible for determined leaders like Carlos Salinas in Mexico to deal with the problem in a different way, by introducing a new policy which dislodges a preceding policy and which meets the needs of society rather than of hostile interests, initially at least. The Latin American leaders capitalized on the widespread perception of economic crisis, used patronage power to place supporters in key appointments, sidelined hostile party leaders and trade unions; in short, they pulled all the levers that their formal positions granted them in order to break stalemates and face down rent seekers.

Perhaps we can draw from Grindle's analysis the inference that when a policy sell-by date does arrive, the best way to bring about the termination of an exhausted policy may be by superseding it with a new one that is supported by new ideas and new supporters; by trumping the old policy, in other words, rather than by a frontal assault on it, the latter a drastic option that few leaders will undertake (DeLeon, 1978; Frantz, 2002; Sato, 2002). Thus terminating a policy becomes, paradoxically enough, an issue for the beginning and not the end of the policy cycle, since advocating a new policy will generate more reforming energy than opposing an old one.

Might we go a step further than Grindle herself goes, and propose a policy version of the Second Law of Thermodynamics, in which policies are inevitably subject to entropy? Does every policy, and not just the particular policies that Grindle discusses, come with a sell-by date, and do we have to resign ourselves to the expectation that the same heroic forces that are currently defending cash transfers and health policy in Brazil – the political actors who established the policy, and also the new interest groups that the policy itself has created (families benefiting from the *Bolsa Escola* programme, health service users) – will degenerate into reactionary obstacles to a new and more appropriate policy? Hofman *et al.* might endorse that view: they suggest that one of the lessons of Indonesia's experience is that 'institutions and policies come with an expiration date.'

However, the experience of microfinance suggests that policy entropy, or 'exhaustion', is not inevitable. The same interest groups digging their heels in to resist any diminution of their privileges are, from a different point of view, sources of feedback that policymakers can use to maintain or rescue the congruence of their policies. Institutions, after all, do sometimes renew themselves: the counter-reformation in the Catholic Church is one celebrated historical example. And for policymakers just as for prelates, the incentive is that adaptation based on feedback preserves congruence with the changing policy environment, without which the old policy risks being swept away by a new and more congruent one.

Where does this leave us? Durability turns out to be more important, and more interesting, than we thought it was in Chapter 1. We saw that a policy needs to have a (preferably broad) coalition behind it to survive for any length of time. However, we also saw that durability turns out to be a two-edged sword: policies have the same propensity to go bad as to stay good. To prevent policy decay, at the very outset policymakers need to minimize the influence of potential coalition members whose interests are hostile to policy objectives. Following that, policymakers need to ensure that policy coalitions become feedback mechanisms that facilitate adaptation, rather than ossifying into entrenched associations of rent-seekers.

Figure 9.1 presents the policy trajectories that we have discussed in this section.

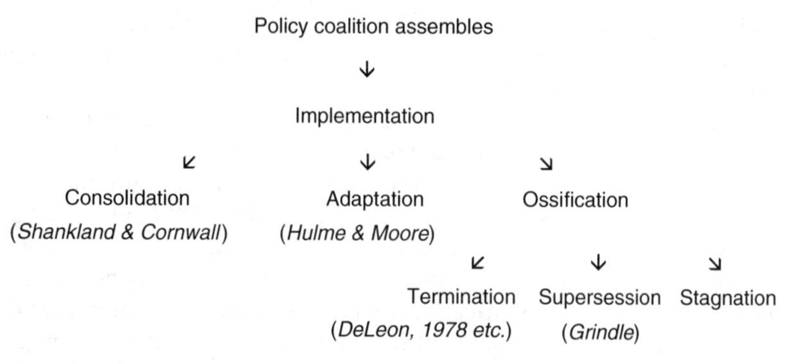

Figure 9.1 Policy duration: a typical implementation trajectory

Design matters: lessons on policy content

Policy and the political environment

Our cases have told us relatively little about the nuts and bolts of policy at the micro-level. The detailed discussion of microfinance models in Hulme and Moore's chapter, where design has mattered critically to financial sustainability, viability and women's empowerment, and likewise the brief but significant discussion of customs reform in Hofman *et al.*'s chapter, throw into relief the decision of our other contributors to concentrate on the non-professional elements of policy success. Perhaps their absence is inevitable in a collection that spans the gamut of development policy, militating against the professional scrutiny that a focus on a single policy area might have allowed. However, we think there are still some useful lessons about the way that policy design at the macro-level interacts with the political environment, including about the way that the political economy of policy is itself amenable to design.

Where should policy 'autonomy' be 'embedded'?

The first lesson is a refinement of what Peter Evans (1995) has called 'embedded autonomy'. Policy design in the tradition that stems from Weber is assumed to require some insulation from political and social influences for the technocrats who design it. Hofman *et al.* argue that insulation along these lines contributed to Indonesia's economic success up to 1997. In the especially complex area of macroeconomics, that insulation is symbolized by the traditional *purdah*, or retreat from day-to-day politics, which the UK Finance minister and his officials are permitted in the run-up to the annual Budget. At the other extreme are those quick and dirty responses to some immediate political need that tend to be stigmatized as 'policy on the hoof'.

However, in another instance of good policy going bad, the same insulation that facilitated Indonesia's success laid it open to failure, Hofman *et al.* tell us, as the crony capitalists captured economic policy unconstrained by any civil society checks and balances. But that does not mean that we should feel nostalgic for the early phase of Soeharto's authoritarian regime. For, admittedly with the wisdom of hindsight, Hofman *et al.* castigate Soeharto for having 'bad policies in good times': for having failed to establish sound institutions, including the institutions of democracy, at a time when windfall oil revenues would have made this relatively easy to do. Moreover, in neighbouring, more-or-less democratic Malaysia[1] and under the roughly contemporaneous Mahathir, the technocrats enjoyed the same insulation from politics. That also goes for their counterparts elsewhere in the region, as Hofman *et al.* note. Those countries are indeed examples of 'embedded autonomy', where technocrats have real autonomy that is qualified by being embedded in a dense network of social ties and which is, among other things, a source of intelligence – or of what we have called 'social learning'. Arguably therefore, our cases show that not just any old form of 'embedded autonomy' will do. 'Social ties', yes; but which ones? After all, macroeconomic policy in Indonesia *did* become embedded after a fashion, but in a small sector of crony capitalists, while its insulation from other groups and political processes fatally weakened policy adaptability.

Thus the 'what' of policy cannot be separated from the 'who whom?' questions of political economy. We have to distinguish between groups which support pro-poor policy and groups that oppose it, in very much the way that Mitlin distinguishes in Chapter 6 between the private companies and politicians that distorted pro-poor housing policy and the residents' groups that tried to keep it on track. In a similar way, because industrial policy in Latin America was not designed to enforce slow phasing out of industrial protection, and there were no countervailing groups to point to that omission, it was possible for industrial interests to lobby for protection to increase beyond reason. That in turn contributed to the replacement of the import-substitution policy by neo-liberal policy, as Grindle outlines in her chapter.

Designing participation

Grasping the importance of distinguishing between groups that support and oppose policy objectives puts us in a position to learn from the history of Brazil's National Health System, perhaps the most significant of all our cases. The institutionalization of support has contributed to its consolidation, as Shankland and Cornwall explain. Enshrined in the Constitution and the Basic Health Law, the Health Councils with their entrenched representation from organized civil society and the regular cycle of Health Conferences at municipal, state and federal levels have been crucial. It may be that policymakers underestimate the extent to which the 'who whom' issues of the distribution of power can be designed in the same way as the 'what' issues of policy content. We will expand on this point when we discuss the importance of institutions later on.

Policy design and policy learning

Design issues are also important in ensuring adaptive capacity in policy. While most of our contributors do not use the language of policy learning in their chapters, the substance of learning is present in most of them. The channels for learning are multiple, and many are not directly related to policy design: the freedom of a critical press, the scope for political debate, the existence of independent research bodies and a host of other attributes of a healthy public sphere are all critical for policy learning. But learning can also be designed for. Brazil's health councils and conferences, and Nampula's district planning processes (Jackson), are as much sources of learning as ways of embedding policy and making it legitimate.

Ideas and coalitions

Whether a nascent policy appeals to an audience that is broad enough to lift it off the ground is a matter of ideas as well as interests (John, 1998). This was clear in Marcus Melo's discussion of Senator Eduardo Suplicy's efforts to gain political support for a basic income grant policy in Brazil. We have seen already that in most of our cases there was a broad and loose coalition of policy champions which shepherded the policies through the necessary parliamentary and other processes. In Brazil it was the fertile suggestion of an economist called José Márcio Camargo that income grants to poor families should be conditional on children going to school which attracted the broad political support that gave the policy the necessary traction.

A further element of design that receives somewhat less attention is clear in Hofman *et al.*'s chapter. This relates to that aspect of design that enhances synergies among different policy instruments (for instance, between sectoral policies and macroeconomic policies), thus increasing the overall human development effects not just of each instrument but of the policy package as a whole. This theme appears as central to the story of Indonesian economic success, and while Hofman *et al.* do not necessarily say so explicitly, the suggestion is that the ability to design with such synergy in mind was itself helped by the existence of a strong, protected and professionally competent team of technocrats.

The political economy must support policy design

In this section we hope to have shown how policy design has interacted with political economy in our cases. Certainly we are obliged to repeat that our emphasis on political economic and institutional dimensions of success ought not to obscure the brass tacks of planning and design which matter greatly to development success; the Weberian insistence on political insulation for the technocratic planners is correct. However, even the best design in the world will only succeed if the surrounding political economy provides, or is designed to provide, a coalition that will support the policy and that will give feedback that will allow the policy to respond to changing circumstances, and hence to endure.

Political economies of success

That 'political economy' which we have just highlighted in relation to policy design can be an all-encompassing concept. Indeed in Chapter 1 we used it to cover everything from leadership to state-society and power relationships. Underlying this broad use of the term, though, are four simple ideas. First, policies cannot be analyzed separately from their social, political and economic contexts. Second, heroic leaders, entrepreneurs and brokers, so often the darlings of policy analysis, must be understood in terms of the networks of which they are a part, and in turn the institutions and social structures within which those networks are embedded. Third, the forms, functions and effects of policies are as much determined by wider socio-economic relationships as they are by the internal dynamics of the policy design process. And finally, for our particular purposes in this collection, 'success' is a question of political economy: not only in its determination, but also in the power relationships that ultimately decide what counts as success in a society.

State-society relations and policy cycles

The cases have reinforced our initial editorial conviction that policy was far from synonymous with state policy, and that successful public policy depends on much more than state action. They depict interaction between the state and a wide range of organized non-state actors which includes social movements, unions, NGOs and business lobbies, and which takes different forms at different stages of the policy cycle. Here we focus on two ways in which state-society interactions contribute to success.

First, they have stimulated a vigorous public debate that has made certain policies imaginable and politically viable. Social movements have been key. The Brazilian cases are clear on this. The progressive democratization of Brazilian society – itself largely a product of social movement pressure (Dagnino *et al.*, 2006) – also made possible new and increasingly inventive forms of mobilization. One of these was the civic movement to impeach President Collor which gave rise to a 'countrywide mobilization' (Melo's phrase) to distribute food to poor people in which NGOs played an important role. 'The Action in Defense of Citizenship for the Fight against Hunger' spawned thousands of local committees across the country. Public awareness of hunger intensified, influencing discussions in Parliament. Melo is convinced that these antecedents were critical in creating an environment in which a basic income transfer programme could become politically attractive. Shankland and Cornwall suggest something similar about Brazil's *movimento sanitarista* (the movement for public health) which brought activists and professionals together and paved the way for a publicly funded, rights-based health system.

This process of policy development is very different from the basically 'top-down' one that Hofman *et al.* and Grindle outline, but not wholly different from the one outlined by Hulme and Moore. The similarity between Bangladesh and Brazil is that income transfers, microfinance and public health provision all alike arose from an initial burst of what Hulme and Moore, quoting Uphoff – who in turn got the idea from Hirschman (1984) – call 'social energy': the creative popular ferment which accompanied democratization in Brazil and independence in Bangladesh. The difference, however, is that Brazil's activists channeled their energy into the state, whereas Bangladesh's channeled it into the voluntary sector: Brazil's activists were as optimistic about government as Bangladesh's were pessimistic.

Such social movement processes not only give more visibility to issues that later become policies. They also create expanding networks of relationships and shared commitments that help sustain the policies that are grounded in those commitments. Moreover, through their subsequent involvement with the policies, the networks develop further links with government reformists (cf. Fox, 1996), and with other activists and professionals outside the core bureaucracy. Shankland and Cornwall argue that this is precisely what occurred in Brazil's health councils, and analyse the process in terms of Peter Haas's concept of 'epistemic communities' – in their case communities that run from council members through to professionals and administrators.

These epistemic communities play various roles. First, they provide a vision of what a fully fledged policy would look like. The case of microfinance (Hulme and Moore) is obvious here, but this also applies to participatory planning in Mozambique (Jackson). Following that, they help to maintain the policy, they provide feedback that can be used for policy adaptations, and they guard against the possibility that the policy will be captured or watered down by others. Mitlin's arguments about the susceptibility of housing programmes to capture by business or political interests reflect her concern that such network-based communities are weak in the field of housing policy, leading to her closing call for policies that promote empowerment.

Networks and the legitimacy of non-state actors

Mitlin's discussion is also helpful because it makes clear that there is always a range of network-based communities that surround policy. Their relative power determines the direction of policy. Hofman *et al.* say the same thing in so many words when they point to the multiple ways in which non-state (or better, non-Soeharto) institutions were weakened, preventing other networks from developing and steering policy away from the increasingly dominant (and closed) networks of the crony capitalists. As so often in this collection, the question 'successful for whom?' arises. We suggest that it is the groups which are able to mobilize networks and influence policy development which will benefit from that policy.

It would seem to follow that the Brazil model of social engagement (development by the people) offers more than the Bangladesh model of social altruism (development for the people, 'of non-poor, for poor', as James Copestake is quoted as saying by Hulme and Moore). The nature of the evidence in this collection means that we can only offer this up as a conjecture on which further research would be worthwhile. However, if we can explore our conjecture, then 'development success' becomes a war of attrition which requires the sustained empowerment of pro-poor actors. That empowerment in turn requires alliances which, however riven by latent tensions (Mitlin), are strong to the extent that they are grounded in prior networks of solidarity and forms of social energy that bind like-minded actors together (Fox, 1996; Hirschman, 1984). Critically, and again as Mitlin suggests, for such alliances to prevail, they must involve both civil society and the state. Civil society actors need to enroll state reformists in their efforts to elicit and sustain particular policies, and reformists need to reach out to civil society.

Thus the state is never the sole actor in any of our cases. That is not a new insight: scholars have recognized it at least since Heclo and Wildavsky (1974) and, more recently, Rhodes' influential writing on networks proceeds from it (1997). But in our cases the state is not always even the leading actor. This is humbling for both elected and appointed state officials in one way. But in another way, it creates the possibility of harnessing the social energy which social movements seem to find easier to tap into than public bodies: the civic mobilization which led up to the substantial commitments to African aid at the G8 Summit of 2005 at Gleneagles in Scotland is a dramatic recent example.

'Dethroning' the state would appear to raise the criticism of legitimacy so often leveled at social movements: by what right do you presume to place yourselves on an equal footing with a legitimate government, especially a democratically elected one? We cannot hope to answer that criticism fully in this chapter. However, we are perhaps entitled to point to Shankland and Cornwall's account of the participatory structures of Brazil's National Health System as adding to rather than supplanting the conventional legitimacy of the state. Certainly those structures may over time degenerate into a glorified rent-seekers' club where an obsession with universal access to health services prevents the service improvements that a market-based system may be better at providing: that would be Grindle's fear. But for the moment they appear on balance to be enhancing the health care available to citizens rather than damaging it.

Varieties of policy and the question of distribution

In our introductory chapter, we suggested that policies that aim to redistribute resources are less likely to be successful, largely because they encounter more resistance. At one level, this may seem an unhelpful observation, as almost all policies have redistributive effects over time. However, our cases appear to endorse the argument that policies that are explicitly redistributive – be this because they transfer the resources of one group to another, because they target significant public spending to particular groups or because they appear to take resources away from a particular interest group – are peculiarly fragile.

This is partly due to the institutional complexities that derive from problems of scale. Any policy that attempts redistribution on a significant scale needs to involve large institutions. Mitlin argues, for instance, that mass housing policy needs the involvement of the state for both resource and legal reasons. In the case of microfinance, any effort to scale up (to step up from a project to a policy, so to speak) has likewise required NGOs to seek funds from new sources. In Indonesia, many of the sectoral and macroeconomic policies had to be resourced by external loans. In all three cases, going to scale drew new players into the institutional network through which policy was delivered, and those players brought with them an additional set of interests, potential conflicts and conditions which complicated policy dynamics.

Merilee Grindle's chapter addresses another related sense in which policy type affects the likelihood of success. Arguing particularly from the experience of education reform, she suggests that policies of expansion have a better chance of succeeding than policies aimed at changing the way a service is provided. This is because expansionary policies (e.g. those aimed at increasing education provision), while benefiting some more than others, do at least bring some benefit to many different groups. Policies that aim to change the mechanisms through which services are delivered and controlled are quite distinct. They offer far less by way of immediate tangible benefits, and generally concentrate heavy costs in a few particular groups (who, furthermore, are often the same groups who benefited from earlier policies of expansion). They generate far more resistance.

Leaders and leadership

Grindle shows that the possibility of overcoming resistance depends greatly on leadership skills, both the ability to negotiate and the ability to force through change in the face of resistance. Likewise, it may be that in conditions of increasing institutional complexity such as those we have outlined, forceful leadership becomes even more important as a way of cutting the Gordian knot of institutions. Certainly leaders appear as important actors in the policy narrative in all our cases, and also as part of the explanation of success in Grindle and Hulme and Moore's chapters. Given that policy is a public matter, leaders are the public faces which those coalitions must have if their ideas are to be implemented as policies.

We have already listed ways in which Grindle's leaders used the levers of power. We need only list, additionally, a couple of the ways in which Muhammad Yunus shaped the development of microfinance in Bangladesh: through inventing it, primarily, but also later on through using his elite position to negotiate its unique statutory position, and later still through reinventing it in the form of 'Grameen II'. Leadership thus emerges as integral to policy success, consistent with other accounts such as Tendler's (1997). Yet it remains hard to theorize and work with, as Melo points out in Chapter 2.

Perhaps it is helpful if we break the identification of leadership with a single leader and think of it as a task, not a person. Individual power is not the exclusive property of leaders who are formally designated as such. Leadership may be 'distributed' (Barry, 1991; Brown and Hosking, 1986), shared relatively equally among several members of a coalition. That seems to have been the case with 'the coalition', as Jackson calls it, which steered participatory planning in Nampula (Chapter 8). Alternatively, leadership may be sequential, with different individuals having more or less power at different stages of policy development, rather in the way that the conch shell in William Golding's *Lord of the Flies* passes from hand to hand to indicate which boy can speak in a meeting. Melo's fine-grained account of Brazil's income transfer policy illustrates this.[2] It was Senator Eduardo Suplicy who put the original idea on the policy table, (he modestly attributes the idea itself to a colleague: see Chapter 2, Note 12), whereupon the economist Camargo refined it in a way that made it attractive to the municipalities (the Mayor of Campinas, Magalhães Teixeira, ran with the ball for a while), and then to the federal government, initially under Cardoso and latterly under Lula.

There are also different categories of leader. One set, exemplified by Suplicy and Yunus, includes those leaders who both help elaborate the initial policy idea and then assiduously promote it. In Burns' (1978) well-known terms, they are 'transformational' leaders, exercising power that derives from their determination and intrinsic skills as policy innovators (see also Rogaly, 1996). They are not necessarily elected or deeply embedded in broader socio-political structures that give them power and legitimacy.

A second category does derive its power from the political base. These are the classic political leaders who populate Grindle's chapter. They resolve conflicts, build policy consensus, and force through policy adaptations which break down the political equilibria that block change. However, it is not a foregone conclusion that they will do any of those things. Melo suggests that their willingness or otherwise depends on their calculation of the political benefits. In Burns' terms, these are the 'transactional' leaders. (Of course some very gifted individuals can be both transactional and transformational leaders: Muhammad Yunus in Bangladesh is an example.)

A third category of leaders are the technocrats. They appear as important players in macroeconomic policy in Indonesia, and in industrial and – even more – education policy in Latin America. Theirs is what French and Raven (1959) have called 'expert power'.[3] They may also have their own networks, particularly professional ones – epistemic communities inside and outside their countries which are also a power base of sorts. Technocratic leaders operate behind the scenes. While this gives them room for manoeuvre, it means that they cannot play a role in resolving political conflicts over policy change. They need the classic political leaders to do that job for them, and to insulate them from political pressures.

Our cases suggest that leadership is particularly important at three policy stages:

- the inception stage, where an individual or individuals get(s) the idea on to the policy agenda (for instance, Suplicy with income transfers in Brazil);
- the implementation stage, where an individual or individuals overcome(s) the opposition of supporters of the old dispensation (Grindle's Latin American leaders);
- an individual or individuals ensure(s) that the policy adapts to changing circumstances, using the coalition as a feedback mechanism (Muhammad Yunus with microfinance in Bangladesh).

Leaders and followers

All this is some way from the railway bookstall picture of the leader as the autonomous, lonely individual taking tough decisions and dragging his followers in his or her wake. Leaders of the kinds we depict may articulate their followers' aspirations better than they can, and they may even persuade their followers that they see their interests more clearly than they do themselves. But their political identity is inseparable from the coalitions whose figureheads they are. Indeed their power evaporates when they become detached from their power bases and identify themselves with other elite figures outside their coalitions. That was the fate of Bishop Abel Muzorewa in the run-up to Zimbabwean independence, of Mikhail Gorbachev in the dying days of the Soviet Union and of Margaret Thatcher after 11 years as the United Kingdom's prime minister. We can contrast that fate with the way that Nelson Mandela in South Africa resisted the apartheid government's attempt to drive a wedge between him and his party, the African National Congress, just before his release from prison in 1990.

This is close to the view of leadership which Melo derives from Fiorina and Shepsle (1989) in Chapter 2. It is clear that Grindle's leaders are not of this type, but it is not clear that the policies they have forced through have been successful. In this collection at least – and once again we stress the limitations of our seven cases – it is the leaders of the kind we have depicted whose coalitions' policies have succeeded.

Perhaps the need for leaders to stay close to followers mitigates the striking fact that all the 'leaders' that we have named in this section are still within the charmed circle of the policy elite: they are 'of non-poor, for poor', in Copestake's words which we quoted earlier. There is nothing in our cases to suggest that individual poor people have directly influenced 'pro-poor' policy (Hulme and Moore have an interesting discussion of 'men's leadership and [poor] women's agency' which bears on this). Lacking all of French and Raven's bases of social power, their route to influence is through collective action, as Mitlin emphasizes in her chapter conclusion, and as Shankland and Cornwall illustrate in their discussion of Brazil's institutionalized health councils and conferences.

Implementation

Given that our definition of success has been a time-based one – we wanted to see policies that have endured and, preferably, survived a change of government – the implementation phase is part and parcel of development success. The chapters suggest several lessons about it.

Complex policies and empowering the powerless

The first lesson concerns policy complexity. Generally, the simpler a policy's implementation process, the greater the chance of success. Macroeconomic policies of the kind that Hofman *et al.* address are easier to implement and sustain than social development policies because the path from design to implementation is short and involves fewer actors.[4] A short path means less resistance, slippage or reworking of the policy. This in fact was one of the arguments used to justify setting up Latin America's social funds. They were designed to minimize the steps from central government to final recipient in order to speed up implementation and limit the diversion of funds (Van Domelen, 2006).

However, for most social sector policies, implementation is a complex process involving multiple actors, intermediaries and interests. Our cases suggest a useful lesson here, one that relates to 'empowerment'. Diana Mitlin argues forcefully in her chapter that a range of actors try to twist policy implementation to their own advantage. Since some of them naturally have more power than others, the extent to which a policy actually addresses human development needs comes to depend on the extent to which the implementation process empowers those who lack power, since they are the very ones at whom pro-poor policy is directed (in Mitlin's case, those who lack secure shelter). Shankland and Cornwall's chapter pulls in the same direction. Brazil's health councils enhanced health system users' ability to insist that access to services should be based on citizenship, not the market.

These observations, which echo those made by Guggenheim (2006) among others, highlight the fact that policy success means keeping implementation processes 'on track', oriented towards human development goals rather than clientelist ones. For this to occur, the progressive empowerment of the groups which are committed to ensuring these human development goals is of signal importance to forestall policy capture and distortion.

Policy success and the institutions of democracy

We included institutions under the heading of implementation in our Chapter 1 framework, so it is convenient to review here what our cases have told us about them. At this stage we do not need to labour their basic importance, which most of our contributors recognize, notably Hofman *et al.* and Grindle. However, our contributors are divided about the special case of the institutions of democracy, so we will spend some time discussing them in this section. It may be an advantage of a cross-national case collection like ours that there is an opportunity to reflect on divisions that may be taken-for-granted assumptions at national level.

Our first group of contributors associates democracy with success. The association is strongest in the two Brazil chapters, which argue that the electoral popularity of income transfers and the institutionalization of civic engagement in the health sector there have done a great deal to keep the income transfer policy and the National Health System on track. But it is also present in the Indonesia chapter. Earlier on we noted Hofman *et al.*'s reading that although prosperity was possible in Indonesia up to 1997 with weak institutions which included Soeharto's 'guided democracy', the Crisis of 1997 was the point at which the institutional and democratic chickens came home to roost.

However, other contributors barely raise even E. M. Forster's celebrated 'two cheers for democracy'. All that Hulme and Moore's social entrepreneurs seem to need from the Bangladesh government is for it to keep out of microfinance's way. They note that the growth of NGOs there, including microfinance NGOs, was a reaction to the early failure of government to respond to the problems that accompanied Bangladesh's independence in 1971. So negative is the view of government that the Grameen Bank, they report, refuses to employ anyone who has been tainted by working in the public sector. Likewise, Mitlin's heart is with 'community democracy' rather than the party political variety, which for her is indelibly clientelistic; while Grindle, for her part, makes no distinction between democratic and authoritarian leaders.[5]

Outside the sometimes wishful thinking of international development agencies, it is the skeptical view of democracy of the latter contributors that is probably the mainstream academic one, as Melo highlights at the start of his chapter. Mushtaq Khan (2005), for example, has used the incontestable fact that rich countries are generally more democratic than poor ones to argue that the electoral competition that stems from democratization in developing countries is very likely to increase the power of patron-client factions, since they are usually better organized to assert their preferences than the atomized majority of poor voters. He exempts from his rule only the high middle-income countries where he sees democracy approximating to the version prevailing in rich countries.

Yet Khan remains explicitly a democrat, as is Grindle among our contributors despite her recognition of some authoritarian leaders' narrow political skills, and even Mitlin and Hulme and Moore's criticisms of democratic politics are contingent rather than fundamental ones. Therefore the challenge is to make democracy work for development, and to see whether the social entrepreneurialism of Chapters 2, 5 and 7 can be replicated in, or transferred to, other countries (from

Brazil), and equally to the public sector[6] (from the NGO sector, where microfinance has been most vibrant).

Constraints on replicating Brazil's state-led success

In canvassing that possibility we must be aware of four specific constraints that our cases suggest, in addition to the general one that 'context matters' with which most of us are familiar by now.

1. Both our positive examples of civic engagement come from a single country, Brazil. Relevant to Khan's critique, one of Brazil's characteristics is that it is a lower middle-income economy, whereas Bangladesh, despite encouraging recent growth, remains low income. (However, so too does Mozambique, whose success with embedding democratic participation in a disadvantaged region Jackson has recorded.)
2. Even if the decision of social activists to go down the NGO path in Bangladesh and the government path in Brazil was fortuitous, rather than a clear-eyed calculation about the potential for a state-led approach to succeed in the two countries (and we have already noted the view that the growth of Bangladeshi NGOs reflected government failure following independence), there may be some 'path dependence' by now (Mahoney, 2003), restricting Bangladesh's freedom to switch to the government path.
3. A replication of the 'social energy' that accompanied democratization in Brazil in the late 1980s will probably be necessary, as that was crucial at the inception of the income transfer policy and the National Health System. We need hardly stress what a tall order that is, although we should note that there are those who believe that some inducement or 'catalyization' is possible (see for example Uphoff, 2000).
4. Great care will be needed to design an institutional structure of participation that will empower the intended beneficiaries of the policy, and prevent the political patrons and rent-seekers from capturing it. This is also a stringent constraint, but at least our Brazilian cases offer encouraging precedents.

It is beyond the scope of our enquiry to say if those formidable constraints can be overcome in any particular country. However, it seems reasonable to say that if in Bangladesh (or elsewhere) a new generation of social entrepreneurs were to arise, share Khan and Grindle's democratic instincts and decide to apply the same energy to the public sector that a previous generation applied to the voluntary sector in Bangladesh, then the success of state-led social development in Brazil is a model that it may be able to adapt.

Policy transfer: entrepreneurs and incentives

Voluntary and coercive transfer: donors as bit players

In discussing policy transfer in Chapter 1, we suggested that it was unlikely that policies imposed through 'coercive transfer' (Dolowitz and Marsh, 2000) would succeed. It may be significant, therefore, that none of the successful policies in this collection seems to have been foisted on the policymakers. Indonesia's macroeconomic policy under Soeharto and economic liberalization in Latin America were broadly 'orthodox', but according to Hofman *et al.* and Grindle they were still developed locally. In Indonesia the 'technocrats' were more influenced, it seems, by their university teachers in the United States than by the IMF or the World Bank, whose views also counted for less in Latin America than political leaders' own deep conviction that change was necessary, as Grindle goes out of her way to emphasize.

Where policies are transferred voluntarily rather than imposed, then political salesmanship will be at a premium: the saying that 'a good product sells itself' does not apply to policies. Here again there is a role for the domestic 'transformational' leader. Eduardo Suplicy, Raúl Prebisch and Muhammad Yunus in Chapters 2, 3 and 5 respectively are examples. They promoted as well as designed the policies with which they are associated.

It is striking how modest is the role that the IMF, World Bank and other donor agencies play in our cases, either for good or for ill, considering their ubiquity in the development literature.[7] This may be because when these agencies promote a policy, their financial power means that they inevitably do so as coercers rather than salesmen. But it may also be – and this is a hypothesis – that large bureaucracies are less good at innovating or persuading than think tanks, research institutes, NGOs and public intellectuals. If there is something to the hypothesis, then apart from the cold water it pours on the late 1990s ambition of the World Bank to turn itself into a 'knowledge bank', it has important implications for knowledge generation to support policy development. Multi-nodal systems of policy innovation which bridge research and policy may be more fertile than bureaucratic monoliths (Stone, 2000, 2002).

Varieties of transfer

Even in our cases of policies that have been adopted voluntarily rather than through coercion, there is still considerable variation in the nature of the transfer. Grindle's account of the transfer of policy ideas in industrial development and education across Latin American governments is closest to the transfer process that Dolowitz and Marsh envisage. Here the transfer is from one national polity and technocracy to another, with other actors, in particular multilateral ones, oiling the wheels.

But we also have two forms of transfer that are outside Dolowitz and Marsh's model. The first is what is probably the paradigmatic case of modern international development policy transfer, microfinance. Its interesting feature is that it has largely bypassed governments, the conventional agents of public policy. The process of transfer has been from its inception and expansion in the Grameen Bank to its adoption by other Bangladeshi NGOs, and then subsequently by international policy circuits, including the World Bank, at which point it entered the pantheon of development orthodoxy. This, however, is a logical consequence of the view of development policy which we espoused in Chapter 1, in terms of policy beneficiaries rather than providers, a view that brings the NGOs which have taken the lead on microfinance within the scope of mainstream development policy.

The second form of transfer was hinted at in the last paragraph when we talked about the expansion of the Grameen Bank and the replication of its activities by other Bangladeshi NGOs. That phase of the development of policy is well discussed under the heading of 'scaling up' in the NGO literature (see for example Uvin *et al.*, 2000), but something like it also occurs in the public sector. Thus Melo describes a process of within-country transfer of the income transfer policy in Brazil, initially across municipalities and subsequently up to federal government, and Jackson describes the difficulties encountered in Mozambique's attempts to scale up Nampula's participatory planning model.

Policy refraction: incentives and congruence

In Chapter 1 we talked about 'policy refraction', where policies are adapted to local conditions rather than adopted wholesale. Our cases have provided two insights into this process. The first concerns incentives. When policymakers are free to adopt or not adopt, incentives matter as much in transferring policies as they do in transferring footballers.[8] Melo's argument in Chapter 2 is that the income transfer policy benefited from a 'bandwagon' effect, with first one municipality after another and then the federal government scrambling on board because of the electoral return which they expected this popular policy to give them. Similarly, the opportunities to make money and win votes were incentives for private companies and politicians to yoke themselves to housing policies in Mitlin's chapter. Arguably it is because such incentives are missing in Mozambique that the Nampula participatory planning experiment has not transferred successfully to other provinces or up to the national level.

The problem here is that the incentive may be so much baggage weighing the policy down. With income transfer in Brazil, making payments conditional on school attendance added a transaction cost, as someone presumably has to monitor attendance, adjudicate on appeals from feckless parents and so on. More problematically, we have seen already how bringing private companies and politicians on board skewed housing provision away from support to community self-help activities. These compromises may have been what made the policies viable, but they came at a cost.

That said, one way or another policies have to be brought in line with the broader incentives and values that structure policymaking. The tremendous transfer and diffusion of microfinance, for instance, has occurred partly because its emphasis on individual repayment and individual entrepreneurship[9] chimed with the broadly neo-liberal discourse that dominates international financial institutions, ministries of finance and social responsibility foundations. The emphasis on women was helpful too. The transfer of import-substituting industrialization policy in Latin America was also aided by its congruence with nationalist ideologies of state-led development that underlay both military and populist governments of the period. Finally, and perhaps most interestingly among our cases, the argument for basic income-guarantee transfers tied to education resonated with the structure of political incentives in Brazil's consolidating representative democracy. It offered a policy with potential vote-winning dividends, and thus became an object of partisan competition as each party tried to leapfrog the others by adopting the policy to reach out to a larger part of the electorate.

The consumers of particular policies are thus at different levels, and so it is not only the impact on beneficiaries that will determine whether they are transferred. The more a policy appeals to other policy stakeholders, particularly powerbrokers, the likelier its transfer into new domains will be. In this sense, once again, design matters.

The policies that travel are not only those whose design increases the likelihood of human development effects, but also whose design makes the policy attractive to its different audiences. The design challenge, here again, is to structure the policy process to empower groups committed to ensuring that the policy stays faithful to its original objectives. Shankland and Cornwall's account of the development of Brazil's National Health System shows that this can be done, even in the face of considerable pressures.

Conclusion: institutionalized social energy

The framework developed in Chapter 1 was more comprehensive than parsimonious. It gave our contributors plenty of room to manoeuvre, but as an explanatory tool it was unwieldy. In the light of our cases and our analysis of them in this chapter, can we identify a shorter list of factors that has greater explanatory power? Based on our cases, the items on that list will all concern the politics of policy, about which our cases have told us more than we expected, and less than we expected about its managerial and professional aspects. In part that emphasis must reflect our contributors' (and their editors') personal preoccupations. We would not want readers to go away with the idea that the professional content or the management of policy don't matter. That is, for one thing, because in individual cases they have mattered a good deal (the content of customs reform in Indonesia, the Grameen Bank's human resource system in Bangladesh). But it is equally because in the actual development practice of governments like Malaysia's and of development agencies (to take an example from outside this collection), we observe the ever-increasing use of the techniques of strategic management – in performance indicators, Poverty Reduction Strategy Papers, logical frameworks and so on. However, it is the political issues that our contributors have given us a mandate to highlight, and we do so now.

Taken as a whole, the cases suggest three main explanatory factors: power, leadership and institutional design. We discuss them now in turn.

Power: organizations and coalitions

The balance of power is central to all seven cases. It creates environments more or less propitious to different policies, and determines which groups and which ideas will prevail. The power of different actors ebbs and flows over the lifetime of a policy. Power over policy has many sources, but two seem to matter a good deal: organization and coalitions. Actors gain power as they become organized: unity is strength, not only in the teachers' and other unions where that motto was coined, but also in squatters' associations, business lobbies and users' committees. Getting organized increases policy leverage.

The ability to develop policy coalitions (which our contributors have variously labeled alliances, epistemic communities, social movements or networks) is also important (cf. Keck and Sikkink, 1998). Our contributors make clear again and again how such coalitions serve as sources of power in policy arguments. In policy tussles, it is effectively coalitions that do the tussling.

Leadership

Second, one cannot read these cases without being impressed by the frequency with which leadership emerges. Policy success is not impersonal, and cannot be understood without referring to named individuals. However, as well as the heroic and lonely figures of popular legend (though they exist), our cases depict two other styles of leadership, which we called 'distributed' and 'sequential'. We also noted three different types of leadership, transformational, transactional and technocratic, variously important at different policy stages. All these styles and types are rooted in the coalitions that they personify and in the environments in which they operate; they do not float freely above them.

Institutional design

Third, while our cases have told us little about the professional content of policy design, they have given us an insight into its institutional architecture. We have seen the importance of conducting pro-poor policy in a way that empowers those who are committed to it (and, by the same token, that relegates those who are opposed). Once more we highlight Brazil's health councils and conferences as the paradigm case of empowerment through institutional design.

Likewise, the policy needs to be designed to provide incentives to individuals and groups whose participation is crucial to realizing a policy, as we saw happening in Brazil when income transfers were linked to school attendance; an example which illustrates that the incentives need not take the form of crude personal inducements.

A model of the stages of policy success

In the light of our cases and our analysis of them, it is possible to identify a schematic account of the stages of policy success which incorporates the above three explanatory factors, and which seems to map quite well on to the cases (Table 9.2). We suggest 'institutionalized social energy' as a label for this account, as long as it is recognized that it is a shorthand for a process whose stages, in terms of Table 9.2, are these:

social energy → idea → coalition → leader → institutionalization → feedback

There are three things listed under 'threats to success' which are not self-explanatory. First, our reference to 'sterile oppositionism' is influenced by Mitlin's account of how the urban housing movement in Mexico shifted from negative resistance to evictions and land tax charges towards active demands. The slogan that encapsulated the shift was '*Protesta con propuesta*': protest with proposal. Sterile oppositionism would mean not going beyond resistance: '*protesta sin* (without) *propuesta*', so to speak.

Second, while we would love to be able to say pithily that policy success comes from inside while failure comes from outside, that would exclude the case of income transfers in Brazil, which had a European origin. However, we have noted that it was adopted voluntarily, just like all our successful policies and in contrast to structural adjustment policies (our chosen example of a 'threat' at Stage One), which notoriously failed partly because they were not 'owned' (McCourt, 2003). The idea need not be indigenous, but the impetus for adopting it must be. The American historian Barbara Tuchman's (1984: 411) incisive rhetorical question – 'What nation has ever been built from outside?' – retains all its force.

Third, since all the policies discussed here were actually implemented, we have had to look beyond our collection for an example of failure to overcome opposition to a policy. Our example (from a distressingly large set of possibilities) is the economic reform failure and the election defeat of President Soglo of Benin in the mid-1990s, at the hands of an informal alliance of trade unions and opposition parties (Kiragu and Mukandala, 2004).

We would draw the attention of conservative-minded readers, who may feel they have had little to show for our enquiry up to now, that despite the 'pro-poor' definition of development which we have espoused in this volume, our 'institutionalized social energy' account turns out to be ideologically neutral, with equal application to policies of any political complexion – including 'anti-poor' ones.

Table 9.2 Institutionalized social energy: an account of the stages of policy success

POLICY STAGE	EXAMPLE	THREAT TO SUCCESS
An upsurge of '*social energy*' ...	Democratization in Brazil (Chapter 2)	Policy lacks popular roots or is imposed (structural adjustment policies)
Generates a policy *idea* ...	Microfinance in Bangladesh (Chapter 5)	
or highlights an existing idea ...	Income transfers borrowed from the Basic Income European Network (Chapter 2)	Sterile oppositionism (Chapter 6)
around which a *coalition* assembles ...	'the coalition' in Nampula, Mozambique (Chapter 8)	Sabotage or competing coalitions (Chapter 6)
which throws up a *leader* who gets the idea on the policy agenda ...	Suplicy in Brazil, Salinas and other Latin American leaders (Chapters 2 and 4)	Leadership is weak (succession of presidents in Venezuela, Chapter 4)
and overcomes opposition from supporters of the old dispensation.	Deliberate weakening of teachers' unions in Latin America (Chapter 4)	Opposition to reform is too strong (Kiragu and Mukandala, 2004)
The coalition is *institutionalized*, empowering beneficiaries and deflecting patrons and rent-seekers ...	Health councils and conferences in Brazil (Chapter 7)	Patrons or rent-seekers capture the policy (partial capture of housing policy, Chapter 6)
and the policy is consolidated through *feedback* to adapt it to changing circumstances.	Innovation in microfinance products in Bangladesh (Chapter 5)	Policy entropy (macroeconomic policy in Indonesia, Chapter 3; universal access education policy in Latin America, Chapter 4)

The distance we have traveled to arrive at this account becomes clear when we compare it with a standard model of the public policy process such as that of Jenkins (1978), with its stages of initiation, information, consideration, decision, implementation, evaluation and termination.[10] In a nutshell, where Jenkins' model is rational, ours is political (which is not to say that 'political policy' is necessarily irrational). However, we hope that our account is not idiosyncratic. In its stress on the social origins of policy ideas and coalitions, it shares much with those accounts that emphasize the sociology of knowledge and the politics of ideas in policy processes (e.g. Bebbington *et al.*, 2006); and in its stress on the multifarious membership of policy coalitions, in which the state is not necessarily the leading member, it aligns itself with Houtzager's (2003) polity approach. This is apart from those writers we have referenced from whom we have drawn inspiration – and not least from the contributors to this volume.

Further research

Research is hydra-headed: we resolve research problems only to see others sprout in their place. The limitations of our research strategy are a specific reason for that happening here. If the results of our enquiry have vindicated our decision to look at development policy through the lens of success, then first and foremost we call for further analyses of success. There are frequently cited examples of 'success' about which we know surprisingly little. Economic growth in Malaysia and Mauritius are two which have been invoked in this collection (there are of course many more examples). We saw in Chapter 1 that it is not clear how much Mauritius owes to a World Bank structural adjustment loan in the early 1980s and how much to the earlier indigenous decision to launch an all-island Free Trade Zone. Nor is it clear how we should compare Malaysia with an account like Hofman *et al.*'s in this volume of growth in neighbouring Indonesia. Such analyses may wish to use the criteria for success (durability etc.) and at least the standard of evidence that we have established here, but they will take our enquiry to a deeper level if they are based on fresh primary research rather than looking sideways at their authors' previous research as our contributors have done (and as we intended that they would).

Paraphrasing Mahatma Gandhi's famous remark, our contributors tend to agree that democratic development 'would be a good idea': they remain democrats at heart even where it is authoritarian success that they discuss (Hofman *et al.* and Grindle). There is even the hope in Jackson's chapter that policy success will strengthen democratic legitimacy. While there may be no statistical correlation between democracy and growth, as Mushtaq Khan has pointed out, we can still seek examples beyond the possibly exceptional case of Brazil where democracy has gone hand-in-hand with development success, bucking the patronage and rent-seeking trend about which authors like Khan and Anne Krueger are so pessimistic. Providing an answer to this second research question of ours will throw light on the very large but very important issue of the relative viability of state-led and NGO-led (not to mention private sector-led) development.

A third research question which our emphasis on development policy in the long run has created, somewhat to our editorial surprise, concerns the trajectory of implementation. Are policies doomed to atrophy, as Grindle implies they must, or are they able to renew themselves, as Hulme and Moore imply that they can? Again, we need examples to supplement Hulme and Moore's account of microfinance in Bangladesh. In this context it will be interesting to see if empowering those who support the objectives of pro-poor reform and using their feedback to adapt policy to changing circumstances is as important as our cases suggest. There may well be other factors that we have overlooked, possibly those factors of professional content or policy management about which we have had so little to say.

The fourth and final question concerns the origin of policy ideas. The creative ferment from which they emerge takes place beneath the policy analysis radar. For example, it took a good number of years for microfinance in Bangladesh to come to the attention of scholars, by which time the gestation was long over. Again in the social capital tradition, we know quite a lot about the social movements from which policy emerges, and at the other end of the policy process we know quite a lot about policies once they are in the public arena. But between those two extremes we know little. It would be very useful to have more accounts that are as close to the data as Melo's and Jackson's are here.

Suggestions for policymakers

We come now to the practical implications of our findings, even though the suggestions we will make come with a health warning because of the nature of our research strategy. Our expanded view of the policy community means that we will address social activists as well as the government and development agency officials to whom recommendations in volumes like this are usually confined.

State officials, both elected and appointed, should develop antennae that will enable them to scan for winners on which to base their policies in the ever-bubbling pot of social ideas and inventions: outside agencies may be more fertile sources than government ministries and departments. Officials will increase the likelihood of their policies materializing and sticking by making common cause with groups outside government who share their commitments, and by giving them a formal institutional role. Such groups can be a sounding board for the appropriateness of policies, allowing running repairs that will keep the policies on course. It is wise to give as few hostages to fortune in the form of concessions to hostile groups as possible.

Social activists should think whether counterparts' success in influencing government policy in Brazil, Mozambique and (for housing policy) Chile, the Philippines and South Africa is a precedent for moving from opposition to constructive engagement – from '*protesta*' to '*propuesta*' – and uniting in a policy coalition with like-minded state officials. The frustrations of working with the state are substantial, but so are the potential rewards. Activists should try to channel at least some of their 'social energy' into state structures, and avoid the vicious circle where dissatisfaction with state corruption and inefficiency leads to setting up parallel structures which further erode state capacity, and so round again.[11] They should stay engaged through implementation, firstly by lobbying to be included in a formal institutional structure that will help ensure that the policy is not hijacked by patrons and freeloaders, and then by giving feedback that will contribute to the policy staying on track rather than atrophying.

Development agencies should consolidate the view to which many of them already subscribe that successful policy largely comes from inside, and in normal conditions cannot be induced by an outside agency – however bitter a pill that may be for some agencies to swallow. Since they are committed to supporting 'what works', they should use their purchasing power to commission studies that will help them understand long-run policy success and pick winners.

For all three alike, it is important to identify the policy leader who at the policy inception stage will be the battering ram that gets a policy on to the statute book. And lastly, the *leaders* themselves should recognize that their role is to personify the policy, and stay close to the people who put them where they are. They should have Mandela and not Muzorewa as their role model.

Celebrating success

In his eulogy for the Irish poet William Butler Yeats, W. H. Auden (1966: 143) said that it was part of a poet's job to teach the free man how to praise.[12] Sober-sided policy analysts as well as ecstatic poets do well to remember that giving credit where credit is due is part of our job. The seven cases in this collection, despite their scrupulous authors' many and proper qualifications, provide serious evidence of policy success on a large scale which has been sustained for a decade or longer, often against the odds, evidence that takes the form of impact on human development and social and political life. Even professional students of development are not immune from the prevailing image of the Third World as a place of famine, fire and flood, and it is salutary to remind ourselves occasionally of what has been achieved in development policy, and to learn and draw inspiration from the reminder. That is the simple thought with which we began this enquiry, and with which we now end it.

Notes

1. Malaysia during the period in question has been variously labeled a 'quasi-democracy' (Zakaria, 1989), 'semi-democracy' (Case, 1995) and, perhaps most expressively, a 'repressive-responsive regime' (Crouch, 1996).
2. However, Melo also warns against the quasi-psychological discussion of leadership in which we are about to indulge.
3. It may be useful to list the items of French and Raven's classic taxonomy of individual power. As well as expert power, they are legitimate power, reward power, coercive power and 'referent power' (an individual's ability to generate respect or affection).
4. The problem may also be compounded by a lack of widely accepted models of social reform (see Chapter 2 on this point).
5. Jackson's chapter is in a third category, as an example of reverse causation where it is his chosen policy that strengthens democracy rather than vice-versa.
6. It is worth noting that Hulme and Moore are as critical of Bangladesh's private banks as they are of the government.
7. Hofman *et al.*'s chapter, with its account of aid amounting to over 30% of government spending in 1967, might seem to be an exception. But even here, Hofman *et al.* say that donor influence on economic policy in that period came partly in the oblique form of Ford Foundation scholarships that allowed the 'technocrats' to study in the US; and of course the IMF's role in the 1997 Crisis remains controversial.
8. We are grateful to Anne-Marie Goetz for suggesting this point (though not the football analogy) at the first of the seminars from which this collection derives.

9 Notwithstanding the emphasis on group solidarity and group-based guarantees, microfinance schemes typically produce individual entrepreneurs, not group-based enterprise, and far less social movements.

10 More recent accounts have challenged systems models like Jenkins', but mostly because they are mechanistic and over-simple, rather than because they are apolitical: see Hill (2005).

11 It is tremendously intriguing to note that just as completed this volume in February 2007, Muhammad Yunus, about whom we have had so much to say, announced that he intended to enter politics in Bangladesh.

12 As with the reference to Paul Simon at the start of this volume, obscurantist copyright restrictions prevent us from quoting Auden's own words as we wanted to do.

References

ACHR, CODI and IIED (2004) *Catalysing pro-poor development, the role of savings and savings organizations: Key issues arising from an international workshop on housing finance and poverty*. Bangkok and London: International Institute for Environment and Development.

Ackerley, B. (1995) 'Testing the tools of development: Credit programmes, loan involvement and women's empowerment', *IDS Bulletin*, 26, 3: 56–67.

Adams, D., D. Graham and J. von Pischke (1984) *Undermining rural development with cheap credit*. Boulder: Westview Press.

Ames, B. (2001) *The deadlock of democracy in Brazil*. Ann Arbor: University of Michigan Press.

Arretche, M. (2003) 'Financiamento federal e gestão local de políticas sociais: O difícil equilíbrio entre regulação, responsabilidade e autonomia', *Ciência e Saúde Coletiva*, 8, 2.

Arretche, M. (2004) 'Federalismo e políticas sociais no Brasil: problemas de coordenação e autonomia', *São Paulo em Perspectiva*, 18, 2.

Arrossi, S., F. Bombarolo, J. Hardoy, D. Mitlin, L. Coscio and D. Satterthwaite (1994) *Funding community initiatives*. London: Earthscan.

Athias, R., A. Shankland and R. Nonato (2004) 'Saber tradicional e participação indígena em políticas públicas de saúde na Região do Rio Negro', in *Estudos de Caso do Olhar Crítico* (CD-ROM edition). Rio de Janeiro: ActionAid Brasil.

Auden, W. H. (1966) 'In memory of W. B. Yeats', in *Collected shorter poems*. London: Faber and Faber, 141–3.

Ballesteros, M. and D. Vertido (2004) 'Can group credit work for housing loans? Some evidence from the CMP', *Policy Notes No. 2004–05*. Manila: Philippine Institute for Development Studies (PIDS).

Bardill, J. (2000) *Report of the mid-term evaluation mission*. New York: UNCDF.

Barry, D. (1991) 'Managing the bossless team: Lessons in distributed leadership', *Organizational Dynamics*, 21: 31–47.

Bates, R. (1981) *Markets and states in tropical Africa*. Berkeley: University of California Press.

Baumann, T. (2004) *Housing finance in South Africa*, mimeo, Cape Town: Bay Research and Consultancy Services.

Baumann, T. and J. Bolnick (2001) 'Out of the frying pan into the fire: The limits of loan finance in a capital subsidy context', *Environment and Urbanization*, 13, 2: 103–16.

Baumann, T., J. Bolnick and D. Mitlin (2004) 'The age of cities and organizations of the urban poor: The work of the South African Homeless People's Organization', in D. Mitlin and D. Satterthwaite (eds) *Empowering squatter citizens*. London: Earthscan, 193–215.

Baumann, T. and D. Mitlin (2003) 'The South African Homeless People's Federation: Investing in the poor', *Small Enterprise Development*, 14, 1: 32–41.

Baumgartner, F. and B. Jones (1993) *Agendas and instability in American politics*. Chicago: University of Chicago Press.

Bebbington, A. (1999) 'Capitals and capabilities: A framework for analyzing peasant viability, rural livelihoods and poverty', *World Development*, 27: 2021–44.

Bebbington, A., M. Woolcock, S. Guggenheim and E. Olson (eds) (2006) *The search for empowerment: Social capital as idea and practice at the World Bank*. Bloomfield: Kumarian.

Belo, A. (1999) *Relatório do conselho consultivo em Mogovolas*. Nampula: DPPF.

Bennett, L., M. Goldberg and P. Hunte (1996) 'Ownership and sustainability: Lessons on group-based financial services from South Asia', *Journal of International Development*, 8, 2: 271–88.

Besley, T. and R. Kanbur (1991) 'The principles of targeting', in V. Balasubramanyam and S. Lall (eds) *Current issues in development economics*. London: Macmillan Education, 69–90.

Bheenick, R. and M. Schapiro (1989) 'Mauritius: A case study of the export processing zone', in *Successful development in Africa: Case studies of projects, programs and policies*. Washington D.C: World Bank Economic Development Institute, Analytical Case Studies No. 1, 97–127.

Biersteker, T. (1995) 'The "triumph" of liberal economic ideas in the developing world', in B. Stallings (ed.) *Global change, regional response: The new international context of development*. Cambridge: Cambridge University Press, 174–97.

Birdsall, N. and A. de la Torre (2001) *Washington Contentious: Economic Policies for Social Equity in Latin America*. Washington, D.C: Carnegie Endowment for International Peace and the Inter-American Dialogue.

Birdsall, N., D. Ross and R. Sabot (1995) 'Inequality and Growth Reconsidered: Lessons from East Asia', *World Bank Economic Review*, 9, 3.

Bohman, J. and W. Rehg (eds) (1997) *Deliberative democracy: Essays on reason and politics*. Cambridge: MIT Press.

Bond, R. and D. Hulme (1999) 'Process approaches to development: Theory and Sri Lankan practice', *World Development*, 27: 1339–58.

Boonyabancha, S. (2004) 'A decade of change: from the Urban Community Development Office to the Community Organization Development Institute in Thailand', in D. Mitlin and D. Satterthwaite (eds) *Empowering squatter citizens*. London: Earthscan, 25–53.

Booth, A. (1988) *Agricultural development in Indonesia*. Sydney: Allen and Unwin.

Booth, A. (1998) *The Indonesian economy in the nineteenth and twentieth centuries: A history of missed opportunities*. London: Macmillan.

Booth, A. (2002) 'Growth Collapses in Indonesia: A Comparison of the 1930s and the 1990s', *Itinerario (European Journal of Overseas History)*, vol. 3/4: 73–99.

Booth, A. and P. McCawley (eds) (1981) *The Indonesian economy during the Soeharto era*. Petaling Jaya: Oxford University Press.

Borowczak, W., E. Collier, D. O'Sullivan, A. Orre and G. Thompson (2004) *Mid-term evaluation report (Moz/01/C01 – Moz/01/001)*. New York: UNCDF.

Bourguignon, F., F. Ferreira and P. Leite (2003) 'Conditional cash transfers, schooling and child labor: Micro-simulating Brazil's *Bolsa Escola* programme', *World Bank Economic Review*, 17, 2: 229–54.

BRAC (2005) *BRAC at a glance September 2005*, http://www.brac.net/ataglance.htm.

Brazil National Congress (1999) *Relatório final*, Brasilia: Comissão Especial sobre Pobreza.

Brown, M. and D. Hosking (1986) 'Distributed leadership and skilled performance as successful organization in social movements', *Human Relations*, 39: 65–79.
Buckley, G. (1996) 'Financing the Jua Kali sector in Kenya: The K-REP Juhudi scheme and Kenya Industrial Estates Informal Sector Programme', in D. Hulme and P. Mosley (eds) *Finance against poverty*, Volume II. London: Routledge, 271–332.
Burns, J. (1978) *Leadership*. New York: Harper and Row.
Case, W. (1995) 'Malaysia: Aspects and audiences of legitimacy', in M. Alagappa (Ed.) *Political legitimacy in South east Asia*. Stanford: Stanford University Press, 69–107.
Chambers, R. (1983) *Rural development: Putting the last first*. London: Longman.
Chambers, R. (1994) 'Participatory Rural Appraisal (PRA): Challenges, potential and paradigm', *World Development*, 22: 1–17.
Chowdhury, A. (1989) *Let grassroots speak: People's participation, self-help groups and NGOs in Bangladesh*. Dhaka: University Press.
Christoplos, I. (1997) 'Public services, complex emergencies and the humanitarian imperative: Perspectives from Angola', in M. Minogue, C. Polidano and D. Hulme (eds) *Beyond the New Public Management: Changing ideas and practices in governance*. Cheltenham: Edward Elgar, 260–77.
Claessens, S., D. Klingenbiel and L. Laeven (2003) 'Resolving systemic crisis: Policies and institutions', *Mimeo*. Washington D.C: World Bank, September.
CMP Bulletin (1998) National Congress of CMP Originators and Social Development Organizations for Low-income Housing, January.
CMP Bulletin (2003) National Congress of CMP Originators and Social Development Organizations for Low-income Housing, July, *SELAVIP*, October 2003: 49–52.
Coelho, D., C. Lubambo and M. Melo (eds) (2005) *Desenho institucional e participação política: Experiências no Brasil contemporâneo*. Rio de Janeiro: Vozes.
Coelho, V., A. Araújo and M. Montoya (2002) 'Deliberative fora and the democratization of social policies in Brazil', *IDS Bulletin*, 33, 2: 65–73.
Cohen, J. and C. Sabel (1997) 'Directly-Deliberative Polyarchy' European Law Journal, vol. 3, no. 4 (December 1997): 313–42.
Cole, D. and B. Slade (1996) *Building a modern financial system: The Indonesian experience*. Cambridge: Cambridge University Press.
Commission for Africa (2005) *Our common interest: Report of the Commission for Africa*, http://www.commissionforafrica.org/english/report/introduction.html, accessed April 25, 2005.
Condy, A. and J. Negrao (1999) *Mozambique Country Report, UNCDF Donor Evaluation 1998–1999*. New York: UNCDF.
Connolly, P. (2004a) 'The Mexican National Popular Housing Fund', in D. Mitlin and D. Satterthwaite (eds) *Empowering squatter citizens*. London: Earthscan, 82–111.
Connolly, P. (2004b) *Housing finance in Mexico*, mimeo.
Copestake, J. (1995) 'Poverty-oriented financial service programmes: Room for improvement?', *Savings and Development*, 19, 4: 417–35.
Cordeiro, S., Cornwall, A. and N. Delgado (2004) *A Luta pela Participação e pelo controle social: O caso do conselho municipal de saúde do Cabo de Santo Agostinho, Pernambuco*. Rio de Janeiro: ActionAid Brasil, Mimeo.

Cornwall, A. (2000) *Beneficiary, consumer, citizen: Perspectives on participation for poverty reduction*, Sida Studies 2, Stockholm.
Cornwall, A. (forthcoming) 'Negotiating participation in a Brazilian Health Council', in A. Cornwall and V. Coelho (eds) *Spaces for change? The politics of participation in new democratic arenas*. London: Zed.
Cornwall, A. (2004) 'New democratic spaces: The politics of institutionalised participation', *IDS Bulletin*, 35, 2: 1–10.
Cornwall, A., J. Romano and A. Shankland (forthcoming) 'Cultures of politics, spaces of power: Brazilian experiences of participation in governance', IDS Working Paper.
Côrtes, S. (1998) 'Conselhos Municipais de Saúde: Avaliações otimistas e pessimistas', *Ciência e Saúde Coletiva*, 3, 1.
Costa, M. (2004) 'Luta pela Reforma Sanitária', in *Sistematizações do olhar crítico* (CD-ROM edition). Rio de Janeiro: ActionAid Brasil.
Costa, R. (2002) 'Descentralização, financiamento e regulação: A reforma do sistema público de saúde no Brasil durante a década de 1990', *Revista de Sociologia e Política*, 18.
Cowen, M. and R. Shenton (1996) *Doctrines of development*. London: Routledge.
Cowen, M. and R. Shenton (1998) 'Agrarian doctrines of development: Part 1', *Journal of Peasant Studies*, 25: 49–76.
Crouch, H. (1996) *Government and society in Malaysia*. Ithaca: Cornell University Press.
Crush, J. (Ed.) (1995) *The power of development*. London: Routledge.
Cummings, J. and D. DiPasquale (1997) 'The spatial implications of housing policy in Chile', mimeo. Boston: City Research.
Curtis, D. (1994) 'Owning without owners, managing with few managers: Lessons from Third World irrigators', in S. Wright (Ed.) *Anthropology of organizations*. London: Routledge, 56–67.
Dagnino, E. (2005) 'Meanings of citizenship in Latin America', Brighton: Institute of Development Studies, Working Paper 258.
Dagnino, E., A. Olvera and A. Panfichi (2006) 'Para uma outra leitura da disputa pela construção democrática na América Latina', in E. Dagnino, A. Olvera and A. Panfichi (eds) *A disputa pela construção democrática na América Latina*. Sao Paulo: Paz e Terra.
Daley-Harris, S. (2005) *State of the Microcredit Summit campaign report*, http://www.results.org.au/information/State%20of%20the%20Campaign%20Report%202005.pdf, accessed December 17 2005.
Daphnis, F. and B. Ferguson (eds) (2004) *Housing micro-finance: A guide to practice*. Bloomfield: Kumarian.
Davies, H., S. Nutley and P. Smith (2000) *What works? Evidence-based policy and practice in public services*. Bristol: Policy Press.
DeLeon, P. (1978) 'Public policy termination: An end and a beginning', *Policy Analysis*, 4: 369–92.
DFID (Department for International Development) (2000) *Realising human rights for poor people*. London and East Kilbride: DFID.
DFID (2005) *Drivers of change*, http://www.grc-exchange.org/g_themes/political-systems_drivers.html, accessed May 25, 2005.
Dick, H. (1985) 'Survey of recent developments', *Bulletin of Indonesian Economic Studies*, 21, 3: 1–23.

Dick, H. (2002) 'State, society and institutional learning: Lessons of the 19–20th centuries', paper presented at International Institute for Social History, Amsterdam, February 25.

DiMaggio, P. and W. Powell (1983) 'The iron cage revisited: Institutional isomorphism and collective rationality in organizational fields', *American Sociological Review*, 48: 147–60.

Dolowitz, D. and D. Marsh (1996) 'Who learns what from whom? A review of the policy transfer literature', *Political Studies*, 44: 343–57.

Dolowitz, D. and D. Marsh (2000) 'Learning from abroad: The role of policy transfer in contemporary policy-making', *Governance*, 13: 5–24.

Domínguez, J. (1996) *Technopols: Freeing politics and markets in Latin America in the 1990s*. University Park, PA: Penn State University Press.

Dornbusch, R. and S. Edwards (eds) (1991) *The Macroeconomics of populism in Latin America*. Chicago: University of Chicago Press.

DPPF (Direcção Provincial de Plano e Finanças) (1998) Video recording of opening meeting of Consultative Council in Meucate DPPF – Nampula.

DPPF (1999) *PPFD project progress report 4*. Nampula: DPPF.

DPPF (2000) *PPFD project progress report 5*. Nampula: DPPF.

DPPF (2005) *Metodologia do PES Orçamento Distrital (execução 2005 e elaboração 2006)*. Nampula: DPPF.

Draibe, S. (2002a) 'Social policies in the nineties', in R. Baumann (Ed.) *Brazil in the 1990s: An economy in transition*. London: Palgrave.

Draibe, S. (2002b) 'The Brazilian welfare state in perspective: Old issues, new possibilities', in J. Dixon and R. Scheurell (eds) *The state of social welfare: The twentieth century in cross-national review*. Westport, Connecticut: Greenwood.

Easterly, W. (2006) *The white man's burden: Why the West's efforts to aid the rest have done so much ill and so little good*. New York: Penguin.

ECIAfrica (2004) *Companion Report: Mozambique – Independent Programme Impact Assessment (PIA) of the UNCDF Local Development Programme*. Woodmead, South Africa: ECIAfrica.

Edwards, M. and D. Hulme (eds) (1992) *Making a difference: NGOs and development in a changing world*. London: Earthscan.

Elson, R. (2001) *Suharto: A political biography*. New York: Cambridge University Press.

Escobar, A. (1995) *Encountering development: The making and unmaking of the Third World*. Princeton: Princeton University Press.

Evans, P. (1995) *Embedded autonomy: States and industrial transformation*. Princeton: Princeton University Press.

Evans, P. (Ed.) (1996) 'State-Society Synergy: Government Action and Social Capital in Development', special supplement to *World Development*, June, 1996, vol. 24, no. 6.

Evans, P. and J. Rauch (1999) 'Bureaucracy and growth: A cross-national analysis of the effects of "Weberian" state structures on economic growth', *American Sociological Review*, 64: 748–65.

FAO, World Bank and IDB (2002) BRAZIL. *Projeto Fome Zero: Report of the Joint FAO/IDB/WB/Transition Team Working Group*: www.fao.org/docrep/005/ac829e/ac829e00.htm, accessed January 26 2007.

Ferguson, J. (1994) *The anti-politics machine: Development, depoliticization and bureaucratic power in Lesotho*. Minneapolis: University of Minnesota Press.

Fernandez, V. (2004) *Housing finance – the case of Chile*. mimeo.

Fine, B. (2001) 'Preface', in B. Fine, C. Lapavitsas and J. Pincus (eds) *Development policy in the twenty-first century: Beyond the Washington consensus*. London: Routledge, x–xvi.

Fiorina, M. and K. Shepsle (1989) 'Formal theories of leadership: Agents, agenda setters and entrepreneurs', in B. Jones (Ed.) *Leadership and Politics*. Lawrence: University Press of Kansas, 17–41.

Foster, C. (2005) *British government in crisis*. London: Hart.

Fox, J. (1996) 'How does civil society thicken? The political construction of social capital in Mexico', *World Development,* 24: 1089–1103.

French, J. and B. Raven (1959) 'Bases of Social Power', in D. Cartwright (Ed.) *Studies in social power*. Ann Arbor: University of Michigan.

Fuglesang, A. and D. Chandler (1987) *Participation as process: What can we learn from Grameen Bank*? Oslo: NORAD.

Fung, A. and E. Wright (eds) (2003) *Deepening democracy: Institutional innovation in empowered participatory governance*. London: Verso.

Gabre-Madhin, E. and S. Haggblade (2004) 'Success in African agriculture: Results of an expert survey', *World Development,* 23: 745–66.

Galli, R. E. (2003) *People's spaces and state spaces: Land and governance in Mozambique*. Oxford: Lexington Books.

Garnelo, L., G. Macedo and L. C. Brandão (2003) *Os povos indígenas e a construção das políticas de saúde no Brasil*. Brasília: PAHO.

Gaventa, J. (2002) 'Introduction: Exploring citizenship, participation and accountability', *IDS Bulletin*, 33, 2: 1–11.

Geddes, B. (1995) 'The uses and limitations of rational choice', in P. Smith (Ed.) *Latin America in comparative perspective: New approaches to methods and analysis*. Boulder, CO: Westview Press.

Gilbert, A. (2002a) 'Power, ideology and the Washington Consensus: The development and spread of Chilean housing policy', *Housing Studies*, 17, 2: 305–24.

Gilbert, A. (2002b) '"Scan globally; reinvent locally": Reflecting on the origins of South Africa's capital housing subsidy policy', *Urban Studies*, 39, 10: 1911–33.

Gilbert, A. (2004) 'Helping the poor through housing subsidies: Lessons from Chile, Colombia and South Africa', *Habitat International*, 28: 13–40.

Goetz, A. and R. Sen Gupta (1996) 'Who takes the credit? Gender, power and control over loan use in rural credit programs in Bangladesh', *World Development*, 24: 45–63.

Gomez, E. and K. Jomo (1997) *Malaysia's political economy: Politics, patronage and profits*. Cambridge: Cambridge University Press.

Gough, I. and A. McGregor (2004) 'Human well-being: Communicating between the universal and the local: Guest editors' introduction', *Global Social Policy*, 4, 3: 275–6.

Gough, I. and A. McGregor (eds) (2007) *Wellbeing in developing countries. From theory to research*. Cambridge: CUP.

Government of Singapore (2004) *The enterprise challenge*, http://www.tec.gov.sg/home.htm, accessed October 14 2004.

Government of the United States (2004) *Vice-President Gore's national partnership for reinventing government*, http://govinfo.library.unt.edu/npr/, accessed October 14 2004.

Graham, C. and M. Naím (1999) 'The political economy of institutional reform', in N. Birdsall, C. Graham and R. Sabot (eds) *Beyond trade offs: Market reforms and equitable growth*. Washington D.C: Brookings Institution/IADB.
Grameen Bank (2005) *Grameen Bank at a Glance March 2005*. http://www.grameen-info.org/bank/GBGlance.htm, accessed May 24 2005.
Grameen Foundation USA (2004) *Annual Report 2004*. Washington D.C: Grameen Foundation USA. http://www.gfusa.org/docs/about_us/GFUSA-AnnualReport2004.pdf, accessed May 24 2005.
Gray, C. (1982) 'Survey of recent developments', in *Bulletin of Indonesian Economic Developments*.
Grindle, M. (2004) *Despite the odds: The contentious politics of education reform*. Princeton, N.J.: Princeton University Press.
Grindle, M. (1997) 'Divergent cultures? When public organizations perform well in developing countries', *World Development*, 25: 481–95.
Grindle, M. (1996) *Challenging the state: Crisis and innovation in Latin America and Africa*. Cambridge: Cambridge University Press.
Grindle, M. (1986) *State and countryside: Development policy and agrarian politics in Latin America*. Baltimore, MD: Johns Hopkins University Press.
Guest, D. (1997) 'Human resource management and performance: A review and research agenda', *International Journal of Human Resource Management*, 8: 263–76.
Guggenheim, S. (2006) 'Crises and contradictions: Understanding the origins of a community development project in Indonesia', in A. Bebbington, M. Woolcock, S. Guggenheim and E. Olson (eds) *The Search for empowerment: Social capital as idea and practice at the World Bank*. Bloomfield: Kumarian, 109–44.
Gulhati, R. (1990) 'Who makes economic policy in Africa and how?', *World Development*, 18: 1147–61.
Gulhati, R. and R. Nallari (1989) *Successful stabilization and recovery in Mauritius*. Washington D.C: World Bank Economic Development Institute, Analytical Case Studies No. 5.
Haas, P. (1992) 'Epistemic communities and international policy coordination: Introduction', *International Organization*, 46, 1: 1–35.
Haggard, S. and R. Kaufman (eds) (1992) *The politics of economic adjustment*. Princeton, N.J: Princeton University Press.
Hanlon, J. (1991) *Mozambique: Who calls the shots*? Bloomington IN: Indiana University Press.
Hanlon, J. (2001) *Killing the goose that laid the golden eggs*. Maputo: Metical.
Hanlon, J. (2002) 'Bank corruption becomes site of struggle in Mozambique', *Review of African Political Economy*, 91: 53–72.
Hanson, M. (1995) 'Democratization and decentralization in Colombian education', *Comparative Education Review* 39, 1: 101–19.
Hardoy, J. and D. Satterthwaite (1989) *Squatter citizen: Life in the urban Third World*. London: Earthscan.
Hardoy, J., D. Mitlin and D. Satterthwaite (2001) *Environmental problems in Third World cities*. London: Earthscan.
Harrison, G. (1998) 'Marketing legitimacy in rural Mozambique: The case of Mecufi district, northern Mozambique', *Journal of Modern African Studies*, 36, 4: 569–91.
Hashemi, S. (1997) 'Those left behind: A note on targeting the hardcore poor', in G. Wood and I. Sharif (eds) *Who needs credit? Poverty and finance in Bangladesh*. Dhaka: University Press Limited, 249–57.

Hashemi, S., S. Schuler and A. Riley (1996) 'Rural credit programs and women's employment in Bangladesh', *World Development,* 24: 635–53.
Heaver, R. and A. Israel (1986) *Country commitment to development projects.* Washington D.C: World Bank Discussion Paper No. 4.
Heclo, H. and A. Wildavsky (1974) *The private government of public money: Community and policy inside British politics.* London: Macmillan.
Hedrick-Wong, Y., B. Kramsjo and A. Sabri (1997) 'Experiences and challenges in credit and poverty alleviation programs in Bangladesh: The case of Proshika', in G. Wood and I. Sharif (eds) *Who needs credit? Poverty and finance in Bangladesh.* Dhaka: University Press, 145–70.
Heller, P. (1996) 'Social capital as a product of class mobilization and state intervention: Industrial workers in Kerala, India', in P. Evans (ed.) *State-society synergy: Government and social capital in development.* Berkeley, CA: University of California Press, 48–85.
Hennessy, P. (1993) *Never again.* London: Jonathan Cape.
HIID (1995) *Prospects for manufactured exports during Repelita VI – Report to the Department of Industry and Trade, Republic of Indonesia.* Jakarta: Harvard Institute for International Development.
Hilderbrand, M. (2002) 'Capacity building', in C. Kirkpatrick, R. Clarke and C. Polidano (eds) *Handbook of development policy and management.* Cheltenham: Edward Elgar, 323–32.
Hill, H. (1996) *The Indonesian economy since 1966.* Cambridge: Cambridge University Press.
Hill, M. (2005) *The public policy process.* Harlow: Pearson Longman.
Hirschman, A. (1981) 'Policymaking and policy analysis in Latin America – A return journey', in A. Hirschman, *Essays in trespassing: Economics to politics and beyond.* Cambridge: Cambridge University Press.
Hirschman, A. (1984) *Getting ahead collectively.* New York: Pergamon.
Hoff, K. (2003) 'Paths of institutional development: A view from economic history', *World Bank Research Observer,* 18, 2: 227–48.
Hoff, K., A. Braverman and J. Stiglitz (eds) (1993) *The economics of rural organization: Theory, practice and policy.* New York: Oxford University Press.
Hofman, B., E. Roderik-Jones, and K. Thee, (2004) 'Indonesia: Rapid growth, Weak institutions', paper presented at 'Scaling up poverty reduction: A global learning process and conference', Shanghai, May 25–27, 2004.
Houtzager, P. (2003) 'Introduction: From polycentrism to the Polity', in P. Houtzager and M. Moore (eds) *Changing Paths: International development and the new politics of inclusion.* Ann Arbor: University of Michigan Press, 1–31.
Houtzager P. with J. Pattenden (2003) 'Coalition building from below', in P. Houtzager and M. Moore (eds) *Changing Paths: International development and the new politics of inclusion.* Ann Arbor: University of Michigan Press, 88–118.
Huchzermeyer, M. (2003) 'A legacy of control: The capital subsidy for housing and informal settlement intervention in South Africa', *International Journal of Urban and Regional Research,* 27, 3: 591–612.
Hulme, D. and P. Mosley (1996) *Finance against poverty, Volumes I and II.* London: Routledge.
Human Sciences Research Council (2004) *Fact Sheet: Poverty in South Africa.* Pretoria: Human Sciences Research Council.
Hyden, G., J. Court and K. Thee (2004) *Making sense of governance: Empirical evidence from 16 developing countries.* Boulder, CO: Lynne Rienner.

IDB (Inter-American Development Bank) (2000) *Economic and social progress in Latin America, 2000 Report.* Washington D.C: IDB.

Ikenberry, G. (1990) 'The international spread of privatization policies: Inducements, learning and "policy bandwagoning"', in E. Suleiman and J. Waterbury (eds) *The political economy of public sector reform and privatization.* Boulder, CO: Westview.

Independent, The (2005) 'New BB Governor to turn central bank into a pro-people institution', *The Independent* May 4 2005. http://www.independent-bangladesh.com/news/apr/24/24042005bs.htm, accessed May 24 2005.

IBGE (Instituto Brasileiro de Geografia e Estatística) (2005) *Pesquisa nacional por amostra de domicílios: Acesso e utilização dos serviços de saúde.* Rio de Janeiro: IBGE.

Jackson, D. (2001) *Discussion document: What's new about the Nampula Model? How can it be extended nationally?*, Nampula: Internal PPFD discussion document.

Jackson, D. (2002) 'Local governance approach to social reintegration and economic recovery in post-conflict countries: The view from Mozambique', paper presented at UNCDF/UNBCPR/ Institute of Public Administration Conference on 'A Local Governance approach to Post Conflict Recovery'.

Jackson, D. and D. Lambo (2003) 'Capacitação institutional e formação para planificação distrital: Experiências e desafios', in J. Macuane and B. Weimer (eds) *Governos locais em Moçambique: Desafios de capacitação institutional,* Maputo: Imprensa Universitária (UEM), 145–59.

Jain, P. and M. Moore (2003) *What makes microcredit programmes effective? Fashionable fallacies and workable realities.* IDS Working Paper 177. Brighton: Institute of Development Studies.

Jenkins, W. (1978) *Policy analysis.* London: Martin Robertson.

Jiron, M. and G. Fadda (2003) 'A quality of life assessment to improve urban and housing policies in Chile', Paper presented to the *World Bank Urban Research Symposium* 2003. Washington D.C: World Bank.

John, P. (1998) *Analysing public policy.* London: Pinter.

John, P. and H. Margetts (2003) 'Policy punctuations in the UK: Fluctuations and equilibria in central government expenditure since 1951', *Public Administration,* 81: 411–32.

Johnson, J. and S. Wasty (1993) *Borrower ownership of adjustment programs and the political economy of reform.* Washington D.C: World Bank Discussion Paper No. 199.

Johnson, S. (1999) 'Gender impact assessment in microfinance and microenterprise: Why and how', *Development in practice* (mimeo).

Jomo K. S. (ed). (1998) *Tigers in trouble: Financial governance, liberalization and the crises in East Asia.* London: Zed.

Jones, David (1974) 'The tribune's visitation', in David Jones, *'The sleeping lord' and other fragments,* London: Faber and Faber, 42–58.

Jones, B., F. Baumgartner and J. True (1998) 'Policy punctuations: US budget authority 1947–1995', *Journal of Politics,* 60: 1–33.

Kabeer, N. (1998) *'Money can't buy me love'? Re-evaluating gender, credit and empowerment in rural Bangladesh.* Brighton: Institute of Development Studies, Working Paper 363.

Kabeer, N. (2002) *We don't do credit: Nijera Kori social mobilization and the collective capabilities of the poor in rural Bangladesh*. Dhaka: Nijera Kori.

Kaufmann, D. (1999) *Governance redux: The empirical challenge*, http://www.worldbank.org/wbi/governance/pubs/govredux.html, accessed June 17 2004.

Kaufman, R. and J. Nelson (eds) (2004) *Crucial needs, weak incentives: Social sector reform, democratization and globalization in Latin America*. Baltimore: Johns Hopkins University Press.

Keck, M. and K. Sikkink (1998) *Activists beyond borders: Advocacy networks in international politics*. Ithaca: Cornell University Press.

Kenward, L. (2002) *From the trenches*. Jakarta: CSIS.

Khan, M. (2005) 'Markets, states and democracy: Patron-client networks and the case for democracy in developing countries', *Democratization*, 12: 704–24.

Khandker, S. (2005) 'Microfinance and poverty: Evidence using panel data from Bangladesh', *World Bank Economic Review*, 19: 263–86.

Killick, T. (1998) *Aid and the political economy of policy change*. London: Routledge.

Kiragu, K. and R. Mukandala (2004) *Pay reform and policies report*. Paris: OECD Development Assistance Committee.

Korten, D. (1980) 'Community organization and rural development: A learning process approach', *Public Administration Review*, 40: 480–511.

Kothari, U. and V. Nababsing (1996) *Gender and industrialization: Mauritius, Bangladesh, Sri Lanka*. Port Louis: Editions de l'Océan Indien.

Krueger, A. (1974) 'The political economy of the rent-seeking society', *American Economic Review*, 64, 3: 291–303.

Labra, M. (2001) 'Política e saúde no Chile e no Brasil. Contribuições para uma comparação', *Ciência e Saúde Coletiva*, 6, 2: 361–76.

Labra, M. and J. St. Aubin de Figueiredo (2002) 'Associativismo, participação e cultura cívica: O potencial dos conselhos de saúde', *Ciência e Saúde Coletiva*, 7, 3: 537–47.

Larrañaga, O. (1997) 'Educación y superación de la pobreza en América Latina', in J. Zevallos (Ed.) *Estrategias para reducir la pobreza en América Latina y el Caribe*. Quito, Ecuador: United Nations Development Programme.

Leach, S. and C. Collinge (1998) *Strategic planning and management in local government*. London: Pitman.

Lemos, M. and J. De Oliveira (2004) 'Can water reform survive politics? Institutional change and river basin management in Ceará', *World Development*, 32: 2121–37.

Leonard, D. (1991) *African successes: Four public managers of Kenyan rural development*. Berkeley, CA: University of California Press.

Levy, F. (2002) *Apex institutions In microfinance*, CGAP Occasional Paper 6, http://www.cgap.org/docs/OccasionalPaper_06.pdf, accessed May 24 2005.

Lewis, D., A. Bebbington, S. Batterbury, A. Shah, E. Olson, M. Siddiqi and S. Duvall (2003) 'Practice, power and meaning: Frameworks for studying organizational culture in multi-agency rural development projects', *Journal of International Development*, 15: 541–57.

Lindblom, C. (1959) 'The science of muddling through', *Public Administration Review*, 19: 79–88.

Llanto, G. *et al.* (1998) *A study of housing subsidies in the Philippines: Report submitted to the Housing and Urban Development Coordinating Council (HUDCC).* Manila: Office of the President.

Locke, E. and G. Latham (1990) *A theory of goal-setting and task performance.* New York: Prentice-Hall.

Machel, S. (1985) *Samora Machel: An African revolutionary, Selected speeches and writings.* London: Zed.

Macintyre, A. (2002) *The power of institutions: Political architecture and governance.* Ithaca: Cornell University Press.

MAE (Ministério da Administração Estatal) (2003) *Lei dos orgãos locais.* Maputo: MAE.

Mahoney, J. (2003) 'Long-run development and the legacy of colonialism in Spanish America', *American Journal of Sociology,* 109: 50–106.

Mahoney, J. and R. Snyder (1999) 'Rethinking agency and structure in the study of regime change', *Studies in comparative international development,* 34, 2: 3–32.

Mainwaring, S. (1999) *Rethinking party systems in the third wave of democratization: The case of Brazil.* Stanford: Stanford University Press.

Maio, M. and S. Monteiro (2005) 'Tempos de racialização: O caso da "saúde da população negra" no Brasil', *História, Ciências, Saúde – Manguinhos,* 12, 2.

Mansur, M. (2001) *O financiamento federal da saúde no Brasil: Tendências da década de 1990,* Master's Dissertation, Escola Nacional de Saúde Pública. Rio de Janeiro: FIOCRUZ.

Matin, I. and D. Hulme (2003) 'Programmes for the poorest: Learning from the IGVGD in Bangladesh', *World Development,* 31: 647–65.

Matin, I., S. Rutherford and M. Maniruzzaman (2000) *Exploring client preferences in microfinance: Some observations from SafeSave.* CGAP Focus Note 18, http://www.cgap.org/docs/FocusNote_18.html, accessed May 24 2005.

Mayoux, L. (1995) *From vicious to virtuous circles? Gender and micro-enterprise development.* Geneva: United Nations Research Institute for Social Development.

Mayoux, L. (1998) *Women's empowerment and micro-finance programmes: Approaches, evidence and ways forward.* Milton Keynes: Open University Development Policy and Practice Working Paper No. 41.

McCourt, W. and D. Eldridge (2004) *Global human resource management: Managing people in developing and transitional countries.* Cheltenham: Edward Elgar.

McCourt, W. (2005a) *Path dependence and history in the Malaysian civil service.* University of Manchester: Management, Governance and Development Working Paper No. 12.

McCourt, W. (2005b) *Patrons versus Weberians in the Sri Lankan civil service.* University of Manchester: Management, Governance and Development Working Paper No. 13.

McCourt, W. (2003) 'Political commitment to reform: Civil service reform in Swaziland', *World Development,* 31: 1015–31.

McCourt, W. (2002) 'New Public Management in developing countries', in K. McLaughlin and S. Osborne (eds) *The New Public Management: Current trends and future prospects,* London: Routledge, 227–42.

McCourt, W. and A. Ramgutty-Wong (2003) 'Limits to strategic human resource management: The case of the Mauritian civil service', *International Journal of Human Resource Management,* 14: 600–18.

McVey, R. (1992) 'The case for the disappearing decade,' paper delivered at the Conference on Indonesian Democracy in the 1950s and 1990s, Monash University, December 1992.

Melo, M. (2005) 'O sucesso inesperado das reformas de segunda geração: Federalismo, reformas constitucionais e política social', *Dados – Revista de Ciências Sociais*, 48, 3.

Melo, M. (2003) 'When institutions matter: The politics of administrative, social security and tax reform in Brazil', in B. Schneider and B. Heredia (eds) *Reinventing Leviathan: The political economy of administrative reform in developing countries'*. University of Miami: North-South Center Press.

Melo, M. (1993) 'Anatomia do fracasso: Intermediação de interesses e a reforma das políticas sociais na Nova República', *Dados – Revista de Ciências Sociais*, 36, 1.

Melo, M. and F. Rezende (2004) 'Decentralization and governance in Brazil', in J. Tulchin and A. Selee (eds) *Decentralization and democratic governance in Latin America*. Washington: Woodrow Wilson Center.

Mendes, E. (1998) *O sistema de serviços de saúde no Brasil*. Brasília: PAHO.

Mintrom, M. (1997) 'Policy entrepreneurs and the diffusion of innovation', *American Journal of Political Science*, 41: 738–70.

Mitlin, D. (2003) 'Finance for shelter: Recent history, future perspectives', *Small Enterprise Development*, 14, 1: 11–20.

Moser, C. (1998) 'The asset vulnerability framework: Reassessing urban poverty reduction strategies', *World Development*, 26: 1–19.

MPF (Ministério do Plano e Finanças)/DNPO (1997) *Planificação distrital: Estudo e recomendações*. Maputo: MPF.

MPF/MAE (1998) *Plano distrital de desenvolvimento – Orientações para elaboração e implementação*. Maputo: MPF.

MPF/MAE (2002) *Manual 2 o ciclo anual de planificação e orçamentação*. Maputo: MPF.

Mulgan, G. and D. Albury (2003) *Innovation in the public sector*. London: Cabinet Office.

Naipaul, V. S. (1972) 'The overcrowded barracoon', in *'The overcrowded barracoon' and other articles*. London: André Deutsch, 255–86.

Nasution, A. (1985) 'Survey of recent developments', *Bulletin of Indonesian Economic Studies*, 21, 2: 1–23.

Nasution, A. (1995) 'Survey of recent developments', *Bulletin of Indonesian Economic Studies*, 31, 2: 3–40.

Navarro, J. (2002) *Quienes son los maestros? Carreras e incentivos docentes en América Latina*. Washington D.C: Inter-American Development Bank.

Navarro, J., M. Carnoy and C. de Moura Castro (n.d.) 'Education reform in Latin America and the Caribbean', Washington D.C: Inter-American Development Bank, Background Education Strategy Paper No. 1.

Nelson, J. (2000) 'Reforming social sector governance: A political perspective', in J. Tulchin and A. Garland (eds) *Social development in Latin America*. Boulder CO: Lynne Rienner.

Nelson, J. M. (ed.) (1990) *Economic crisis and policy choice: The politics of adjustment in the Third World*. Princeton, N.J: Princeton University Press.

Netherlands Ministry of Foreign Affairs (2000) *The sectoral approach*. The Hague: Sectoral Approach Support Group.

Nunberg, B. (1997) *Rethinking civil service reform: An agenda for smart government.* Washington D.C: World Bank.

NZ Institute of Economic Research (2002) *New Zealand public sector innovation: Practical prospects based on experience*, http://www.treasury.govt.nz/innovation/nzier-nzpsi.pdf, accessed on April 20 2005.

Ogu, V. I. and J. E. Ogbuozobe (2001) 'Housing policy in Nigeria: towards enablement of private housing development' *Habitat International,* 25: 473–92.

Olaia, J. (2003) Interview during July 2003.

Oliveira, F. (2002) *Saúde da população negra: Brasil, ano 2001*, Brasília: PAHO.

O'Rourke, K. (2002) *Reformasi: The struggle for power in post-Soeharto Indonesia.* Crows Nest, NSW: Allen and Unwin.

Ortiz, E. (1996) *FONHAPO Gestión y desarrollo de un fondo público en apoyo de la producción social de vivienda.* México City: Habitat International Coalition.

Parsons, W. (1995) *Public policy: An introduction to the theory and practice of policy analysis.* Cheltenham: Edward Elgar.

Pearson, S. and E. Monke (1991) Introduction, pp. 1–7 in Pearson, Scott: Walter Falcon; Paul Heytens; Eric Monke & Rosamund Naylor, 1991, *Rice Policy in Indonesia.* Ithaca & London: Cornell University Press.

Peet, R. (2002) 'Ideology, discourse and the geography of hegemony: from socialist to neoliberal development in postapartheid South Africa', *Antipode,* 34, 1: 54–84.

Perkin, E. and J. Court (2005) *Networks and policy processes in international development: A literature review.* London: Overseas Development Institute, Working Paper 252, http://www.odi.org.uk/RAPID/Publications/Documents/WP252.pdf, accessed November 12 2005.

Peters, T. and R. Waterman (1982) *In search of excellence: Lessons from America's best-run companies.* New York: Harper and Row.

Peterson, P. and M. Rom (1990) *Welfare magnets: The case for a national welfare standard.* Washington D.C: Brookings Institute.

Pierson, P. (1994) *Dismantling the welfare state: Reagan, Thatcher and the politics of retrenchment.* Cambridge and New York: Cambridge University Press.

Pijnenburg, B. (2004) *Keeping it vague: Discourses and practices of participation in rural Mozambique.* Wageningen: Wageningen University, doctoral dissertation.

Pinto, J. (1998) 'Innovation in the production of public goods and services', *Public Administration and Development,* 18: 387–97.

PKSF (2002) *Microcredit programs in Bangladesh: Giving a chance to the poor.* http://www.pksf-bd.org/Microcredit_bangladesh.htm, accessed May 24 2005.

PKSF (2004) *Annual Report 2004.* http://www.pksf-bd.org/annual_report2004/annual_report_cont.html, accessed May 24 2005.

Pompe, S. (2002) 'Court corruption in Indonesia: An anatomy of institutional degradation and strategy for recovery', Draft World Bank Report.

Porio, E. with C. S. Crisol, N. Magno, D. Cid and E. Paul (2004) 'The CMP: An innovative social housing programme in the Philippines and its outcomes', in D. Mitlin and D. Satterthwaite (eds) *Empowering Squatter Citizens.* London: Earthscan, 54–81.

Prawiro, R. (1998) *Indonesia's struggle for economic development: Pragmatism in action.* Kuala Lumpur: Oxford University Press.

PREAL (Programa de Promoción de la Reforma Educativa en América Latina y el Caribe) (2001) *Lagging behind: A report card on education in Latin America,* Washington D.C: PREAL (November).

Prebisch, R. (1950) *The economic development of Latin America and its principal problems.* New York: United Nations.

PREM (Poverty Reduction and Economic Management) Sector Unit – South Asia Region (2005) *The economics and governance of non governmental organizations (NGOs) in Bangladesh.* Consultation draft. Washington D.C: World Bank. http://www.lcgbangladesh.org/NGOs/reports/NGO_Report_clientversion.pdf, accessed May 24 2005.

Pressman, J. and A. Wildavsky (1973) *Implementation.* Berkeley, CA: University of California Press.

Preston, P. (2006) 'No president's man', *Observer,* October 15, 2006.

Pritchett, L. and M. Woodcock (2004) 'Solutions when the solution is the problem: Arraying the disarray in development', *World Development,* 32: 191–212.

Pryer, J., S. Rahman and A. Rogers (2005) 'Work-disabling illness as a shock for livelihoods and poverty in Dhaka slums, Bangladesh', *International Planning Studies,* 10, 1: 69–80.

Rawlings, L. (2004) 'A new approach to social assistance: Latin America's experience with conditional cash transfer programmes', Washington, D.C: World Bank, Social Protection Discussion Paper Series 0416.

Reimers, F. (1999) 'Education, poverty and inequality in Latin America', Cambridge, Mass: Harvard Graduate School of Education.

Rhodes, R. (2000) 'The governance narrative: Key findings and lessons from the ESRC's Whitehall programme', *Public Administration,* 78: 345–63.

Rhodes, R. (1997) *Understanding governance: Policy networks, governance reflexivity and accountability.* Buckingham: Open University Press.

Rhyne, E. (2001) *Mainstreaming microfinance: How lending to the poor began, grew and came of age in Bolivia.* Bloomfield, CT: Kumarian Press.

Riker, W. (1986) *The art of political manipulation.* New Haven: Yale University Press.

Robinson, M. (2002) *Microfinance revolution Volume 2: Lessons from Indonesia.* Washington D.C: IBRD/The World Bank.

Rodrik, D. (1999) 'Where did all the growth go? External shock, social conflict and growth collapse', *Journal of Economic Growth,* 4, 4: 385–412.

Rodrik, D. (ed.) (2003) *In search of prosperity: Analytic narratives on economic growth,* Princeton, N.J: Princeton University Press.

Rodrik, D., A. Subramanian and F. Trebbi (2004) 'Institutions rule: The primacy of institutions over geography and integration in economic development', *Journal of Economic Growth,* 9, 2: 131–65.

Rogaly, B. (1996) 'Micro-finance evangelism, "destitute women" and the hard selling of a new anti-poverty formula', *Development in Practice,* 6, 2: 100–12.

Rojas, E. and M. Greene (1995) 'Reaching the poor: Lessons from the Chilean housing experience', *Environment and Urbanization,* 7, 2: 31–50.

Roll, M. (2004) *Between political development and effective poverty reduction: Decentralised governance in rural Mozambique in times of the new development architecture.* Bielefeld, Germany: University of Bielefeld, M. Phil. dissertation.

Romeo, L. (1999) *Decentralised development planning: Issues and early lessons from UNCDF-supported Local Development Fund programmes*, 'Taking risks' background papers.

Romeo, L. (2000) 'Systems experimentation in support of decentralization reforms', in H. Kammaier and H. Damaine (eds) *Decentralization, local governance and rural development*. Bangkok: AIT.

Rondinelli, D. (1993) *Development projects as policy experiments: An adaptive approach to development administration*. London: Routledge.

Sabatier, P. (1988) 'An advocacy coalition framework of policy change and the role of policy-oriented learning therein', *Policy Sciences*, 21: 129–68.

Sachs, J. (2005) *The end of poverty: Economic possibilities for our time*. New York: Penguin.

Samuels, D. (2003) *Ambition, federalism and legislative politics in Brazil*. New York: Cambridge University Press.

Sarrar, S. (2005) 'Libya acts in HIV row with Bulgaria', *The Guardian*, April 13: 17.

Sato, H. (2002) 'Abolition of leprosy isolation policy in Japan: Policy termination through leadership', *Policy Studies Journal*, 30: 29–46.

Scanlon, K. and C. Whitehead (2004) 'Cross country trends in tenure and finance', in European Mortgage Federation (Ed.), *Hypostat 2003: European Housing Finance Review*. Brussels: European Mortgage Federation, 14–20.

Schieflebein, E. and J. Tedesco (1995) *Una nueva oportunidad: El rol de la educación en el desarrollo de América Latina*. Buenos Aires: Santillana.

Schwarz, A. (1994) *A nation in waiting: Indonesia in the 1990s*. London: Allen and Unwin.

Scott, J. (1998) *Seeing like a state: How efforts to improve the human condition have failed*. New Haven: Yale University Press.

Sen, B. and D. Hulme (eds) (2006) *The state of the poorest 2005/2006: Chronic poverty in Bangladesh – Tales of ascent, descent, marginality and persistence*. Dhaka/BIDS and Manchester: IDPM/Chronic Poverty Research Centre, www.chronicpoverty.org, accessed May 24 2005.

Sen, G. (1992) 'Social needs and public accountability: The case of Kerala', in M. Wuyts, M. Mackintosh and T. Hewitt (eds) *Development policy and public action*. Oxford: Oxford University Press, 253–77.

Shahiduzzaman (1999) 'PKSF: A success story', *Bangladesh Observer*, 30 July 1999. http://www.pksf-bd.org/ass.html, accessed May 24 2005.

Shankland, A. and R. Athias (2007) 'Decentralization and difference: Indigenous peoples and health system reform in the Brazilian Amazon', *IDS Bulletin*, Vol. 38, 1 (forthcoming).

Shotton, R. (2000) *Note on financing in decentralization, local governance and rural development*. Bangkok: AIT.

Siebel, H. (2003) 'History matters in microfinance', *Small Enterprise Development*, 14, 2: 10–12.

Silva, P. (2003) 'Serviços de saúde: O dilema do SUS na nova década', *São Paulo em Perspectiva*, 17, 1.

Simon, P. (1973) 'Something so right', in Paul Simon *There goes rhymin' Simon*. Los Angeles: Warner Records.

Sinha, S. (2005) *Microfinance in South Asia: A common heritage and common challenges*, Presentation made to the World Bank Conference on Microfinance in South Asia, 6 December 2005. http://siteresources.worldbank.org/INTINDIA/Resources/SanjaySinha_ppt.pdf, accessed January 15 2006.

Smets, P. (2002) *Housing finance and the urban poor: Building and financing low-income housing in Hyderabad, India*. Amsterdam: Vrije University.

Smith, W., C. Acuña and E. Gamarra (eds) (1994) *Democracy, markets and structural reform in Latin America*. New Brunswick, N.J: Transaction.

Srinivas, P. and D. Sitorus (2004) 'State-owned banks in Indonesia', in G. Caprio, J. Fiechter, R. Litan and M. Pomerleano (eds) *The future of state-owned financial institutions*. Washington D.C: Brookings Institution Press, 123–80.

Stallings, B. (1992) 'International influence on economic policy: Debt, stabilization and structural reform,' in S. Haggard and R. Kaufman (eds) *The politics of economic adjustment*. Princeton, N.J: Princeton University Press.

Stiglitz, J. and S. Yusuf (eds) (2001) *Rethinking the East Asian miracle*. New York: Oxford University Press.

Stone, D. (2000) 'Non-governmental policy transfer: The strategies of independent policy institutes', *Governance*, 13, 1: 45–62.

Stone, D. (2002) 'Using knowledge: The dilemmas of "bridging research and policy"', *Compare*, 32, 3: 285–96.

Suplicy, E. (2002) *Renda de cidadania: A saída é pela porta*. São Paulo: Cortez Editora.

Suryadinata, L. (1979) *Political thinking of the Indonesian Chinese 1900–1995: A source book*. Singapore: Singapore University Press.

Tabor, S. (1992) 'Agriculture in transition', in A. Booth (ed.) *The oil boom and after: Indonesian economic policy*. Oxford: Oxford University Press, 161–203.

Tazi, H. (ed.) (2005) *Performance and transparency: A survey of microfinance in South Asia*. Washington D.C: Microfinance Information Exchange, Inc.

Tendler, J. (1997) *Good government in the tropics*. Baltimore: Johns Hopkins University Press.

Tendler, J. and S. Freedheim (1994) 'Trust in a rent-seeking world: Health and government transformed in Northeast Brazil', *World Development*, 22: 1771–91.

Tesoro, J. (2000) 'Indonesia learns the ropes of press freedom', *Unesco Courier*, February, 43–5.

Thee, K. (ed.) (2003) *Recollections: The Indonesian economy 1950s–1990s*, Indonesia Project, ANU and ISEAS, Singapore 2003.

Thee, K. (1992) 'The investment surge from the Asian newly-industrializing countries into Indonesia', *Asian Economic Journal*, 6, 3: 231–64.

Thee, K. (1989) 'Industrialization in India and Indonesia', in *Itinerario*, 13, 1.

Thomas, J. and M. Grindle (1990) 'After the decision: Implementing policy reforms in developing countries', *World Development*, 18: 1163–81.

Tichy, N. and M. Devanna (1986) *The transformational leader*. New York: Wiley.

Timmer, C. (1981) 'The formation of Indonesian rice policy', in G. Hansen (Ed.) *Agricultural and rural development in Indonesia*, Boulder, CO: Westview, 33–43.

Timmer, C. (2004) 'Operationalizing pro-poor growth', Indonesia Case Study, Presentation at the World Bank East Asia PREM group, March.

Todd, H. (1996) *Women at the center: Grameen Bank borrowers after one decade*. Boulder: Westview Press.

Tokman, V. (1989) 'Policies for a heterogeneous informal sector in Latin America', *World Development*, 17: 1067–76.

Tomlinson, R. (2002) 'International best practice, enabling frameworks and the policy process: A South African case study', *International Journal of Urban and Regional Research*, 26, 2: 377–88.

Tuchman, B. (1984) *The march of folly: From Troy to Vietnam*. London: Michael Joseph.

Tullock, G. (1967) 'The welfare costs of monopolies, tariffs and theft', *Western Economic Journal*, 5: 224–32.

Tullock, G. (2005) *Public goods, redistribution and rent seeking*. Cheltenham: Edward Elgar.

Turner, J. (1976) *Housing by people*. London: Marion Boyers.

Turner, B. (1986) *Building community: A Third World case book*. London: Habitat International Coalition.

UNCDF (United Nations Capital Development Fund) (2006) *A decade of support to local planning and financing in Mozambique*. UNCDF Website.

UNESCO (United Nations Economic, Scientific and Cultural Organization) (2000) *World Education Report 2000*. Paris: UNESCO.

UN-Habitat (2001) *Istanbul plus 5: Thematic Committee, report by the South African government*, 6–8 June, mimeo.

UN-Habitat (2003) *The challenge of slums: Global report on human settlements 2003*. London: Earthscan.

UN-Habitat (2005) *Financing urban shelter: Global report on human settlements 2005*. London: Earthscan.

Uphoff, N. (1992) *Learning from Gal Oya: Possibilities for participatory development and post-Newtonian social science*. Ithaca: Cornell University Press.

Uphoff, N. (2000) 'Demonstrated benefits from social capital: The productivity of farmer organizations in Gal Oya, Sri Lanka', *World Development*, 28: 1875–1900.

Uvin, P., P. Jain and L. Brown (2000) 'Think large and act small: Toward a new paradigm for NGO scaling up', *World Development*, 28: 1409–19.

Van der Berg, S., R. Burger, R. Burger, M. Louw and D. Yu (2005) *Trends in poverty and inequality in South Africa*. Stellenbosch: Stellenbosch Economic Working Papers 1/2005, University of Stellenbosch.

Van Domelen, J. (2006) 'Social capital in the operations and impacts of social investment funds', in A. Bebbington, M. Woolcock, S. Guggenheim and E. Olson (eds) *The search for empowerment: Social capital as idea and practice at the World Bank*. Bloomfield: Kumarian, 177–203.

Vatikiotis, Michael R. J. (1993) *Indonesian politics under Suharto: Order, development and pressure for change*. London: Routledge.

Viegas, A. (1999) Personal communication (interview).

Wade, R. (1990) *Governing the market: Economic theory and the role of government in East Asian industrialization*. Princeton, N.J: Princeton University Press.

Wallis, J. (1999) 'Understanding the role of leadership in economic policy reform', *World Development*, 27: 39–53.

Weimer, B. (1999) 'Abstaining from the 1998 local Government elections in Mozambique: Some hypotheses', *L'Afrique Politique*, 125–54.

Weimer, B., L. Cabral, and D. Jackson (2004) *Aid modalities, flow of funds and partner structures: Experiences and recommendations for ASPS II*. Maputo: Danida.

West, H. (2005) *Kupilikula: Governance and the invisible realm in Mozambique*. Chicago: University of Chicago Press.

Weyland, K. (1995) 'Social movements and the state: The politics of health reform in Brazil', *World Development*, 23: 1699–1712.

Wie, T. (Ed.) (2003) *Recollections: The Indonesian economy 1950s–1990s*. Singapore: Institute of South East Asian Studies.

Williamson, J. (1990) 'What Washington means by policy reform', in J. Williamson (Ed.) *Latin American adjustment: How much has happened?*. Washington D.C: Institute for International Economics.

Williamson, J. (1994) *The political economy of policy reform*. Washington D.C: Institute for International Economics.

Wolf, L., E. Schiefelbein and P. Schiefelbein (2000) 'El costo-efectividad de las políticas de educación primaria en América Central, Panamá y República Dominicana: Un estudio basdo en la opinión de expertos', in J. Navarro, K. Taylor, A. Bernasconi and L. Tyler (eds) *Perspectivas sobre la reforma educativa*. Washington D.C: U.S. Agency for International Development, Inter-American Development Bank and Harvard Institute for International Development.

Woo, W., B. Glassburner and A. Nasution (1994) *Macroeconomic policies, crises, and long term growth in Indonesia 1965–90*. Washington D.C: World Bank.

Wood, G. (1992) 'Introduction', in B. Kramsjo and G. Wood *Breaking the chains: Collective action for social justice among the rural poor in Bangladesh*. London: IT Publications, 1–34.

Wood, G. and I. Sharif (1997) 'Introduction', in G. Wood and I. Sharif (eds) *Who needs credit? Poverty and finance in Bangladesh*. Dhaka: University Press, 27–58.

World Bank (2004a) 'IBRD program document for a proposed programmatic loan to the amount of US$100 million to the United Mexican States for affordable housing and urban poverty sector adjustment loan', Report no. 27627–MX. Washington D.C: World Bank.

World Bank (2004b) *Project appraisal report for the Bolsa Familia Project – Report 28544–BR*. Washington D.C: World Bank.

World Bank (2005) *World Development Report 2006: Equity and development*. New York: Oxford University Press.

World Bank (2003a) 'Indonesia and poverty: Sector background', *Social policy and government*, The World Bank Group, 2003, http: //www.worldbank.org/eapsocial/countries/indon/pov1.htm, accessed July 24 2003.

World Bank (2003b) *World Development Report 2004: Making services work for poor people*. New York: Oxford University Press.

World Bank (2002) 'Poverty update', Jakarta: World Bank Office, June.

World Bank (2000) *World Development Report 2000/01: Attacking poverty*. New York: Oxford University Press.

World Bank (1998a) *Assessing aid: What works, what doesn't, and why*. Washington D.C: World Bank.

World Bank (1998b) 'Indonesia in crisis: A macroeconomic update'. Washington D.C: World Bank.

World Bank (1993a) *The East Asian miracle: Economic growth and public policy*. New York: Oxford University Press.

World Bank (1993b) *World Development Report 1993*. New York: Oxford University Press.

World Bank (1989) *Strategy for growth and structural change*. Washington D.C: World Bank, Report No. 7758-IND, May 3.

World Bank (1979) *Growth patterns, social progress and development prospects*. Washington D.C: World Bank, Report No. 2093-IND, February 20.

World Bank (1968) *Economic development of Indonesia*. Washington D.C: World Bank report No. AS-123a, February 12.

World Bank Brazil (2001) *Assessment of the Bolsa Escola Programme*. Brasilia: World Bank Report No. 20208-BR.

WHO (World Health Organisation) (1995) *World Health Report 1995: Bridging the gaps*. Geneva: WHO.

WHO (2005) *World Health Report 2005: Make every mother and child count*. Geneva: WHO.

WHO (2006) *World Health Report 2006: Working together for health*. Geneva: WHO.

Zakaria, H. (1989) 'Malaysia: Quasi-democracy in a divided society', in L. Diamond, J. Linz and S. Lipset (eds) *Democracy in developing countries: Asia*. Boulder, CO: Lynne Rienner, 347–81.

Zaman, H. (2004) 'Microfinance in Bangladesh: Growth, achievements, and lessons' in World Bank *Scaling up poverty reduction – Case studies in microfinance*, Washington D.C: CGAP/World Bank, http://www.cgap.org/docs/CaseStudy scalingup.pdf, accessed December 17 2006.

Zaman, H. (n.d.) 'Microfinance in Bangladesh: Growth, achievements and lessons', in World Bank *Scaling up poverty reduction – Case studies in microfinance*. http://www.cgap.org/docs/CaseStudy_scalingup.pdf, accessed May 24 2005.

Zeller, M., Schreider, G., J. Von Braun and F. Heidhus (1997) *Rural finance for food security for the poor (Food Policy Review 4)*. Washington D.C: International Food Policy Research Institute.

Subject Index

Name Index